Psychoticism as a Dimension of Personality

Psychoticism
as a Dimension
of Personality.

Hans J. Eysenck and
Sybil B.G. Eysenck

HODDER AND STOUGHTON
LONDON SYDNEY AUCKLAND TORONTO

MIDDLEBURY COLLEGE LIBRARY

RC
512
E97

11/1977
Psych

Everything conceptualisable is constructive and not derivable in a logical manner from immediate experience. Therefore we are in principle completely free in the choice of those fundamental conceptions upon which we base our picture of the world. Everything depends on this alone: to what extent our construction is suitable for bringing order into the apparent chaos of the world of experience.

A. Einstein

ISBN 0 340 20919 4

Copyright © 1976 H.J. Eysenck and S.B.G. Eysenck

All rights reserved. No part of this publication may be reproduced or transmitted in any form or by any means, electronic or mechanical, including photocopy, recording, or any information storage and retrieval system, without permission in writing from the publisher.

Printed in Great Britain for
Hodder and Stoughton Educational, a division of Hodder and Stoughton Ltd, London, by The Pitman Press, Bath.

Computer Typesetting by Print Origination, Bootle, Merseyside L20 6NS.

Contents

Introduction

In some ways, this is an unusual book. In the first place, it introduces a concept which, if not entirely novel (we have been working on it since the early 'fifties, and publishing on it regularly over the past few years), is yet so unorthodox and contrary to much current theorizing that few psychiatrists or personality theorists have shown much interest in it. And in the second place, this concept spans such a wide field that readers expert in one area may find themselves relatively inexpert in others. Thus we deal with psychometric problems of test construction, with the elaboration of genetic models and their testing by biometrical analysis, with experimental laboratory studies of certain personality correlates, with the relationship between psychiatric diagnoses and personality variables, with theories of criminality, with the psychological interpretation of the Lie scale, and various other topics which at first sight seem to have very little relation with each other. The fact that the concept of *psychoticism* brings all these variegated topics together in one theoretical framework is, for us, a good argument for taking the concept seriously; it does, nevertheless, make it difficult to write a book with some pretensions at cohesion, and it does raise problems about the level at which the different chapters should be written. It even raises doubts about the inclusion of certain chapters— how much interest would a psychiatrist be expected to show in the psychometric details of test construction, or the experimentalist in the refinements of biometrical genetical analysis? In short, of course, the answer is that there has probably been too much specialization in these different fields, and that it may be salutary for experts in these different areas to view their specialities from novel and somewhat different points of view. Whether we have been able to make such a course palatable must of course remain doubtful; that it is desirable we hope the reader will agree after looking through what we have written.

The concept of psychoticism only makes sense within the context of a dimensional theory of personality, and of the extension of that theory to the psychiatric field; such a theory runs counter to the categorical disease-concept theory of clinical diagnoses which dominates psychiatry. Our first chapter therefore discusses these alternative points of view, and suggests that the evidence which is currently available supports the dimensional view, rather than the categorical one. This is probably more readily conceded in relation to neurotic disorders, where the concepts of neuroticism and extraversion-introversion have become quite widely accepted, not only as dimensions of personality, but also as characterizing psychiatric groups normally diagnosed anxiety states, reactive depressives, psychopaths, hysterics, obsessive-compulsives, etc. It is less likely to be accepted in the field of the functional psychoses, where the notion of a categorical difference seems intuitively much more likely. We argue that here too the evidence suggests continuity rather than discontinuity, and that just as the neurotic disorders are at one extreme of a dimension of (normal) personality, so also are psychotic disorders at one extreme of another dimension of (normal) personality. It is the purpose of this book to assess the validity of this hypothesis, and to elaborate the nature of the concept of *psychoticism.*

In chapter 2 we take a look at the genetic literature, particularly twin studies and studies of adopted children, and attempt to show that genetically there are close relations between the different functional psychoses, i.e. mainly schizophrenia and manic-depressive illness (whether unipolar or bipolar); it also appears that these genetic links extend to psychopathy and criminality (and perhaps to alcoholism). This apparent reversion to the discredited notion of *Einheitspsychose* does not, of course, mean that there are no very real differences between different psychotic disorders; what is suggested is rather that underlying these differences there is also an important unity, and it is the purpose of the concept of psychoticism to try and elaborate the nature of that unity. The genetic evidence not only suggests the feasibility of this attempt; it also provides us with specific hypotheses for testing.

Chapters 3, 4 and 5 deal in some detail with the construction of the psychoticism (P) scale, and chapter 6 deals with the construction of the Junior P scale. It may seem slightly over-elaborate to go in such detail into the mechanics of scale construction, but there are good reasons for doing so. The development of the finished scale contains, in part, the justification for its validity; the sequence of factorial studies which led us to test, reject or accept individual items as part of the scale is a vital part of the information which alone can enable the reader to judge its adequacy. We would argue that for most published scales there is too little information given on these aspects of test construction to make judgment easy. We have preferred, if anything, to err in the opposite direction.

There is also another important point. Various psychologists and psychiatrists have used intermediate forms of our final scales (the PEN, the PI) for studies which we have quoted in later chapters; the adequacy of these studies could not be judged without some detailed knowledge of the differences between these various scales, and the stages of development at which they were constructed. The differences between the scales are not very marked, but they are sufficient to change considerably the intercorrelations of the P and the E (extraversion) and N (neuroticism) scales; this in turn explains some of the findings with the earlier scales which are unlikely to be replicated with the later ones.

We hope that a look through these consecutive studies will bring home to the reader a point about factor-analytic procedure, and test construction generally, which is often obscured in textbooks and popular accounts of the methodology. To what extent do published scales mirror some inexorable law of nature, and to what extent are they just arbitrary results of predetermined notions? Neither view is tenable by itself. Clearly the hypothesis that certain types of items correlate together to define a separate factor approaching the nature of 'psychoticism', as conceived on a partly intuitive basis, is borne out; such items do exist and can be discovered, and shown to correlate together. So far we would seem to be dealing, if not with an inexorable law of nature, yet with some regularity in nature which is worth documenting and measuring. However, our choice of items can create a factor which is independent of other major dimensions of personality, such as N and E, or it can produce slight correlations, positive or negative, with either. This choice of items is in part subjective, and in the hands of the investigator. Our early scale of P correlated positively with N (although not very highly), just as in the development of the N and E scales early measures showed a slight negative correlation between the two. Omitting just one or two items having loadings on both scales, and substituting other items not having such double loadings, make it possible to produce scales which effectively correlate zero with each other. It is impossible, and indeed meaningless, to say that our decision to aim at uncorrelated scales may go counter to nature, and is therefore arbitrary. Concepts like P, E and N are just that—concepts; they are not discovered but invented, just like all other scientific concepts (gravitation, intelligence, mass), and the criterion by which they must be judged is not absolute truth (itself a concept without philosophical standing), but scientific usefulness. Slightly oblique factors are a nuisance as far as mathematical treatment and conceptualization are concerned, and if it is possible to correct this fault (which arises in any case from the quite arbitrary selection of the original items) by slight changes in the choice of items, then it seems desirable that such changes should be made—as long as this does not alter the conceptual nature of the scale. Thus the construction of a scale embodies both lawful and objective decisions, and somewhat arbitrary and subjective choices. Readers have a right to see in detail the bases for our decisions.

Chapter 7 deals with a fundamental question in the identification of psychoticism—is it true that psychotics have greatly elevated P scores, as compared with normals and neurotics? This chapter reviews some of the earliest results; the last chapter adds some more recent evidence. On the whole the answer is that psychotics have higher P scores than normals and neurotics; that the P scores of psychotics are higher for those whose disorders are more severe than those with less severe symptoms; and that the P scores of psychotics are lower after successful treatment. Furthermore, psychotics show similar performances on laboratory tests as do high P scorers, as opposed to normals and low P scorers, respectively. These findings seem to justify the labelling of the factor as one of psychoticism.

Chapter 8 continues the investigation of social correlates of P with an investigation of criminality and psychopathy. As already noted, psychopathy and criminality appear on the fringes of the genetically-determined psychotic core of symptoms, and it would seem that members of these groups should also have high P scores on the average. This is indeed so; the work on criminality gives some of the strongest evidence for the meaningfulness of psychoticism as a dimension of personality. There is furthermore some evidence to show that drug addiction and other antisocial activities, related to criminality, are also correlated with high P scores.

We next go on to chapter 9, in which we make an attempt to consider certain theoretical concepts which have been suggested to underlie psychoticism. No definite causal theory can at the moment be put forward in this field, but arousal has been linked with schizophrenia in many theoretical efforts, and it seemed worthwhile to look at this concept in connection with P. The evidence does not suggest that arousal can explain the major facts known about P, and we next consider hormonal differences related to the concept of *maleness*, as possibly suggesting cues for a more viable theory. The fact that males have much higher P scores than females suggests that the androgen/oestrogen balance may be involved, but in the absence of any decisive experiments in this connection we are forced to leave this theory as suggesting further work, rather than as capable of explaining the known facts in any definitive manner.

Chapter 10 deals with the inheritance of P, and is based on our own work with large samples of twins. We have made use here of recent advances in the biometrical genetical analysis of such data, and we believe that the results are of considerable importance. We show, in fact, that genetic factors are responsible for 81 per cent of all the reliably measured differences in P between subjects, that all the important genetic factors involved are additive, and that between-families environmental variance plays little or no part in the causation of such differences. Additionally, we show that the genetic model which best fits our data is identical with that which best fits the known facts regarding schizophrenia. These are important findings, suggesting that the term *psychoticism* may with justice be applied to our factor.

Throughout the preceding chapters, we have noted that psychotic groups are characterized not only by an elevated P score, but also by an elevated Lie score. Psychopaths, behaviour disorders and other criminal and antisocial groups, however, do not have such high L scores. In chapter 11 we discuss in detail the construction, validation and meaning of the Lie scale, and also furnish some information regarding its heritability. We believe that no data on personality questionnaires are properly interpretable without some information of the subject's Lie-scale scores, and it also seems that this scale measures not only dissimulation, but in addition gives information concerning a personality trait of conformity, orthodoxy, or conservatism which may rank as another dimension of personality.

The last chapter deals with a series of more recent empirical studies of psychoticism, subdivided into three sections—clinical, experimental, and correlational. The clinical studies reinforce the earlier conclusions regarding the high P scores of psychotics, as compared with neurotics and normals: the fact that not only schizophrenics but also in some studies endogenous depressives have high P scores, and that within the psychotic group P correlates with severity of disorder. The important point is added that P+ respond poorly to psychotherapy and behaviour therapy, as compared with P− neurotics. In the experimental section, tests are reported of hypotheses linking P with poor preservation of set, poor vigilance, and high originality and creativity, as shown in unusual associative responses. And in the correlational section, it is shown that P correlates along predicted lines with other personality inventories, such as the Minnesota Multiphasic Personality Inventory (MMPI), the Cattell 16PF, the Foulds Hostility scale, etc. Other correlates, e.g. ratings, are also considered. On the whole, they bear out our interpretation of P, and the various trait components of P. In particular, P is found to be related to toughmindedness, and indeed there is evidence to show that this relationship is in large part the product of genetic factors.

Finally, a brief set of Conclusions summarizes the major findings elaborated throughout this book, some of which have already been mentioned in this Introduction. There is a large number of Tables and Figures in the various chapters; these are used partly to condense data, but also to make clearer the argument. Dimensional theories are particularly in need of diagrammatic representation, and although theories requiring more than two dimensions are difficult to illustrate in this manner, we have done the best we could.

After twenty-five years of work on this concept, how do we feel about it now? On the whole, we feel that what was at first a most unlikely candidate has turned out to be exceptionally promising. It always seemed to us that among the major dimensions of personality there was a gap beside the well-established E and N factors; we now feel that this gap has been filled, and we note with particular satisfaction that our concept falls in line with a variety of other suggestions for that role. In particular, psychoticism would seem to be the obverse of a concept of superego as used, for instance, by Cattell; this relates it to a whole series of empirical and factorial studies which will be well known to students of personality. In spite of this set of relationships, however, our factor would seem to span a much wider area than primary factor constructs such as superego, or empathy, or hostility, to name only some of those which are combined in P. It is too early to say much more about P, particularly as most of the work on it has been done in our laboratories, or by people directly or indirectly connected with us; clearly only the widest use of the P scale by many other people and departments can decide whether the usefulness we like to see in this concept can be discerned by others also. It is reassuring, however, to find that replications of some of our work in countries as distant from England as Iran, Nigeria, India and Czechoslovakia have successfully duplicated findings of ours on nationals tested in these varied countries. This book essentially sets out the facts about psychoticism as they are known to us in the summer of 1975; it is very much hoped that much more will be known about this concept, and that in particular research will enable us to formulate a stronger causal theory than is possible at present. However that may be, we are not dissatisfied with the growth of our baby to date; we have seen him through adolescence, now the tasks of manhood are before him. We trust they will be duly carried out successfully.

Sybil B.G. Eysenck
Hans J. Eysenck
Institute of Psychiatry,
1st July, 1975

1

The dimensional model of personality

The concept of psychoticism as a personality dimension makes sense only within a dimensional system of personality description, and when the possibility of adding such a dimension to those of E and N was first mooted (Eysenck, 1952a, 1952b) this was of course fully recognized. The main difference between categorical, typological (in the old sense), or diagnostic systems, on the one hand, and dimensional systems on the other is of course the question of continuity; in this case, the question of whether psychotics as a group are differentiated from normals in an absolute, categorical, qualitative manner, such that all psychotics possess some characteristic which is possessed by no one in the normal group, or whether the characteristics which differentiate normals from psychotics are infinitely graded, giving rise to all sorts of intermediate personalities from one extreme to the other. Psychiatrists seldom deal with this problem in any systematic fashion. In their continued use of psychiatric diagnoses, which presuppose discontinuity, they seem to adhere to the categorical system, but they also often talk about intermediate types, about incomplete dominance and about schizoid characters or schizophrenia-form behaviour, as if recognizing the existence of continuity. Officially, textbooks would appear to hold the discontinuity view, but all practising psychiatrists recognize the impossibility of fitting reality into this Procrustes bed of diagnostic nomenclature and use verbal formulations which, in fact, approximate to a dimensional view.

What is clearly needed would seem to be a statistical method which could decide between these two models in a logical fashion. Such a method was designed with precisely this problem in mind and designated 'criterion analysis' (Eysenck, 1950a). It was used first to establish the validity of the concept of continuity with respect to neurosis (Eysenck, 1950a) and then applied later on to the study of psychosis (Eysenck, 1952b). The specific problem which formed the subject matter of this paper originated with a review of Kretschmer's theory of schizothymia-cyclothymia (Eysenck, 1950b), and historically it might be said that the concept of psychoticism in fact originated with this review. It will be remembered that Kretschmer's theory of personality (1948), which was very influential at one time, postulated a dimension of personality ranging from schizophrenia to manic-depressive illness, via the rather less psychiatrically ill groups of schizoids and cycloids, and the normal sub-variants Kretschmer called dystonics and syntonics (Figure 1). This dimension of personality resembles, in its descriptive aspects, Jung's extraversion-introversion dimension, except that Jung thought that at the extremes of his dimension there were located hysterics and asthenics, i.e. neurotic rather than psychotic groups. Both authors failed to see that their hypotheses of one dimension of personality in reality required a second dimension as well; in

1

Kretschmer's case, if psychotic groups form both extremes of his personality dimension, then clearly there must be an additional dimension of personality, orthogonal to the first, bringing together the two psychotic groups, and contrasting them with normality. This hypothesis is of course based on the belief that for two groups to be called 'psychotic' they must share in common something which sets them both off from the rest of the population; this something cannot be discontinuous if at the same time we place these two groups at the two ends of a continuum. Similarly, Jung's postulation requires to be supplemented by the postulation of another continuum of neuroticism, orthogonal to his typological continuum of extraversion-introversion, for the same reason. This, of course, raises the additional question of whether psychoticism and neuroticism are, in fact, identical dimensions, or whether they are quite separate; this question we shall return to later on.

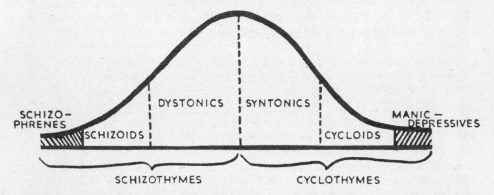

Figure 1   Diagrammatic representation of Kretschmer's theory of psychotic continuity with normality (from Eysenck, 1970a)

Let us now consider the method of criterion analysis, with special application to the question of the continuity or discontinuity of normal and psychotic states. (The method itself is, of course, of perfectly general applicability.) Let the line AB in Figure 2 represent the normal—psychotic continuum, and let the line I, I' cut off at point X that part of the continuum containing mental states conventionally diagnosed 'psychotic' by psychiatrists. (The distribution of the total population has been tentatively included in the figure in the form of a normal curve of distribution. As the actual form of the distribution is irrelevant to the argument, which merely hypothesizes a continuous distribution, any other form of rectilinear or curvilinear distribution might be substituted for the normal form without affecting the argument.) Let n objective psychological tests $(a,b,c...n)$ be given to the two populations separated by the line I, I', i.e. to a normal group and to a psychotic group. (The term 'normal' here means nothing but 'not under psychiatric care for mental disorders'; it does not imply anything more positive than this absence of demonstrable and demonstrated mental disorder.) Let us assume that each of these n tests distinguishes significantly between the normal and the psychotic groups. (In actual practice, $n + x$ tests would have to be given in all, so that tests not distinguishing at the chosen level of significance could be rejected.)

Now let us divide the normal group into two parts, by making a cut at point L

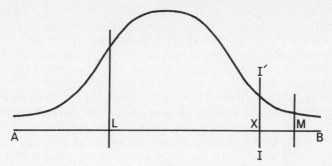

Figure 2   Diagrammatic representation of dimensional theory of psychiatric abnormality. The segment of the curve to the right of X represents the psychiatrically abnormal, divided at M into the more and less abnormal. The segment to the left of X represents the psychiatrically normal, divided at L into the more and less normal

on the line AX; similarly, let us make a cut at point M on the line XB, thus subdividing the psychotic group also. (Points L and M may be anywhere between A and X and X and B, respectively; there is no implication that they should divide the respective populations into equal halves.) On the hypothesis that AB represents a true continuum, we have now divided both the normal and the psychotic groups into two parts, one of them more normal, the other more psychotic. Group AL is more normal than LX; group XM is more normal than group MB. If AB is a true continuum (the hypothesis to be tested), and if each of our *n* tests is related to that continuum in a linear fashion (supplementary hypothesis), then it would follow that on these *n* tests, group AL would differ from group LX in the same way that group AX differed originally from group XB. Similarly, group XM would differ from group MB in the same way that AL differed from LX.

We may put these arguments in a form which permits of their being tested. If tests *a* and *b* differentiate significantly between groups AX and XB, then it would follow according to our hypothesis that they should differentiate also between AL and LX. Similarly, they should differentiate between XM and MB. This deduction, unfortunately, does not permit of any direct test, as there is no known method of determining points L and M, and therefore of differentiating the groups under discussion. However, we can transform the concept of 'differentiate' into the concept of 'correlate' and test our hypothesis in this fashion. If on tests *a* and *b* the normal group does better than the psychotic group, it would follow, as explained above, that group AL should do better on both tests than group MB. But these statements are synonymous with saying that for both the normal and the psychotic groups separately, there should be a positive correlation between tests *a* and *b*.

This argument can be extended to *n* tests and implies as one consequence that tests which differentiate significantly between normals and psychotics should give positive intercorrelations when these correlations are run for the normal or the psychotic groups separately. Here then we would have a possible test of our hypothesis. But we can refine this test a little by pointing out that not only should these correlations be positive, but also that they should be proportional to the power of each test to differentiate between the normal and psychotic groups originally. We may express this differentiating power in terms of a biserial correlation for each test with the normal—psychotic dichotomy, denoting the column of n correlations between tests and criterion, the criterion column $(C_{n,p})$. We may then say that the average of the intercorrelations of a test with all the other tests in the battery, for either the normal or the psychotic group, should be proportional to the correlation of that test with the criterion, i.e. the normal—psychotic dichotomy.

Instead of averaging correlations, it would appear more suitable to perform a factor analysis on the intercorrelations between our n tests. Let us assume that we extract two factors from each of our two matrices, the sets of intercorrelations for the normal and the psychotic groups respectively, which we may call F_n and F_n' for the normal and F_p and F_p' for the psychotic group. It would follow from our hypothesis and our selection of tests that F_n and F_p should be proportional to each other and to our criterion column, $C_{n,p}$. Here, then, we have reached the final and crucial test. We have made a hypothesis as to the existence of a general factor underlying the pattern of variances and covariances of test performances of normal and psychotic groups and deduced certain consequences which would follow if our hypothesis were true and which would not follow on any tenable counter-hypothesis. In so far as these deductions are verified, we may consider our hypothesis as supported; in so far as these deductions are not verified, we may consider our hypothesis as disproved.

A similar procedure could, of course, be used to test (simultaneously) Kretschmer's original hypothesis, i.e. that there exists a continuum from schizophrenics to manic-depressives, passing through various kinds of 'normal' personalities. What would be required here would be a set of tests which discriminate between schizophrenic and manic-depressive patients; the criterion column in this case would consist of the biserial correlations of each test with this new column. Apart from these changes, the procedure as outlined above is applicable to just the same extent as it is in respect to our first hypothesis; on the basis of Kretschmer's hypothesis we would expect factors F_a' and F_p' to be proportional to each other and also to the new criterion column, $C_{s,d}$.

Both hypotheses can be tested at the same time, using n tests which differentiate significantly (using Fisher's F test) between the three groups involved: the normal schizophrenic and manic-depressive. The two criterion columns, $C_{n,p}$ and $C_{s,d}$, could then be calculated quite easily by running point biserial correlations between each of the n tests and the normal vs. psychotic dichotomy for $C_{n,p}$ (using the combined schizophrenic and manic-depressive groups to form the psychotic group), and by running point biserial correlations between each of the n tests and the schizophrenic—manic-depressive dichotomy for $C_{s,d}$. Product-moment correlations would then be run between the n tests for the normal and the psychotic groups separately, thus giving us two separate matrices. These, when factor analysed according to either the centroid or the summation method, or indeed any of the current methods, should result in two factors each, F and F', which would be proportional to each other and to the respective criterion columns.

This method was used in an experiment which employed one hundred volunteers, fifty schizophrenic patients and fifty manic-depressive patients. All were voluntary patients; none were long-term or deteriorated.

Great care was taken to include in the two groups (schizophrenic and manic-depressive) only cases about whom there could be little doubt as to their proper provenance, and even after they had been tested care was taken to follow them up for a period of several months to see if there had been any change in their condition which would lead to a change of diagnosis. A number of such changes did in fact occur, sometimes as much as six or eight months after testing, and such cases were immediately discarded. While this precaution probably served to purify the two groups in question, there can be no doubt that we were only partly successful in reaching 100 per cent reliable and valid diagnoses; if the patients had been followed up over a period of ten years and re-diagnosed after that lapse of time, it is highly likely that many more would have been diagnosed under some other category than that originally chosen. All that can be claimed is that our schizophrenic group probably contained more schizophrenics than our manic-depressive group, and conversely, that our manic-depressive group contained more depressives than our schizophrenic group. For the purpose of our demonstration this is sufficient, and it will be noted, in support of this view, that there were significant differences on a variety of objective tests between these two clinical groups. In other words, the null hypothesis is not tenable with respect to our final clinical groups.

A set of fifteen separate laboratory tests was given to our subjects, from which ninety separate scores could be calculated, of which the majority differentiated significantly between the groups. Many of these tests were taken from Kretschmer's book, in order to provide a fair test of his hypothesis. For these tests predictions exist as to the likely direction of differences between the psychiatric groups; in fact, these expectations were not on the whole borne out and we will not here enter into a detailed discussion of this disproof of Kretschmer's hypothesis. A more important point arising is that manic-depressives on the whole deviated more from the normals than did schizophrenics. A third point of interest is that tests which had in the past discriminated neurotics from normals did not on the whole discriminate psychotics at all well from normals; this point, of course, is relevant to the problem of the number of dimensions necessary in our system, a point which will be discussed later.

With respect to the criterion analysis of the data, results were exceptionally clear-cut. Two sets of factor saturations were obtained from the normal and the psychotic groups respectively; when the respective factors were correlated in turn, they were found, as required by the hypothesis, to be remarkably alike, with correlations of .87 and .77 respectively. The next deduction requires that the first factors extracted (F_n and F_p) should both be proportional to $C_{n,p}$. The respective correlations are .90 and .95. The hypothesis that psychotic states do, in fact, form a continuum with normal mental states thus receives very strong support. Last, we can test the specifically Kretschmerian hypothesis which requires that $F_n{}'$ and $F_p{}'$ should both be proportional to $C_{s,d}$. The correlations in question in fact were quite insignificant (.01 and −.09) and it is clear that the hypothesis is not supported. There is no evidence in our data for schizothymia-cyclothymia as a separate dimension of personality. The data are not at variance with an alternative hypothesis, namely that in both the normal and the psychotic groups there exists a factor of (possibly) extraversion-introversion which is identical from group to group, but which does not differentiate between schizophrenics and manic-depressives. This alternative hypothesis is mentioned as a possibility; we shall later on discover some support for it. The data so far discussed do not support it directly, as we have no independent evidence for the relevance of E.

This study is the only one which would appear to bear directly on the issue of continuity and discontinuity; there is other, indirect evidence which we shall be discussing later on. It would not be correct to infer from one single, limited study that the conclusion of continuity is necessarily correct; clearly, replications are required before any far-reaching claims can be made. Nevertheless, the results are exceptionally clear-cut and decisive, and unless there are any errors in the logic underlying criterion analysis we may provisionally accept the conclusion suggested by this study.

While this study is the only one which has applied a rigorous criterion to the problem of continuity, there are several studies by Cattell and his associates which powerfully support the conclusion reached. The argument here is somewhat different, and not perhaps as convincing; nevertheless, it is difficult to see how the results obtained could have been found had there been any really deep and absolute dividing line between psychotics and normals. Cattell's concern has been with the problem of whether psychotics, when tested with the same objective tests used on normals, would show identical (or at least very similar) patterns of correlations, generating the same major factors. Cattell, Dubin and Saunders (1954) and Cattell and Tatro (1966) did find that this was indeed so, and Cattell, Delhees and Nesselroade (1971) came to the same conclusion on a group of normals and psychotics analysed jointly. The evidence is discussed at some length in Hundleby, Pawlik and Cattell (1965) and Cattell and Scheier (1961), and the reader who wishes to go into the details of these very large-scale studies is referred to these sources (see also Cattell and Schmidt, 1972). The last-named source book also gives evidence on the similarity of factors in normals and neurotics, again supporting the criterion analysis results reported by Eysenck (1950a). There are many interesting differences in the approaches of our respective Departments to the problems of classification, personality, factor analysis and diagnosis, but on the empirical plane, our results, although independently arrived at and using quite distinct methods, have in the great majority of cases been in excellent agreement. We shall later on discuss some of the differences in methodology; here let us only note that Cattell's findings strongly support our own with respect to the question of continuity or discontinuity of psychosis with normality.

While these studies cannot give results which are to be regarded as conclusive, we may perhaps for the moment be justified in assuming that they do support the dimensional view with respect to psychosis and neurosis, and we will use these hypotheses in next turning to our other major problem, namely whether these two dimensions are orthogonal or colinear.

Wolpe (1970) has reviewed a large body of clinical and experimental evidence suggesting that these two large groups of disorders are relatively separate. As he summarizes his survey: 'The evidence from genetic, physiological and behavioural studies adds up to the conclusion that neurosis and schizophrenia are behavioural disorders with separate and probably entirely unrelated etiologies. The genetic factor in schizophrenia does not coincide with that of neurosis. Several physiological features have been found in schizophrenics that are absent in normal people and neurotic patients. In particular, there is evidence of an abnormality of autonomic reactivity in schizophrenics that persists even in remission. The behavioural differences between the two conditions are many. The early symptoms of schizophrenia are characteristic and distinctly not neurotic. Neurotic behaviour is much more responsive to external stimulus conditions and is lastingly modifiable by conditioning procedures in a way that schizophrenic behaviour is not. There is also notable difference in response to selected performance tests' (p. 179). He contrasts this view with that held by many psychoanalysts, namely that the development of schizophrenia is functionally related to the neuroses and that transitions occur between one and the other (e.g. Arieti, 1956).

We shall review systematically some of the more experimental supports for this belief that neurotic and psychotic disorders and dimensions are essentially unrelated; for the moment, let us consider one additional point. Let us consider diagnosis, a system which is based on the categorical view of mental disease. If mental disorders were truly categorical in essence, and if psychosis were but a continuation of neurosis, then we would expect reliability of diagnosis within and between these two groups to be similarly high (or low); but this is not so. Reviews of the evidence (Kreitman, 1961; McGuire, 1973) demonstrate that between-groups reliability (psychosis *vs.* neurosis) usually centres around the 80 per cent level, while within-group reliability falls to 50 per cent or less on the average. This suggests a break between neurosis and psychosis, rather than a continuum. The evidence from diagnosis is of course not decisive, but it adds another point to those enumerated by Wolpe. Let us now turn to a systematic series of studies carried out in our laboratories. These have made use of the two methods of multivariate analysis most relevant: discriminant function analysis and factor analysis. Let us first of all consider discriminant function analysis (Slater, 1960).

In this method, *n* groups are tested or measured by means of *m* tests or measurements, and the analysis discloses the number of significant latent roots, which cannot exceed $n-1$ or $m-1$, whichever is the smaller, but which may not reach either value. Thus if a neurotic, a psychotic and a normal group are tested by means of at least three tests, the method may result in two, one or no significant latent roots; this would correspond to a statement that the results require two or one dimensions (or, of course, when none of the latent roots are significant, that the groups cannot be distinguished by means of the tests chosen). This method is preferable in many ways to factor analysis, as fewer assumptions are made and more acceptable tests of significance are available; interesting comparisons between the two methods, used on the same set of data, are presented by Slater (1960) and yet another comparison by Eysenck and Claridge (1962).

Let us consider in a slightly more formal way the two alternative hypotheses between which we wish to decide. These are presented in Figure 3a and Figure 3b. The one-dimensional view, shown in 3a, presents the hypothetical distribution of scores on the single hypothesized variable of normality-neurosis-psychosis, of three groups of people, respectively diagnosed as normal, neurotic and psychotic. The two-dimensional view, shown in 3b, presents along the abscissa a normality-abnormality dimension, and along the ordinate a psychosis *vs.* neurosis dimension. Given that we have three such groups, appropriately diagnosed, and a number of questionnaire scales or objective laboratory tests which discriminate between the groups, we can perform our analysis, determine the number of significant latent roots required and decide whether the one-dimensional or the two-dimensional model fits reality better.

A programmatic study by Lubin (1951) has been discussed in some detail in Eysenck (1952a). Four dexterity tests from the General Aptitude Battery of the US Employment Service were applied to fifty normal, fifty psychotic and fifty neurotic subjects (*Ss*), and the results analysed by means of discriminant function analysis. Two significant latent roots were found, and the means of the three groups

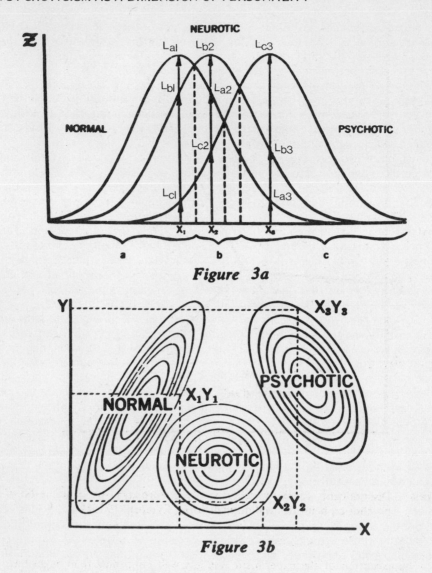

Figure 3 a One-dimensional model of relation between normal, neurotic and psychotic subjects
b Two-dimensional model of relation between normal, neurotic and psychotic subjects (from Eysenck, 1955b)

were found to lie in the two-dimensional space thus generated, as shown in Figure 4. The two variates jointly correlated with the criterion to the extent of .78; 71.3 per cent of the *S*s were correctly identified by these extremely simple and objective

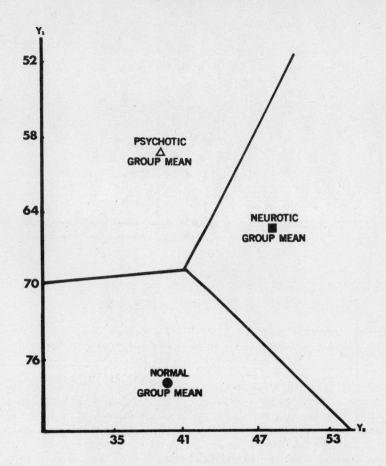

Figure 4   Discriminant function analysis of performance on four tests of psychotics, neurotics and normals (from Eysenck, 1955a)

tests. The execution of the experiment was less well controlled than might have been desired and made its repetition with a better choice of tests desirable. Two such repetitions are in fact available.

S.B.G. Eysenck (1956a) used 123 normals, 53 neurotics and 51 psychotics; all of them were administered six objective tests and a discriminant function analysis was performed. Two significant latent roots were again discovered, and Figure 5 shows the distribution of scores on the two axes corresponding to these two variables. Again it was found that 71 per cent of the Ss could be correctly identified on the basis of these tests; it was also suggested that the amount of misclassification shown in the study was due in large measure to faults in the criterion rather than in the tests and their combination. Devadasan (1964) has replicated Eysenck's study on an Indian population with very similar results.

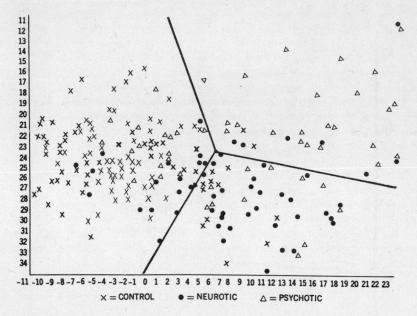

Figure 5 Discriminant function analysis of psychotic, neurotic and control (normal) subjects (from S. B. G. Eysenck, 1956a)

Eysenck (1955a) published a similar but smaller study in which twenty normals, twenty neurotics, and twenty psychotics were tested on four tests. Again, two significant latent roots were found and the results are shown in detail in Figure 6. The number of correct classifications was 65 per cent, using one criterion and 75 per cent using another; again we find much the same proportion of cases misclassified as in the two studies mentioned above. Two cases, marked A and B in the Figure, had been classified as 'neurotic' by the psychiatrists; their scores fell

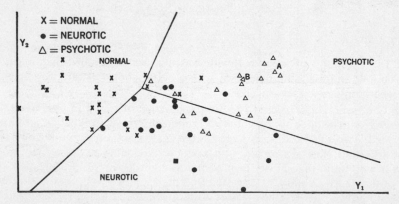

Figure 6 Distribution of scores of twenty normals, twenty neurotics and twenty psychotics on two canonical variates (from Eysenck, 1955a)

right into the psychotic cluster. They therefore count as misclassifications. Yet when they were readmitted to the hospital later on, the revised diagnosis was 'psychotic'. Here again, therefore, it may be suspected that much of the unreliability in the diagnosis is in fact due to unreliability in the criterion.

Factor analysis has given similar results, too, in the sense of requiring two rather than one dimension to accommodate neurotic and psychotic symptoms. Trouton and Maxwell (1956) used forty-five rated items on a random sample of 819 patients at the Maudsley and Bethlem Royal Hospitals, intercorrelated these items and factor analysed the resulting matrix. Two clear-cut factors of neuroticism and psychoticism emerged; their nature can best be seen from Figure 7, which is taken from Eysenck (1960). (A third factor opposes schizophrenic to manic-depressive symptoms, while a fourth factor is labelled 'inactivity-withdrawal', and may be related to introversion.) Factor scores were calculated for the members of various diagnostic groups and their means plotted (Figure 8). The oblique line running across the diagram gives a complete separation of the psychotic from the neurotic diagnoses. Patients with psychotic diagnoses tend to have elevated factor scores; patients with neurotic diagnoses are all below any of the psychotic groups on psychotic factor scores.

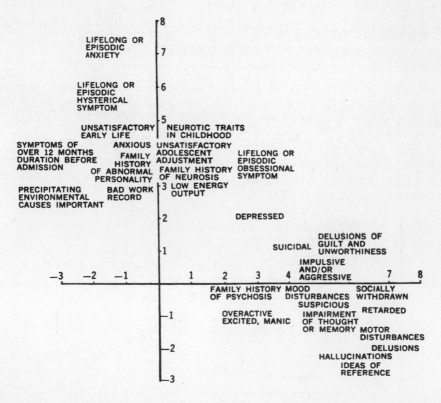

Figure 7 Factor analysis of forty-five rated items on a random sample of 819 psychiatric patients (from Trouton and Maxwell, 1956)

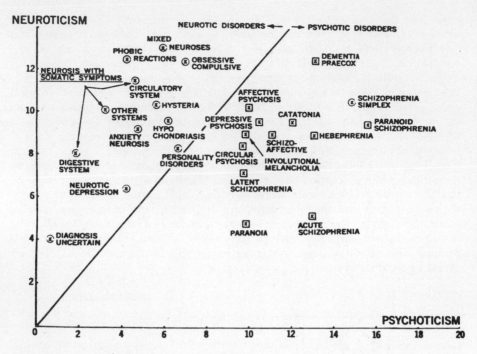

Figure 8 Means of factor scores for various diagnostic groups (from H.J. Eysenck, 1960)

Table 1 and Figure 9 give the individual scores of seventy neurotic patients, thirty psychotics and twenty normals, in order to show that the effects noted above are not artifacts produced by diagnostic grouping. There is one psychotic patient, marked B, whose score falls well into the neurotic group; on readmission he was rediagnosed 'neurotic'. There are two neurotics, labelled A in the diagram, whose scores fell well into the psychotic group; on readmission to the hospital these were rediagnosed as psychotic.

TABLE 1 Statistical summary of data in Figure 9

DIAGNOSIS	NORMAL	NEUROTIC	PSYCHOTIC	TOTAL
NORMAL (×)	19	1	0	20
NEUROTIC (●)	2	60	8	70
PSYCHOTIC (△)	0	4	26	30
	21	65	34	120

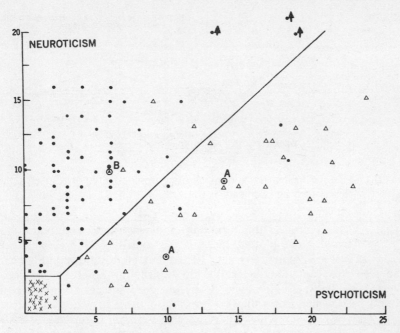

Figure 9 Individual scores of seventy neurotics, thirty psychotics and twenty normals. Normals are designated by crosses, neurotics by circles and psychotics by triangles (from H. J. Eysenck, 1960)

Cattell's work agrees well with the main conclusion to be drawn from the above-mentioned studies; he concludes his survey of his own studies by saying that 'psychoticism is a direction of abnormality distinct from neuroticism and anxiety. As a result, neurotic-contributory factors are not psychotic-contributory; that is, the neurotic-contributory factors discriminate between neurotics and normals and between neurotics and psychotics, but they do not discriminate between psychotics and normals'. Figure 10 shows the profiles of neurotics and psychotics, as compared with normals on the sixteen questionnaire factors which Cattell recognizes; the marked differences will be obvious. Cattell adds in a footnote to this figure: 'The objective test evidence . . . confirms that psychotics are not significantly different from normals on factor M, Non-Conformity, F(Q)II, Anxiety, and F(Q)I, Introversion.' Cattell's work is far too extensive to allow of summary here, but the agreement with our own studies is reassuring (Cattell and Scheier, 1961, p. 112).

Even studies purporting to prove the unidimensional theory reveal, when properly analysed, the clear-cut existence of two factors. Consider the case of the Bühler, Bühler and Lefever (1949) 'Basic Rorschach Score'. These authors recognize four levels of personality integration, ranging from normal through neurotic and psychopathic to psychotic. Proceeding rather in the manner familiar from the construction of the MMPI, they constructed a compound measure of Rorschach indices which would give optimal differentiation between various clinical and diagnostic groups; this measure had a reliability of .83. The authors claim that clinical groups characterized by increasing severity of illness do, in fact, have

13

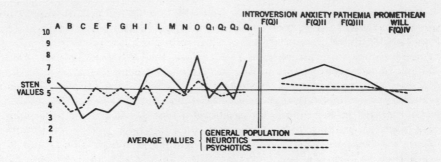

Figure 10 Scores of neurotics and psychotics, respectively, on Cattell's factors (from Cattell and Scheier, 1961)

increasingly higher scores on this test, thus validating a single-continuum type of theory. H.J. Eysenck has plotted eight of the constituent scores of the Basic Rorschach against level scores (Eysenck, 1970a); the result is shown in Figure 11. It will be seen that, far from being linearly related, the observed function is a curvilinear one between score and level; on these indices level-two patients (neurotics) have higher scores than do level-four patients (psychotics); indeed, on some of these, psychotics actually have lower scores than normals! It is apparent that Bühler *et al.* have thrown together in one 'score' indices having quite different regressions on neurotic and psychotic disorders, which is statistically impermissible and psychologically misleading; some indices show neurotics to have high scores, but not psychotics, while on others psychotics have high scores, but not neurotics. These data support, rather than contradict, those of the other studies cited.

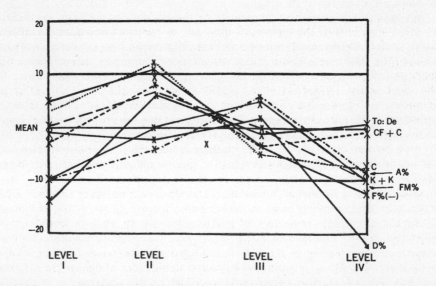

Figure 11 Curvilinear relation between 'basic Rorschach score' and normal–neurotic–psychopathic–psychotic dimension (from Eysenck, 1970a)

Perhaps even more convincing than statistical studies are genetic observations and experiments, such as those reported by Cowie (1961) from the Institute of Psychiatry at the Maudsley Hospital. She argued that if it is true that psychotic and neurotic disorders are orthogonal to each other, then we would expect that the children of psychotic parents should not show any greater degree of neuroticism than would the children of normal parents. Conversely, the unidimensional theory would have clear implications genetically regarding the higher degree of neuroticism to be expected in the children of psychotic parents. In actual fact, the children were found, if anything, to be less neurotic than the children of normal parents—a finding which supports the two-dimensional hypothesis, and which may also serve as a warning to those who would overstress the importance of environment in giving rise to neurotic disorders—it is difficult to imagine a more severe stress to a child than having a psychotic parent. Her results are thus particularly important in that they give support to the two-dimensional theory from a direction quite different from those discussed thus far. Provisionally, at least, we must conclude that the unidimensional theory, in spite of its widespread and almost axiomatic acceptance by psychoanalysts, finds no support in the experimental or statistical literature; all serious studies in the field contradict the assumptions on which this theory is built.

The possibility might, of course, have to be considered that the unidimensional theory might be rephrased so as to fit the facts. It might be suggested, for instance, that the relation between the two major types of mental disorder was unidimensional but nonlinear. Unless the actual relation were more precisely specified, however, such a view could not be said to have much value, as it could obviously not be verified or falsified. In any case, it would still not account for the results obtained by Cowie. Nor is there any indication that such a restyled version of his theory would be acceptable to Freud. As the evidence stands at present, it clearly contradicts any form of unidimensional theory actually held by past or present writers.

We shall not attempt here to evaluate all the evidence available on the question of the dimensional *vs.* the categorical approach, or the agreement between different scales in defining the major dimensions. Instead, we shall discuss briefly an attempt to align the MMPI system with that proposed here. Several such attempts have been made in the past (Goorney, 1970; Hundleby and Connor, 1968; Corah, 1964), but the most recent (Wakefield *et al.*, 1974) is not only the most interesting and sophisticated but also the most relevant to our general thesis and will, therefore, be presented here. The results reported have implications for the general development of the argument which will be taken up in later chapters.

Wakefield *et al.* write: 'In order to demonstrate the relationship (between the three dimensions of Eysenck's personality theory and the empirically developed MMPI), nine of the ten clinical scales are considered as measures of points in Eysenck's three-dimensional framework. (The Mf scale is not so considered.) MMPI scales that are commonly held to measure neuroticism are Hs, D and Hy (Meehl, 1956; Gough, 1946). Indicators of psychoticism are Pa, Pt and Sc (Winter and Stortroen, 1963; Ruesch and Bowman, 1945). The Si scale (Drake, 1946) was originated as a measure of the non-clinical introversion-extraversion dimension of personality. The Ma scale has been considered an indicator of neurosis (e.g. Rousell and Edwards, 1971). Also, persons who score high on this scale tend to be outgoing and energetic (Carson, 1969). For these reasons, the Ma scale is considered to measure both the neuroticism and extraversion dimensions of Eysenck's theory.

The Pd scale is associated with psychoticism and supposedly measures psychopathic character disorders (Carson, 1969). However, the failure of the MMPI to discriminate between such character disorders and psychosis has been noted (Affleck and Garfield, 1960). High scores on this scale also indicate a tendency to "act out" (Carson, 1969). This scale is considered to measure both psychoticism and extraversion' (p. 414).

Wakefield *et al.* present a Figure to indicate the conceptual placement of these nine MMPI scales in Eysenck's three-dimensional personality theory; this is reproduced as Figure 12. The correspondence between the empirical relationships among the MMPI scales and their theoretical placement, as indicated in the Figure, was tested by a procedure suggested by Wakefield and Doughtie (1973). This procedure involves the specification of the relative lengths of interpoint distances from the theory and comparing each theoretically ordered pair of distances with the empirically ordered magnitudes of the distances in factor space. To illustrate this approach, when the scales are intercorrelated for a given population and the matrix of intercorrelations is factor analysed, a factor space is created in which each scale can be plotted as a point in *n*-dimensional space. The distances between these points can be measured (or rather calculated) and should follow a certain pattern as set out in Figure 12. Thus, among the three neurotic scales there are three distances (A—B, A—C, B—C). Since the scales measure variations of the same construct, neuroticism, the distances among them should be relatively short. Similarly, the three interpoint distances among the psychotic scales should likewise be short. In contrast, there are nine interpoint distances from the three neurotic scales to the three psychotic scales; these should be of middling length. Last, there are two long distances, from Si to Ma and from Si to Pd. There are six short distances, twenty-two middle distances and two long distances implied in the prediction; the test is applied to the observed distances. Each of the six short distances should be shorter than each of the twenty-two middle distances; this yields 132 ordered pairs of distances. Further, both of the long distances should be longer than each of the

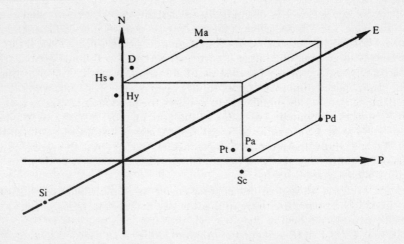

Figure 12 Conceptual placement of nine MMPI scales in Eysenck's three-dimensional personality theory (from Wakefield *et al.*, 1974)

twenty-two middle distances. This yields forty-four more ordered pairs of distances. Thus, from the theoretical structure presented in the Figure, there can be derived a total of 176 ordered pairs of distances.

The test was carried out on 205 married couples who took the MMPI; the distance check was carried out independently on the males and females. Rejection of the null hypothesis at the .01 level requires 104 correct orders out of the 176 possible ones. For the males, 111 of the distances were as hypothesized, for the females 134; both are therefore very significant statistically, with the females giving results very much more in accord with prediction (significantly so). Why there should be a sex difference is not clear. The authors comment on the results achieved; they believe that a particularly interesting aspect 'of the correspondence between the MMPI and the three personality dimensions is the support it gives Eysenck's dimensional conception of personality. The MMPI was not developed to correspond to Eysenck's personality theory. The actual geometric correspondence between the inventory and the theory suggests that the theory has a reality apart from the test construction skills of the theorist' (p. 419). However that might be, clearly there is considerable agreement between personality and psychiatric symptomatology and both sets of data can be ordered by reference to the same theoretical model.

This conclusion was strengthened in a later paper by the same authors (Wakefield *et al.*, 1975) in which they repeated the same type of analysis on a new sample of 100 adults. The analysis was carried out twice, using the ten clinical scales and the three validity scales of the MMPI, but scoring the scales either for overlapping items only, or for non-overlapping items of each scale only. They argued that if the overlapping items represent valid variances, they must represent variance that the scales containing them share (or in the case of oppositely scored items, variance that is shared negatively). If the overlapping items of two scales represent the shared variance, the unique variance of each scale should be represented by the non-overlapping items. By virtue of their appearing on only one scale, these items must not measure the shared aspects of the criteria employed to select items for the scales. For example, items that are scored for both the Hy and D scales measure some more general factor or trait that includes the criteria for both scales—that is, neurosis or N. Items that appear on only one of these scales do not measure N in general, but rather a particular variation within the general trait. If this argument be accepted, the analysis of the overlapping item scales should confirm, and indeed improve upon, the previous analysis; analysis of the non-overlapping item scales should fail to confirm the previous analysis. In fact, of the 176 distances computed, 141 were in the correct order for the overlapping scales, only 93 (not significantly different from chance) for the non-overlapping scales. This new study therefore strongly confirms, and extends the scope of the previous one; results from the MMPI can be interpreted very clearly in terms of the dimensional model here advocated.

Does the evidence quoted in this chapter enable us to derive any conclusions? Clearly it would be premature to claim that the two main points at issue had found a definitive answer. We believe that the evidence indicates with some force that psychotic and normal states present a continuum, rather than a clear-cut separation between healthy or normal and psychiatrically abnormal, showing all sorts of intermediate variations. We also believe that the evidence indicates with some force that psychotic and neurotic states are not situated along the same continuum, but are independent of each other. These beliefs do not contradict orthodox psychiatric teaching, although they do make an attempt to bring these questions to a sharper point than is customary, in psychiatric writings. Many psychiatrists write at times as if they believed in discontinuity between normal and abnormal and in the relation between neurosis and psychosis, while at other times they write as if they believed the opposite. It is only by stating the issues precisely, and attempting to put them in a quantitative and experimental framework, that we can hope to come to any meaningful conclusion.

When this is done, we see that diverse methods of testing give substantially similar answers. The conclusions from factor analysis result in similar answers to those from discriminant function analysis. Although quite independently conceived and carried out along quite different lines, using different tests, different populations, and different methods of analysis, the work of Cattell and Eysenck, done in different countries, comes to remarkably similar conclusions. Similarly, work in India has replicated work done in the UK and in the USA. In judging the outcome of these studies, the amount of replication and agreement should not be forgotten.

It is of course possible that all the methods used, and all the models put forward, show some common fault or drawback which has not become obvious; such a possibility always exists. However, until such a fault is actually demonstrated mathematically, or until new evidence is brought forward to contradict our conclusion, we believe that the burden of the evidence so far justifies us in believing that the concept of psychoticism has sound backing in so far as the two major premises in question are concerned.

2

The genetic model of psychoticism

Psychiatry began with the concept of the *Einheitspsychose*; that is, of a unitary type of psychotic illness which could take all sorts of forms, but was fundamentally one and the same under all these protean manifestations. Later on, differential diagnosis was based on the concepts of different psychotic syndromes, such as schizophrenia, manic-depressive illness, etc. The question remains whether there is in fact anything common to all psychotic disorders of the functional variety (psychoses caused by obvious physical irritants and stimuli, like senile psychoses, paresis, etc., are clearly irrelevant here). If there is no common ground, then the concept of psychoticism is clearly ruled out of court (as is that of psychosis!). The derivation of the concept from such figures as that illustrating Kretschmer's hypothesis (Figure 1) makes the assumption that because both schizophrenia and manic-depressive disorder are labelled 'psychosis', they must have something in common. This may not be so, of course; it is conceivable that each type of disorder is caused by some quite specific inherited defect, and that these defects show no overlap at all. This problem is crucial to our theory, and this chapter will be devoted to a discussion of the evidence.

Looking first of all at the current position in psychiatry, with particular reference to diagnosis, we would have to conclude that there is very little support for the view of completely separate diseases. There is, as we have already seen, much unreliability in psychiatric diagnosis, particularly *within* the psychotic or neurotic field; there is some reliability *between* these two groups of disorders. Such unreliability extends to changes in diagnosis with time; many patients are re-labelled after a few years of residence in a mental hospital, or on leaving a hospital and re-entering it (or another hospital) after some time. Even more convincing is the work of the UK–US Diagnostic Unit, which has shown that diagnosis in these two countries depends far more on the nationality of the psychiatrist than on the symptomatology of the patient; Americans tend to diagnose five times as many patients as 'schizophrenic' compared with British psychiatrists of comparable experience (Cooper *et al.*, 1972). Many patients who would have been diagnosed as manic-depressive, as endogenous depressive, as personality disorder, or psychopaths in Britain would be diagnosed as schizophrenic in the USA. Such differences in point of view, and such errors on one side or the other, are almost inconceivable if these two sets of disorders are indeed quite separate, having no causal connection at all with each other.

This is not a very strong argument, but it is nevertheless suggestive. All the evidence for the separateness of these two conditions comes essentially from psychiatric diagnosis; if that evidence fails to suggest anything other than relatively close agreement in symptomatology between the two states, and the impossibility of clear distinction, then the alternative view becomes that much more likely. However, much stronger evidence is available from genetic studies, carried out over several decades in the attempt to answer precisely this question, and it is to a consideration of these studies that we must turn next. No effort has been made to cover what is an outstandingly complex and rich literature; it has been reviewed in detail, with many expert discussions, in Kaplan (1972). Other relevant sources are Rosenthal (1970), Reed *et al.* (1973), Shields (1973), and Gottesman and Shields (1972b).

First of all, let us consider certain genetic consequences of the theory of genetic specificity of schizophrenia and contrast them with the consequences expected in terms of the theory of a general factor of psychoticism. Consider, for example, Ödegard's report (1963) on 202 successive patients with psychotic disorders; he found, among the first-degree relatives of his schizophrenics, forty-five schizophrenics, which is expected on the specificity theory, but also forty non-schizophrenic psychoses, which is unexpected and clearly counter to the theory. Already Rüdin (1916) had reported that among the parents of schizophrenic patients there were to be found many manic-depressive patients, and Schulz (1940) who studied fifty-five couples with affective psychosis found among their children a higher incidence of schizophrenia than that reported in all children of parents one of whom was in fact schizophrenic! Misdiagnosis and differential fertility have been suggested as possible reasons for part of these findings. Data from twins tend to support schizophrenic specificity (Kringlen, 1967a,b) although, as Planansky (1966b) points out, 'the twin partner of a typical schizophrenic may develop practically any clinical type of schizophrenic psychosis . . . no documented case of a non-schizophrenic psychosis has been reported'. Atypical psychoses, as studied in detail by Kraulis (1939), led him to the conclusion that when schizophrenia, manic-depressive illness, and atypical psychoses were concentrated in certain families, these psychoses might be considered part of a single, independent syndrome. These studies, and many others of a similar kind reviewed by Planansky (1972), suggest the existence both of specificity and of generality; either theory by itself is supported very strongly, and any realistic model requires to take into account both mechanisms.

The families of schizophrenics not only show an increase in the probability of psychotic, particularly schizophrenic, disorder; but they also show an increased incidence of minor psychosocial defects. Ödegard (1963) reported that relatives of psychotic probands were classified as psychopaths, criminals, or alcoholics in some 10 per cent of all cases. Planansky (1972) comments that: 'It might be tempting to interpret the uniformity as an expression of a biological homogeneity, invoking, perhaps, a polygenic hypothesis. However, a concept of a single genetic mechanism underlying all endogenous psychoses and their associated disorders would lead to the ancient doctrine of single mental disease. Such concept would render the search for genetic specificity redundant, but would also preclude all discovery.'

As we shall see, a proper model based on all the facts need not have such calamitous consequences! Of particular interest in this connection is the close relationship between schizophrenic disorder and psychopathic behaviour: 'The psychopathic personalities are the most persistently reported group among close relatives of schizophrenics; and certain forms of these vaguely defined disorders appear to be, not only structurally, but also developmentally, connected with schizophrenic psychosis.' Planansky traces the history of this association from

Kahlbaum (1890) through Kraepelin (1913) to Delay *et al.* (1957) and Schafer (1951) and summarizes the empirical literature by saying that: 'There is an abundance of reports concerning incidence of schizoid psychopathic personality in families of schizophrenic probands.' Mostly, these studies have started from the psychotic proband (Essen-Möller, 1941; Planansky, 1966b), but of equal interest are studies starting at the other end, using psychopathic probands (Meggendorfer, 1921; Riedel, 1937; Stumpfl, 1935). These studies have dealt with so-called schizoid psychopathic personalities; however, there is also a considerable agglomeration of non-schizoid psychopathic personalities in relatives of schizophrenics (Rüdin, 1916, Medow, 1914). The most important study in this field is Heston's (1966) in which children of schizophrenic mothers were removed immediately after birth and raised by foster parents. Nine out of forty-seven children were diagnosed sociopathic personalities with antisocial behaviour of an impulsive kind, and with long police records. Only four of these forty-seven children developed schizophrenia, demonstrating that the incidence of non-psychotic to psychotic abnormalities is very high in the progeny of schizophrenics, under conditions when direct environmental determination is ruled out. (It should perhaps be added that Heston found other behavioural abnormalities in some twenty additional cases.) Reisby (1967) is another author who found an excess of sociopathic children among the offspring of schizophrenic mothers. Gottesman and Shields (1972a) found an excess of psychopaths among the co-twins of schizophrenic probands.

These findings are of particular interest in view of the close relationship we have found between criminality and high scores on psychoticism (S.B.G. Eysenck and H.J. Eysenck, 1970b); the evidence just cited indicates that, in this respect, hereditary studies of schizophrenia also demonstrate a close relationship between psychosis and criminality. Planansky (1972) summarizes his extensive review by saying: 'Thus, the search for the boundaries of schizophrenic phenotype focused on a minimal but still specific single trait, derived either from the clinical picture of the psychosis, or from a theoretical construct of essential psychopathology, may be in vain. Selection of pathognomonic functions for the detection of minimal, specific psychopathology is difficult, considering that even in frank acute psychotic states, disruption of conceptual thinking, considered exclusive for schizophrenia, was also found in patients with nonschizophrenic diagnoses as well as in some neurotics.'

This conclusion is strongly supported by experimental studies on over-inclusiveness of thinking and retardation (Salzman *et al.*, 1966; Payne and Hewlett, 1960); retardation tests discriminated between schizophrenics and manic-depressives, on the one hand, and between neurotics and normals on the other, suggesting an experimental basis for the general factor of psychoticism; over-inclusiveness strongly characterized some schizophrenics, but by no means all. As the authors say, 'perhaps the most striking fact in the present study is the heterogeneity of the schizophrenic group'. These two findings are supported by many other experimental studies (Eysenck, 1973b).

It is interesting that neurotic disorders, very much required by our dimensional hypothesis, are not imbricated genetically with schizophrenia to any considerable extent; as Planansky (1972) points out, the 'ordinary symptom neuroses seem to occur rarely in the parents of schizophrenics' (Alanen, 1966); Cowie (1961) found no increase in neurotic disorder over the normal in the children of psychotics. These studies, as well as the experimental ones of H.J. Eysenck (1952b, 1955a) and S.B.G. Eysenck (1956a) leave little doubt about the orthogonality of the neurotic and psychotic dimensions.

If we have to conclude from this hurried survey of empirical studies that the evidence favours a general factor of psychoticism, rather than sharply segregated schizophrenic and manic-depressive illnesses, we must add that there is quite strong evidence for the existence of more sharply demarcated subtypes within the schizophrenic diagnosis. Experimental studies such as those of Payne and Hewlett (1960) carry perhaps most conviction, but genetic evidence is also strong (Ödegard, 1963; Kringlen, 1967a,b; Slater, 1947, 1953; Rosenthal, 1963); curiously enough, this does not seem to extend to the level of primary symptoms, e.g. thought disorder. Perhaps a combination of the experimental and the genetic method would give more convincing evidence; thought disorder as clinically assessed tends to be an all-or-none affair rather than a quantitatively graded characteristic, and the inclusion of tests of over-inclusiveness and other modes of thought disorder might help to objectify the assessment.

Our concept of psychoticism probably has most similarity to that of unspecific vulnerability of Welner and Strömgren (1958). Their data, and those of Faergemann (1963), are well in accord with such a notion of a general factor, predisposing persons to psychosis in varying degree, and inherited as a polygenic character; this predisposition would extend into the psychopathic and criminal, antisocial field, but not into that of the dysthymic neuroses. However, it seems likely that this modern version of the *Einheitspsychose* theory may have to be supplemented by a theory of specific genes giving rise to special subvarieties of psychotic behaviour. The evidence does not make it entirely clear whether such subvarieties would be coextensive with such broad categories as schizophrenia and endogenous depression, or whether we should postulate rather a large number of more sharply delineated categories normally subsumed within these great groups of psychotic disorders. Our own preference, based on the existing evidence, is in favour of the latter alternative; but, clearly in the absence of genetic research specifically directed at the solution of this problem, it is impossible to come to any firmly based conclusion. What we think can be said with some confidence is that a general factor of psychoticism, quantitatively varied and strictly independent from the general factor of neuroticism, reconciles many of the reported findings, both from the experimental and from the genetic literature, and is not essentially contradicted by any findings yet recorded.

It might be retorted that the recently established notions of reactive and process types of schizophrenia (translations of the rather older notions of malignant and benign schizophrenia) seem to contradict these conclusions. This is not so; we may point out that there appears to be a marked correlation between this particular continuum (for it is difficult to accept the notion of a categorical distinction) and that of extraversion-introversion (Armstrong *et al.*, 1967). Critics of the dimensional system often fail to realize that, in dealing with a particular axis or factor, all other axes or factors must also be taken into consideration. In saying that two people are both six feet tall, we do not imply that they are also equal in weight or hirsuteness or drinking habits; similarly, two people equal in psychoticism are not therefore equal in neuroticism, extraversion-introversion, or intelligence. These orthogonal factors may determine, to a very marked extent, the particular expression of a person's degree of psychoticism. In any case, as Planansky (1972) points out: "Since no unequivocal correlations could be established to support a genetic division of schizophrenia in relation to the type of onset and characteristics of the preclinical phase, the "reactive-process" classification would hardly describe two biologically different groups, although it may be useful as an empirical means for the prediction of the length of stay in hospital.'

In summary, we may perhaps say why in our view the evidence is so inconclusive, and why such very diverse deductions have been made from it by experienced and well-trained individuals. In the first place, psychiatry has been too slow to divest itself of inappropriate medical, categorical notions of disease entities; as long as we deal with such diagnostic categories which are demonstrably not well matched to the observations made by clinicians and which are notorious for their unreliability, so long will all our studies be saddled from the beginning with an impossibly heavy weight of unnecessary, unrealistic, and invalid preconceptions. If we agree to reject this notion, or at least regard it as an hypothesis to be proved or disproved rather than as a God-given and immovable shibboleth, then we are likely to remove from our research a major stumbling block which has hitherto succeeded in blocking all realistic research in this field.

In the second place, and granted that some model embodying the notion of a continuum rather than of categorical disease entities is preferable, then more attention should be paid to the simple logical and mathematical requirements of such a model; attention has been drawn to some quite elementary faults in the Kretschmer and Jung models, faults which are clearly traceable to the exclusively verbal way in which these and other psychiatric writers treat what are essentially geometrical and topological problems.

In the third place, proper statistical procedures should be employed in deciding factual questions of this kind, i.e. both the continuum/category and the 'number of continua needed' problem. Criterion analysis, discriminant function analysis, and factor analysis are all available for use, instead of the customary 'clinical' type of survey, whose subjectivity and lack of validity have so often led to contradictory and inconclusive results. The proper task of the clinician is clinical work; research requires more objective methods of quantification and of proof, transcending those which may suffice for purely clinical purposes.

In the fourth place, there has been a tendency in psychiatric work to disregard not only statistical methods of analysis, but also psychological methods of data gathering. Subjectivity of data processing has been compounded by subjectivity of data collection; reliance has too often been placed on such methods as the interview, in spite of its notorious fallibility, and on devices elaborated on an interpretive basis, such as the Rorschach and the TAT test, in spite of their known lack of reliability and validity (Zubin *et al.*, 1965). Until the data collected are of an objective nature, replication of research will not in the nature of things be possible, and we will continue to be beset by contradictory and meaningless results.

In the fifth place, even when objective laboratory tests are used, their choice is only too often arbitrary and almost accidental. It is suggested that the choice of such tests, whether psychological (such as tests of eye-blink conditioning, vigilance, or sensory thresholds) or physiological (such as tests of sedation thresholds, autonomic arousal, or habituation) should be in terms of quite specific theories, and such tests should be used within the context of the hypothetico-deductive method.

In the sixth place, we would draw attention to the possibilities opened up by the use of the continuum hypotheses and objective, experimental tests of applying the new and very powerful methods of biometrical genetics. It also becomes possible in this way to get away from the use of inpatients in psychiatric hospitals (on whom most of the work reviewed in this book is based) and to extend genetic studies to non-patients. The advantages of such an extension are very great; not only do they allow us to use much more refined and rigorous statistical methods of genetic analysis, but also they get rid, once and for all, of the curious and too little considered errors of sampling involved in dealing with mental patients. The selection of such patients introduces factors which are largely unknown and which cannot easily be controlled (if at all); it is well known how selection can distort existing relations, and create non-existing ones. It is not of course suggested that we give up the study of patients; it is merely suggested that this might be supplemented by the study of non-patients differing in degree of psychoticism, neuroticism, and extraversion-introversion.

It is our belief that the existing evidence, unsatisfactory and partial as it is, is converging on to some kind of dimensional system of the kind posited, and that such a scheme, buttressed by some rather specific hereditary factors responsible for specific symptom-sets, is adequate to represent a large mass of data collected in a great variety of different circumstances, different countries, using different methods, and by different people. We do not believe that the same could be said of

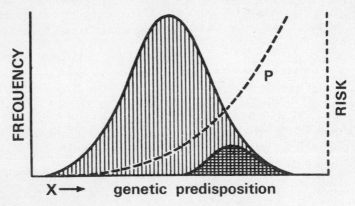

X   Genetic predisposition

|||| Frequency distribution in the population

P   Likelihood of being affected at a particular level of x

▦   Frequency distribution of affected individuals

Figure 13   Model of the diathesis-stress theory of psychiatric disorder—the Edwards (1969) model (from Shields, 1971)*

*One of the reasons for psychiatric misdiagnosis, or unreliability of diagnosis, is not so much that cases are erroneously assigned to the wrong dimension, but rather that arbitrary standards are applied as to the cut-off point along a dimension. Thus the difference between 'schizophrenia' and 'schizoid state' along the abscissa in our Figure is quantitative, and the common practice of using qualitative terms to make out an arbitrary point of division almost ensures the kind of unreliability in diagnosis which is in fact found. Shields and Gottesman (1971) have shown by having case histories classified by different, experienced judges, that the major difference between them was the broadness or narrowness of their concept of schizophrenia; it seems to make much more sense psychometrically to ask judges to locate each case along a continuum, i.e. rate it in terms of *degree* of psychoticism, rather than to ask them to make a categorical judgement.

any other scheme currently available, largely because their authors tend to restrict themselves to certain parts of the evidence and leave out of account other parts which would not be easy to get into their schemes. Most frequently omitted are psychological studies, particularly those using objective measures; also frequently omitted are animal studies, such as those demonstrating the inheritance of autonomic arousal differences (Eysenck and Broadhurst, 1964). It seems unfortunate that it is precisely the most reliable and valid studies which suffer this fate; their occasional lack of 'face validity' should not deter the seeker after truth from considering the potential contribution which they can make to the general problem discussed in this book.

Our model seems most closely related to models proposed by Ödegard (1972) and by Shields (1971) and Gottesman and Shields (1972a, b, 1973). Shields quotes a figure, reproduced as Figure 13, which illustrates both his and our own theory. The base line represents the genotype of our concept of P; the size of the shaded area is determined by the frequency of the condition in the population. The distribution need not be normal, of course, but has been drawn like this for purposes of illustration. Those affected will vary in their genetic predisposition; in the population as a whole the majority will have a negligible risk of actually developing psychotic disorders, while a few are almost destined to do so. The actual state of psychotic disorder is of course only partly determined by genetic predisposition (probably to the extent of 60 per cent of the total variance); there is a powerful environmental component. Thus this theory is often known as the diathesis-stress theory, giving pride of place to genetic predisposition, but also recognizing the importance of environmental stress.

The genetic predisposition not manifested in actual disease, i.e. that part of the figure, not cross-hatched, would correspond to P, except that P inevitably measures the phenotype, and is thus only partly and indirectly related to the genotype. It is possible that the correlation between genotype and phenotype is stronger for the personality concept P than for the psychiatric disorder of psychosis, for the simple reason that the stress component which transforms the predisposition into an actual breakdown in the latter plays little part in the former; however, this is of course a matter for research, and cannot necessarily be assumed to be true. (Our own work, to be reviewed in a later chapter, suggests a heritability of .81 for P.)

Next to the cross-hatched group of actual psychoses in the Figure would come individuals who carry a diathesis for mental illness by virtue of being the identical or fraternal twins of schizophrenics, or their parents or children, but who nevertheless have escaped developing such an illness themselves. A large number of writers have shown that quite frequently (certainly much more frequently than would be expected by chance) such individuals develop so-called 'schizoid states', disorders of conduct, psychopathic or criminal behaviour, or neurotic symptoms of one kind or another (Bleuler, 1931; Cadoret, 1973; Essen-Möller, 1941; Hoffmann, 1921; Inoue, 1970; Kahn, 1923; Kallmann, 1938; Kringlen, 1967 a,b; Mosher *et al.*, 1971; Rosenthal and Van Dyke, 1970; Slater, 1953; Tienari, 1963). Cadoret (1973), who has reviewed these studies, concludes that 'monozygotic twins discordant for schizophrenia were found to have a high proportion of individuals with significant character abnormalities or neurotic symptoms. . . .A comparison of families of nuclear schizophrenic probands and schizophreniform probands showed that character abnormalities seemed to be more associated with nuclear schizophrenia' (p.684). Similarly, Mednick *et al.* (1974), who studied over two hundred

Danish school children who had a high risk of becoming schizophrenic, found not only that many of these developed mental illness, but also that a sizeable subgroup had evidenced antisocial behaviour. We thus have a second criterion group (in addition to manifest psychotics), namely character disorders, psychopaths and sociopaths, and some kinds of criminals; these would be adjacent (in theory at least) to the individuals in the cross-hatched group of psychotics in the diagram.

Such a group has been called (by Kety *et al.*, 1968) 'schizophrenia spectrum disorders'. In their studies of the relatives of schizophrenic adoptees, they found that the excess of abnormality in biological parents and half-siblings was not one of schizophrenia, but rather inadequate, borderline schizophrenic conditions, etc. Among the parents there was an excess of criminality and character disorders, which were called 'extended spectrum disorders'. As Shields and Gottesman (1973) point out, 'although it may well be that some persons with a general predisposition to schizophrenia may also be prone to develop social problems and character disorders, it would be misleading to consider all delinquents as suffering from schizophrenia spectrum disorder, or the genetic predisposition to schizophrenia to be no different from that to delinquency' (p.169). We shall consider the relation between criminality and P later on; as we shall see, there is certainly a fairly close relationship, but no identity. There are several other studies giving results similar to those of Kety *et al.* (1968), i.e. indicating marked abnormalities in adoptees from psychiatrically disturbed biological parents. Among these studies, particular interest attaches to those by Bohman (1972), Cunningham *et al.* (1975), Goodman *et al.* (1963), Hutchings and Mednick (1973), Offord *et al.* (1969), and Rosenthal *et al.* (1968). These studies are as important as twin studies in revealing the importance of genetic factors in a broad-spectrum psychotic disability.

Of particular interest is the most recent of this series of studies, reported by Stephens *et al.* (1975) and Kay *et al.* (1975). In their papers, they compare the psychiatric morbidity occurring in the close relatives ($n = 332$) of patients showing nuclear forms of schizophrenia with that of a control group ($n = 201$), and consider their findings in relation to the concept of the schizophrenic 'spectrum'. They conclude that the 'spectrum disorders' most likely to be biologically related to schizophrenia are personality disorders of non-neurotic type; they also conclude that their results do not fit in well with models of dominant inheritance of schizophrenia, mediated by a single major gene. They attribute the excess of personality disorders and heavy drinking in the families of schizophrenics to a combination of polygenic inheritance and environmental influences. It is interesting that while both schizophrenia and non-neurotic personality disorders were more common in the parents and sibs of schizophrenics than in the controls, neurosis was in fact less common. This lends support to our separation of the neurotic from the psychotic continuum. The authors conclude that 'the nearest it is possible to get at present to identifying those cases related to schizophrenia among all other conditions is through the presence of the non-neurotic personality disorder. This group of disorders, though itself somewhat heterogeneous, is one most strongly associated with schizophrenia in our material, and appears most likely to be biologically related to schizophrenia' (p.107). This grouping of psychopathic, antisocial conduct with schizophrenia is very much in line with our general theory.

It will have been noted that we have used work on schizophrenia in most of the foregoing discussion, rather than work on manic-depressive illness; the main reason for this has been, of course, that far more work has been done on the former illness.

Another important factor has been the continuing argument as to whether psychotic (endogenous) depression could be validly distinguished from neurotic (exogenous) depression (Lewis, 1934). Most modern work suggests that such a differentiation is indeed required by the data (Eysenck, 1970c; Kendell and Gourlay, 1970; Kiloh and Garside, 1965; McConaghy, Joffe and Murphy, 1967; Spicer *et al.*, 1973). This would range endogenous depression clearly with psychosis, exogenous (reactive) depression with neurosis. Unfortunately the diagnosis presents many difficulties, and in addition many psychiatrists are still not convinced by the arguments brought forward, and refuse to make such a distinction. Some psychiatrists, when asked to make the distinction, go by severity of illness rather than by the criteria worked out by Kiloh and Garside (1965) and others, thus hopelessly confusing the issue. Furthermore, as we have already noted, American psychiatrists subsume most of what would be diagnosed as endogenous depression in the US under the all-inclusive term 'schizophrenia'. For all these reasons our concept of P probably comes closer to schizophrenia than to endogenous depression; it finds its closest analogue in the American concept of schizophrenia. In England, we would probably have to combine schizophrenia and endogenous depression diagnosed according to the criteria mentioned above, to find the group of patients characterizing the extreme of our P dimension. Further work on this point is required before we can be sure of our ground, although some studies, to be discussed later, suggest that this suggestion has some basis in fact. Certainly the observation that schizophrenic probands in addition to significantly more numerous schizophrenic relatives, also have significantly more relatives suffering from other psychoses (Karlsson, 1973) suggests that our hypothesis is not without support.* For the purpose of this book we shall include it as part of our general theory, and see later on how our measure of P groups schizophrenic and manic-depressive patients.

Our theory concerning the genetic model of psychosis is probably closest to that adopted by Gottesman and Shields (1972 a,b) for schizophrenia. We have already explained why we believe that the concept of 'psychoticism' can and should be extended beyond schizophrenia to include other forms of psychosis, but this is not an essential part of our theory; it would be quite possible to restate it in terms of the broader conception of schizophrenia current in the USA, taken together with the postulates of schizophreniform psychoses and schizoid states. This conception would include many of the affective psychoses, endogenous depressions and manic-depressive diagnoses used in the UK. We have cited empirical support for our more inclusive view, but if this should prove too broad on genetic grounds the more restricted view would of course have to be adopted, possibly with a renaming of the factor to indicate this restriction. This whole question is probably at the moment insoluble, and discussions concerned with it are largely verbal arguments about the use of words; our concept will have to be defined in operational terms to be of any

---

*There are of course many odd observations which are difficult to reconcile with any particular hypothesis about the relation of the major functional psychoses. Thus Powell *et al.* (1973) found that while manic-depressive parents had both manic-depressive and schizophrenic children (in the ratio of 2:3!), schizophrenic parents had no manic-depressive children, only schizophrenic ones. It is possible to postulate reasons for this odd state of affairs, but none of these are convincing at the moment. On the other hand, concordance studies (e.g. Elston *et al.*, 1973) of DZ psychotic twins show much greater concordance for 'any psychosis' than for schizophrenia specifically (44% *vs.* 10% on personal inverview); this speaks strongly for our view.

theoretical and practical use, and for the time being we do not feel that the evidence is strong enough to exclude non-schizophrenic psychoses of the kind indicated from our genetic circle of psychotic disorders.

While we support a polygenic theory of psychosis, we do not feel that the two alternative theories held by recognized workers in the field (monogenic and heterogenic theories) could not be made to fit the data by suitable modifications. Monogenic theories (Slater, 1958; Slater and Cowie, 1971) clearly require major additional hypotheses (lowered penetrance, the existence of potentiators or modifiers, themselves probably genetic in nature, etc.) which effectively translate such a theory into a polygenic one (particularly if the polygenic theory postulates major single-gene effects). Genetic heterogeneity theories come in many different forms; one such model which would not essentially differ from that indicated by the facts would postulate a small percentage of clinical cases produced by different dominant and recessive loci, another larger set due to symptomatic phenocopies, with the great majority segregants in a normal distribution of psychotic diathesis. Granted, then, that these alternative theories could be fitted to the data by major surgery, we still feel that a polygenic theory fits the bill with the least amount of change.

Gottesman and Shields (1972 a,b) point out that polygenic models can be divided into two groups: those postulating continuous phenotypic variation, and dependent on a large number of underlying genes all of whose effects are equal (or roughly so); and those postulating quasi-continuous variation and/or threshold effects (Thoday, 1961, 1967). They seem to favour the latter alternative: 'encouraged by the demonstration that the genes in polygenic inheritance need not be and often are not roughly equal in their effects on the phenotype, and bolstered by our clinical observations on what appears to be "excess" similarity between pairs of affected relatives on the simpler equal effects assumption, we hazard the speculation that there are a few genes of large effect in the polygenic system underlying many schizophrenias. In other words, we view the etiology of schizophrenia as being due to a weighted kind of polygenic system with a threshold effect. Some of the heuristic implications of our speculations about high-value genes in the polygenic system underlying schizophrenia include a focusing on partitionable facets of the syndrome such as catatonia, paranoid features, protein polymorphisms in brain and blood, and neurophysiology, on the chance that family studies will reveal one or more of the high-value genes' (p.331). This view is remarkably similar to that presented by Eysenck (1972a), based on much the same reasoning, but in ignorance of the additional material presented later by Gottesman and Shields in their monumental study. (See also Kringlen, 1967 a,b, 1968, on the degree of association of the specific form of illness between proband and co-twin.) We would thus be dealing with a large number of roughly equal genes producing what we have called 'psychoticism', or what Gottesman and Shields would probably call 'schizotype'; in addition there would be major genes dictating the form of schizophrenic breakdown (in their scheme) and additionally the possibility of endogenous depressive breakdown (in our scheme).* It is perhaps obvious that

*It would be quite wrong to suppose that general schizophrenia, and the various major forms of symptomatology, are culture-specific, and in some way due to environmental pressures characteristic of certain countries or socio-economic regimes. Lin and Sartorius (1974) have shown that very similar syndromes are found in nine countries highly differentiated in cultural and socio-economic background.

while these speculations are based on a large supply of empirical fact, they cannot at the present time be disproved nor can alternative theories be ruled out. This need not prevent us from having a theoretical model in mind to direct further research; it should prevent us from taking the correctness of the model for granted.

One important direction which such research might take is in relation to the previous personality of schizophrenics, i.e. before their psychotic breakdown. Gottesman and Shields (1972 a,b) found that in their work 'the previous personality of a schizophrenic is not always obviously schizoid'. (See also Bleuler, 1911; Slater and Roth, 1969.) They go on to argue that 'if we accept the genetic factors in schizophrenia and assume that they are similar in most cases, the observation suggests that it is not merely a tendency to be schizoid that is inherited and in some way causally related to schizophrenia, but something more besides. In addition it suggests that not all genes get "switched on" until certain psychosomatic states are reached. The schizoid personality is clearly an important contributory factor; and, however central to or independent of the main diathesis we may regard it, it is one which is probably under considerable genetic control' (p.251). This notion of 'schizoid personality' corresponds quite well with our concept of 'psychoticism', and accordingly would embody the general level of polymorphic genes of small value, superimposed on which would be the one (or more) genes of large effect. MMPI data given by Gottesman and Shields (1972 a,b) also suggest the similarity of the 'schizoid state' to full-blown psychosis, but at a lower level of elevation of the relevant scales.

We may summarize the main points of our hypothesis, in somewhat simplified form. We postulate that there is a polygenic personality trait, psychoticism, largely composed of genes of small value whose actions are additive, $g_a, g_b, g_c, \ldots g_n$. The number of active genes determines the degree of psychoticism which a person demonstrates, in interaction with environmental factors not yet discovered. These polygenic constituents make up the abscissa of our Figure 13 and determine the probability, p, of being affected by a psychotic illness. In addition we have a small number of genes of large effect, $g_A, g_B, g_C \ldots$ which may or may not be present to add to the sum of the genes of small value, and which, if present, determine the precise nature of the disorder—catatonia, paranoia, hebephrenia, simple schizophrenia, and possibly manic-depressive psychosis, monopolar depression, etc. A person who has a large number of genes of small value, but none of the genes of large effect, would be psychotic without demonstrating any of the classical syndromes; such persons may indeed be in the majority and create the well-known difficulties in diagnosis of sub-varieties of psychosis. When the number of genes of small value is less than that required for a proper psychosis to develop, or when external stress has not been sufficient to provide for effective interaction in producing this state, we have individuals demonstrating varying degrees of 'schizoid state' or schizotype—psychopaths, sociopaths, criminals, drug addicts, etc. When genes of large effect are present (usually only one) we get the classical pictures discussed in textbooks of psychiatry, provided there is a sufficient number of genes of small value to push the individual sufficiently far along the abscissa in our Figure. In the absence of sufficient numbers of such genes, or in the absence of an external event of sufficient stress value, we would obtain a non-psychotic individual with behavioural symptoms reminiscent of paranoia or some other sub-variety of psychosis (suspicious, hostile, etc.), but at a sub-clinical level. We believe that this theory accounts for all the well-documented facts in this field, and combines the advantages of several of the classical theories. As pointed out before, this does not guarantee its correctness, but may entitle it to serious consideration.

The general hypothesis here put forward may account for one of the puzzles of genetic explanations of schizophrenic disorders. Given the manifestation rate of schizophrenia in the population, and also the reduced fertility of the schizophrenic patient, how can we explain the fact that the disorder remains so common without postulating an unlikely mutation rate? Huxley *et al.* (1964) have suggested that the schizophrenic genotype may carry with it certain biological advantages, such as for instance an increased immunity against virological invasion, and Carter and Watts (1971) have recently obtained support for this view by demonstrating significantly reduced incidence of accidents and viral infections in schizophrenics' relatives. However, it does not seem likely that these factors are able to carry the whole burden, and it may very well be that there are certain psychological characteristics which have biological utility and which also form part of the general psychoticism factor postulated in our theory. Thus the schizophrenic genotype would be maintained by biologically advantaged high P scorers, even though excessively high P, manifested in psychosis, is biologically disadvantageous. This view has been argued forcefully by Claridge (1972), and it finds some support in the psychological literature.

Claridge postulates that the characteristics in question may have something to do with cognitive and selective attentional aspects of behaviour, 'seen at the psychological level as styles of thinking in the normal individual and as thought disorder in the schizophrenic patient. Like anxiety, such behaviour clearly has important survival value during the evolution of man, though, again like anxiety, perhaps only at certain optimum levels' (p. 5).

Essentially, what is being postulated is some form of the theory often quoted by reference to Dryden's deplorable rhyming couplet from *Absalom and Achitophel*:

'Great wits are sure to madness near allied,
And thin partitions do their bounds divide.'

In other words, there are certain 'cognitive styles' and other types of thought processes which characterize high P scorers; these are advantageous in non-clinical form, but become disadvantageous when carried beyond a certain point, issuing finally in schizophrenic thought disorder. Such a view of creativity and originality being allied with madness goes back to Aristotle, who pointed out that 'famous poets, artists and statesmen often suffer from depression or insanity, as for example Ajax; in more recent times such tendencies are found in Socrates, Empedocles, Plato and many others, particularly among the poets'. Seneca also expressed the same thought: 'Non est magnum ingenium sine mixtura dementiae.' Later, the French encyclopaedist Diderot expressed the view that genius and insanity touched each other in the personalities of great men: 'the one is incarcerated and put in chains, the other has monuments erected to him'. Schopenhauer, the famous German philosopher, also pointed out that 'genius is closer to insanity than to the average type of intelligence'. A detailed discussion of the frequency of clear mental pathology in great poets, artists, statesmen and other 'geniuses' is given by

Kretschmer (1929); there seems little doubt about the reality of some such connection.*

Systematic study of the problem would, of course, be more impressive than anecdote; unfortunately there has not been very much of this. Ellis (1904) found that of 1,030 people selected from the Dictionary of National Biography 4.2 per cent were demonstrably insane; this is a rather higher percentage than would be expected, particularly when one considers the extreme burden which manifest insanity would impose on anyone aspiring to become sufficiently famous to be included in the Dictionary. Juda (1953) investigated the lives and medical histories of 113 artists and 181 men of science, chosen by experts in their fields of achievement. She found psychosis in 4.8 per cent of the scientists, and in 4.0 per cent of the artists. These figures resemble Ellis's, and are in excess of the population figures. What is of particular interest, however, is the extraordinary number of psychopathic personalities in both groups—27.3 per cent among the scientists, 19.4 per cent among the artists! These psychopaths were usually of the schizoid type, rather than secondary psychopaths; in other words, they would be classified among the schizophrenic *Erbkreis* group. These results prove little, other than that many, or even most, of the people who show high achievement in art and the sciences are reasonably 'normal'. However, most of the probands were first-class scientists and artists, not in the 'genius' class. It might be thought that the slight excess of psychotics, and the large percentage of psychopaths, suggest a definite admixture of P in this group, with explicit psychotic behaviour reducing the chances of the person so afflicted from achieving the success that might have been compatible with his abilities. Pickering (1975), from his analysis of the data, suggests that 'a psychological illness may appear to increase the range of association of ideas. . . On the other hand, a disturbance of the mind is in no way associated with wisdom, the ability to make a sensible choice' (p.297). Storr (1972) goes a little further, and suggests that many creative people have a schizoid character. These various views are certainly tenable as suggesting a testable hypothesis, even though they cannot be regarded as proven.

However well supported, such historical studies do not constitute proper evidence for our hypothesis. There are, however, more recent formal studies of the problem. Claridge has divided these into two main groups.

The first group in question is concerned with the relationship between creativity and personality traits in psychiatrically normal individuals. A distinction is often made in recent work between the classical 'convergent' type of problem solving widely used in IQ tests, and the 'divergent' type of thinking required to solve problems of an open-ended kind (even though, of course, these two abilities are by no means entirely separate, but correlate quite highly). Creativity, which is believed to be measurable by means of such divergent tests, is conceived as involving the ability to take conceptual leaps in the face of minimal information, to see remote connections between apparently unrelated items, and to retain a flexible approach in the solution of problems. When we look at the personality characteristics of

---

*If there is anything in this notion, then one would expect that the frequent association between schizophrenia and low intelligence could not be due to genetic causes. Jones and Offord (1975) have shown that IQ and schizophrenia are independently transmitted, using a comparison of proband-sibling and within-sibling IQ correlation as their methodological tool; they found little difference, both correlations being similar to those usually found for sibling-sibling correlations.

persons judged to be high in creative talent, both in the arts and sciences, we find that such people differ in certain important respects from the general population, and that they resemble psychotic individuals in some ways.

The only study which includes P as a variable directly is one by Farmer (1974). Using forty students as his sample, Farmer also administered a battery of divergent-thinking tests, and factor analysed the resulting matrix of intercorrelations; also included in the matrix were scores on E, N, L and Little's Person Orientation index, which on *a priori* grounds was thought to be opposed to P. The divergent-thinking tests fell into two main groups, 'fluency' and 'originality'. On the 'fluency' factor, P had only a small loading of .24. On the 'originality' factor, P had a loading of .74, and Personal Orientation a loading of −.66. Thus there is here some evidence that originality (as defined by the tests used) is indeed correlated with P. The number of cases involved is too small to allow us to consider this experiment more than suggestive, but it will be seen to align well with other evidence to be considered presently. In these other studies, unfortunately, no tests of psychoticism were used.

MacKinnon (1962) used the MMPI on a group of architects and found not only that all the scales were elevated to a varying degree, but also that there was a small but positive correlation between rated creativity and Sc (schizophrenia) and Pd (psychopathic deviate). In another study of architects, MacKinnon contrasted the performance on a word-association test of a group judged by other architects to be exceptionally original and creative in their work, and another group judged to be more orthodox; both groups were of equal standing professionally. The original architects had far more unusual responses; in fact, the only group tested by MacKinnon which had more unusual responses was a group of schizophrenics!*

Cattell and Butcher (1968) and Cattell and Drevdahl (1955) found a group of eminent research scientists significantly sizothymic (withdrawn), emotionally unstable, self-sufficient, and bohemian; Drevdahl (1956) found that some of these traits also differentiated creative and non-creative students. Cross *et al.* (1967) obtained similar results, contrasting artists with controls; in particular, the artists were low on emotional stability and super ego strength, and especially high in autistic and bohemian tendencies. Using the same scales, McAllister (1968) found that psychotics deviated strongly from controls in sizothymia and autistic tendency. The main difference between the groups appeared to lie in intelligence, with the psychotics low and the artists and scientists high: 'This finding accords well with the conclusion reached by most workers who have examined the trait characteristics of creative thinkers; namely, that while such people emerge as unusual individuals they almost always show the strong intellectual and emotional controls indicative of the integrated personality. Nevertheless, it is of interest that the traits on which the creative thinker does appear to deviate from average are precisely those which, within the range of normal variation, may reflect an increased loading on an underlying personality factor associated with schizophrenia' (p. 6).

---

*This argument makes the implicit assumption that unusual associations are evidence of disturbance of associative ability; this may not be the correct interpretation as far as schizophrenics are concerned. Moon *et al.* (1968) have shown that schizophrenics tend to mishear the stimulus word much more frequently than do normal controls; when this mishearing is controlled for, the difference in remote associations between the groups ceases to be significant. Frequent mishearing in turn may be due to lapses in attention; this too is a well-known symptom of schizophrenia.

One interesting and possibly relevant point relates to age changes. As we shall see later on, P declines with age; if there is any special relationship between P and originality, then we should expect a similar decline in originality with age. There is some evidence from the work of Bromley (1956, 1957), Feifel (1949), Gorham (1956), Yacorzynski (1941) and others that flexibility in assessing different categories of information declines somewhat with age in adulthood (Horn, 1975). This is an important aspect of creativity and originality.

The first group of studies relating schizophrenia and certain 'cognitive style' characteristics of normal persons of known originality or creativity thus lends some support to the notion that high P scorers may possess abilities which are of general use and have survival value. The second group of studies providing some evidence for a continuity between normal and pathological thinking has focused on thought disorder itself. It is suggested that the cognitive style that characterizes the creative process may have similarities to the characteristic loosening of ideational boundaries found in schizophrenia. This has been described as long ago as 1911 by Bleuler, and is now often investigated under the heading of 'over-inclusiveness' (Payne and Hewlett, 1960). As Claridge (1972) points out, it scarcely requires a conceptual leap to see the schizophrenic's tendency to follow irrelevant themes in his stream of thought as an extreme example of divergent thinking, the main difference being that in one case it is an uncontrolled activity and in the other a rationally directed one (p.6).

Studies related to this hypothesis have attempted to find evidence of thought disorder in individuals who are considered genetically predisposed to schizophrenia. Rapaport (1945) showed, for instance, that loosened thinking, as measured by an object-sorting test, was characteristic of pre-schizophrenic patients and non-psychotic subjects judged to be of schizoid personality (high P?). Others, such as McConaghy (1959, 1960), have concentrated in their work on individuals whose predisposition to psychosis could be presumed from the fact that they had a schizophrenic relative. Using an object-sorting test, this author demonstrated a significant degree of allusive thinking (a term he prefers over the more commonly used one of over-inclusiveness) in the parents of schizophrenics. Lidz *et al.* (1963) and Rosman *et al.* (1964) have replicated his results, and Phillips *et al.* (1965) and Romney (1969) have reported that siblings as well as parents of schizophrenics had abnormal scores on tests of thought disorder. Mednick and Schulsinger (1968) provided further confirmatory evidence in their work on children of schizophrenic mothers who, compared with matched controls, showed evidence of loosened thinking, and a high frequency of idiosyncratic responses on continuous association tests.

Claridge (1972) quotes an unpublished study by one of his students, which demonstrates that creative artists tended to produce a high number of unusual sortings, indicative of over-inclusion, on an object classification test; as a group these artists fell between a normal control group and a group of schizophrenic patients. McConaghy and Clancy (1968) found allusive thinking in students to be correlated with allusive thinking in their parents; they also argue that modes of abstraction seen in psychosis are also found generally in the population, that they may be characteristic of creative thinking, and that consequently they may indicate some biological advantage of the schizophrenic genotype.

None of the studies quoted would, in isolation, furnish much proof for the hypothesis of continuity in thinking style between normals and psychotics, and for

33

the additional hypothesis that such styles, found in high P individuals, might be biologically advantageous; when taken together they are at least suggestive that some such generalization might be defensible. The point is not a crucial one for our more general thesis, but we believe that it adds considerably to the meaningfulness and acceptability of the theory.

While thinking styles might be important in giving some biological advantage to high P scorers, it is even more likely that the personality characteristics of the high P scorer may also play a part. The impersonal, egocentric, self-contained personality that emerges from our questionnaires would seem to be exceptionally well positioned to look after himself in our type of society—or indeed, in most other types of society of which we have knowledge. Kipling's famous lines would seem to be appropriate here:

'From the depth of Gehennah to the steps of the throne,
He travels fastest who travels alone.'

This could have been written with the high P scorer in mind! Here again, biographies of famous men often suggest personality characteristics of the kind mentioned; they resemble schizophrenics not only in cognitive style, but also in life style.* It would take us too far to try and document this point in detail, and in any case this view is only advanced as an hypothesis which might account for the observed prevalence of psychotic, especially schizophrenic disorder. Even if closer examination should find this relationship between genius and madness to be mistaken, either in relation to mode of thinking or mode of living, or both, this would not detract from our major theoretical contribution.

---

*It seems quite possible that a person characterized by high originality would require a high P type of personality in order to achieve recognition for his unorthodox ideas. In a world of 'normal science' (to use Kuhn's phrase), the original scientist is bound to have difficulties in gaining adherents for his 'scientific revolution'. Much the same is almost certainly true in 'normal music', or 'normal art', or 'normal architecture'. The possible conjunction of the intellectual style and the personality qualities here posited for the high P scorer may be the outcome of a long history of evolutionary development.

3

The construction of the P scale: Methodology

In this chapter we shall be dealing with methodological problems in the construction of the P scale. Before turning to the actual psychometric procedures used, and their results, it may be useful as a preliminary to discuss briefly what such a scale is intended to be and do, as well as what it is not intended to be and do. In our experience, misunderstandings as to the purpose of scales such as these are rife, particularly among psychiatrists, and clarification may be in order.

It is important to realize that our scales are *not* intended primarily to be used for the purpose of psychiatric classification and diagnosis. There are many reasons for this decision. In the first place, we do not regard the present psychiatric system of diagnosis and classification as possessing any scientific validity; reasons for this view (which we believe would be widely shared by psychiatrists themselves) have been given elsewhere (H.J. Eysenck, 1960). The system is retained for heuristic reasons purely; no underlying theory is postulated, or accepted, by psychiatrists. Such a system, lacking scientific status, cannot provide a useful criterion for the scales designed by proper use of psychometric procedures, and measuring variables having a reasonable theoretical basis. It may be of interest to see what amount of agreement there might be between the two systems, and certain deductions from our theory can be tested with reference to psychiatric groups, but in essence the psychiatric system, being based on categorical discrimination between more or less homogeneous groups, is only partly compatible with the continuous, dimensional system on which our scale construction is predicated.

Even if the psychiatric system were scientifically acceptable, and valid in its application to patients, its lack of reliability would be unacceptable for any serious scientific (research) or applied purposes. A few references to document this assertion have already been quoted; to these might be added many more, such as Ash (1949), Beck *et al.* (1962), Foulds (1955), Mehlman (1952), Sandifer *et al.* (1968), Schmidt and Fonda (1956), Seeman (1953), and Zubin (1967). These studies show poor reliability from one psychiatrist to another; but even when we compare the performance of a psychiatric team in this respect (perhaps more normal under actual clinical conditions), results are far from good. Hunt, Wiltson and Hunt (1953) compared broad diagnoses (neurosis, psychosis, personality disorder were the three categories used) of 681 neuropsychiatric patients diagnosed at two separate institutions. The 54 per cent agreement found is better than chance (which would be approximately 33 per cent), but, as the writers conclude: 'On any absolute evaluative scale. . .this reliability certainly cannot be considered either high or satisfactory' (p. 60).

Follow-up studies show considerable change in diagnosis; Rennie (1953) found that in a twenty-year follow-up study of 200 neurotic patients, approximately 14

35

per cent of the diagnoses had changed from 'neurotic' to 'psychotic'. Others have found even greater change after shorter lapses of time: Masserman and Carmichael (1938) found a change of 25 per cent, for instance. Such changes do not inspire confidence in the reliability of the diagnosis.

In view of the comparisons to be made later between scale and diagnosis, it may be useful to give some slightly more meaningful estimates of the reliability of psychiatric diagnosis in respect to different types of disorder. Spitzer and Fleiss (1974) have re-analysed several previous studies, using as their main statistic the kappa coefficient (Cohen, 1960; Fleiss and Cohen, 1973; Light, 1971). This statistic measures agreement on nominal categories and incorporates a correction for chance; it contrasts the observed proportion of agreement with the proportion expected by chance alone. Kappa may be interpreted as an intra-class correlation coefficient, ranging from 0 (for no agreement extra chance) to 1.0 for perfect agreement. Looking only at those categories which will concern us, we find kappa values, averaged over all the studies surveyed, as shown in Table 2. As the authors remark, 'there are no diagnostic categories for which reliability is uniformly high. Reliability appears to be only satisfactory for three categories: mental deficiency, organic brain syndrome. . .and alcoholism [these three diagnoses are of no concern to us, and have been omitted from the Table]. The level of reliability is no better than fair for psychosis and schizophrenia and is poor for the remaining categories' (p. 344).

TABLE 2   Reliability of psychiatric diagnoses (after Spitzer and Fleiss, 1974)

Disorder (Psychiatric Diagnosis)	Mean Kappa Value
Psychosis	.55
Schizophrenia	.57
Endogenous depression	.24
Manic-depressive illness	.33
Neurosis	.40
Reactive depression	.26
Personality disorder	.32
Anxiety reaction	.45

Spitzer and Fleiss go on to say that, with one exception, 'all the studies summarized here involved diagnosticians of similar background and training. In addition, special efforts were made in some of the studies to have the participant diagnosticians come to some agreement on diagnostic principles prior to the beginning of the study. One would have expected these features of similar background and prior consensus on principles to contribute to good reliability. One can only assume, therefore, that agreement between heterogenous diagnosticians of different orientations and backgrounds, as they act in routine clinical settings, is even poorer than is indicated. . . Further, there appears to have been no essential change in diagnostic reliability over time' (p. 344). We believe that further documentation of our contention would be supererogatory.

Our third reason for not regarding psychiatric classification and diagnosis as the primary area of usefulness of our scales is that even if such a venture fulfilled any useful purpose (which we doubt), it could in the nature of the case only give predictions even lower than the reliabilities indicated in Table 2. An indication of the best that could be achieved, using an inventory concentrating on psychiatric symptoms, and exhaustively validated and constructed with the express purpose of predicting psychiatric diagnosis, is given in a study by Goldberg, using the MMPI (1965). In this study, twenty-nine clinical expert judges made diagnostic judgements for each of 861 MMPI profiles along a neurotic–psychotic continuum, i.e. using a criterion that would be considerably easier to predict than detailed diagnosis. Also used were a variety of actuarial indices, made up of different combinations of scales from the MMPI. The average validity of the clinical judges, under these conditions, was .28; the best of the actuarial indices achieved a validity of .39. Thus even the best and most lengthy inventory, using long lists of symptoms, and extensively used and validated, achieves negligible validities when compared against ordinary, run-of-the-mill psychiatric diagnoses. In the construction of our questionnaire, we have eschewed the use of symptoms, and concentrated on personality features entirely; it does not seem likely that a brief questionnaire of this type could succeed where the MMPI, constructed for the purpose, fails.

Having explained what our scales are not expected to do, and the reasons for our decision, we must try and explain what they are expected to do, and for what purposes they might be useful. The points here made are purely programmatic, and will be given body in the remainder of this book. Essentially what we are trying to do, then, is to help build up a dimensional framework within which the major aspects of personality can be located with some degree of exactitude; our scales are intended to locate a given person within that framework, again with some degree of exactitude. Within the limited degree of validity and reliability shown by psychiatric diagnoses, we would expect that groups of psychiatric patients showing common diagnoses would occupy a relatively limited portion of the *n*-dimensional space which constitutes our system, rather than be distributed at random all over the space. Thus there would be a limited amount of homogeneity associated with some at least of the psychiatric diagnoses; the locus of the mean of all the scores of psychotics (as diagnosed) would lie at a different point from the locus of the mean of all the scores of neurotics (again as psychiatrically diagnosed). Thus we believe that predictions could be made from our general theory as to the position of these loci, with respect to each other and with respect to the framework; such predictions would constitute a partial test of our theories.

This is a far cry, however, from accepting the psychiatric system as a criterion, and validating our own system against it. We would prefer to put it the other way around and say that our system has been built up along psychometric lines which follow the usual scientific practice, and consequently constitutes the criterion against which psychiatric diagnoses can be tested. If there were to be no agreement at all between the two systems, then clearly we would be in error in using psychiatrically meaningful terms (i.e. terms having surplus meaning, not terms having demonstrated validity), and would be better advised to use psychiatrically neutral terms. But even if this contingency should arise our system would still, in our opinion, be preferable to orthodox psychiatric practice, by virtue of its pedigree and by virtue of its objectivity and reliability. However, there is no point in arguing a case which does not arise; as we shall see, there is ample overlap between our system and psychiatric diagnosis. What we wish to insist on, though, is that this gives us interesting information about certain properties of the psychiatric diagnostic system, and the proficiency of psychiatrists to operate it; it does not by itself tell us anything about the validity of this system as compared to our own. It tells us something of importance concerning the spread around its central locus of the patients to whom psychiatrists apply a common diagnostic term, and it tells us something about the relative positions, in n-dimensional space, of the various loci corresponding to the cores of the common psychiatric diagnoses. These are all useful items of information, but they do not validate our system in any sense; they merely show the existing degree of overlap betwen the two systems.

Such overlap is of particular interest because psychiatric diagnosis is largely based on symptoms, while our dimensional framework is concerned with personality. Foulds (1965) makes a sharp distinction between the two; he believes that 'it is important to distinguish between personality traits and attitudes on the one hand, and the symptoms and signs of mental (or personal) illness on the other. These symptoms signal a disruption of the normal continuity of the personality. Such a distinction is a necessary prelude to any further understanding of the interaction between personality and illness which might lead to advances in the diagnosis, treatment, aetiology, and prophylaxis of the mentally ill' (p. 3). We believe that underlying the development of specific symptoms there is a firm core of genetically determined personality traits, and that this in large measure determines the particular disorder to which a patient may fall prey. It is this personality which we are concerned with, much more than the symptoms; in so far as psychiatric diagnosis is largely concerned with the latter, observed agreement between the two systems will demonstrate the relevance and importance of the underlying personality structure for psychiatric illness. As we shall see, there are also important repercussions of personality on treatment, and the patient's reaction to treatment (e.g. Di Loreto, 1971). Thus our system would bring into psychiatry certain types of non-redundant information which might be of considerable importance for all the purposes mentioned by Foulds. By comparison, the information given by the MMPI is wholly redundant, the test having been constructed especially to duplicate and replicate psychiatric diagnosis.

What bearing does this discussion have on our psychoticism factor? As already explained, it is conceived as a continuum, a personality dimension independent of E and N, ranging from normal to psychotic; it is concerned with personality traits and their constellation, not with symptoms which would be inappropriate to a normal population. The main uses of such a factor, and the questionnaire designed to measure such a factor, would be in research into normal groups, in an endeavour to discover objective referents and causal agencies concerned with a person's position on this continuum. A rather different use would be in connection with psychiatrically abnormal groups, not in the attempt to duplicate psychiatric diagnosis, but rather in the attempt to go beyond orthodox psychiatric diagnosis. To take but one example in this field, the orthogonality of the N and P factors makes it likely that some neurotics will have elevated P scores, just as other neurotics will have very low P scores. In view of the personality characteristics of high P scorers, we have predicted that neurotics with high P scores would respond very poorly to any form of psychotherapy or behaviour therapy, by virtue of the lack of empathy and the impersonal and hostile attitude characteristic of high P scorers. Psychiatric diagnosis of 'neurosis' does not and cannot take into account the marked differences between neurotics with respect to other personality variables; our system not only allows this to be done, but insists on its importance. We will return to this point later on when we are discussing the actual research projects which lend colour to these arguments.

We start out, then, with a rather vague idea of the kind of factor we are looking for; we go on to construct, on the basis of available knowledge, personal experience, and subjective intuition, a set of questions which would have the three main properties which we would demand in a measure of P: (1) the questions must correlate together, so as to define a common factor; (2) the questions must discriminate between normals, on the one hand, and psychotic and criminal groups, on the other; (3) the scale must not correlate to any appreciable extent with E and N. It seemed unlikely from the beginning that we would succeed straight off to find a series of questions which would pass these three hurdles satisfactorily; the idea was to start out with a set which while obviously only partly successful could be refined by the exclusion of unsuitable items, and the substitution of more suitable ones. By successive iterations of this kind we were hoping to end up with a useful set of questions which would go some way towards reaching our aim. It seemed likely from the beginning that in the course of this quest our original notions of the nature of P would undergo drastic revision, and indeed our theoretical understanding has grown considerably as successive factor analyses confirmed some of our hunches, and disconfirmed others. In this process every question used embodies a specific theory regarding the nature of the factor, and each successive analysis constitutes an experiment which decides on the fate of these theories.

This use of factor analysis is unusual; most users of the method have employed it in order to discover unities in a previously chaotic or unsurveyed field. As Kelley (1947) has pointed out, 'we may say that there are two occasions for resort to statistical procedures, the one dominated by a desire to prove a hypothesis, and the other by a desire to invent one. This has led to distinct schools of statisticians, both lying within the general field of scientific endeavour' (p. 12). Our aim has usually been that of using statistics, including factor analysis, for the purpose of proving or disproving psychological hypotheses; in this we have been at the opposite pole from such men as R.B. Cattell or J.B Guilford, who have been more concerned with the invention of hypotheses through factor analysis. Cattell (1946) has explicitly rejected this hypothetico-deductive use of factor analysis, on two grounds: '. . . in the first place, personality study has so few other reliable avenues for arriving at, or even suspecting, the basic source traits, that hypotheses are likely to be erratic. In the second place, the mathematical solutions to any set of correlations are so numerous and varied that unless the hypothesis can be stated in very precise quantitative terms the "proof" of it is easy—so as to be worthless' (p. 274). We cannot agree with either of these criticisms.

In the first place, personality study has certain ways of arriving at hypotheses which should not be denigrated. Careful, long-continued observation of the behaviour of normal people, and of the apparent consistencies and regularities of such behaviour, is one such method. Clinical study of people psychiatrically disturbed, or in other ways unusual (such as criminals), is another. Investigation of genetic similarities, as in the studies referred to in the previous chapter, is a third. It is one thing to point out weaknesses in psychiatric nomenclature and diagnostic practices, as we have done; it is quite another to reject all the large body of work done during the past century as completely useless; as Cattell would seem to do. Indeed, we may go back some two thousand years and point to the views of Hippocrates and Galen with respect to the four types of temperament; as we have shown elsewhere, these views in many ways presage our concepts of extraversion and neuroticism, and are still in good accord with much recent work. We must indeed be critical of unsupported speculation, however much honoured this may have been by past writers, and demand proof; we need not, however, go so far as to refuse to test these speculations on the grounds that they are bound to be false and pointless. Cattell's method of starting with a *tabula rasa*, attempting to obtain a random sample of all possible traits making up his 'personality sphere', and then proceeding to isolate source traits by factor analysis, without any guiding hypotheses at all, is one method; it poses innumerable problems, but may lead to important conclusions. Our own method is entirely different in principle, but should lead to identical conclusions if our guiding hypotheses are chosen with care and insight. There can be no guarantee that our hypotheses will be supported by the facts, but equally there is no *a priori* reason why they should be rejected. Both methods have their advantages and their disadvantages; in fact that they both converge on very similar factors or dimensions of personality suggests that the disadvantages are not crucial.

Cattell's suggestion that proof of such hypotheses as ours is easy—'so easy as to be worthless'—does not strike us as particularly well taken. The work here recorded was begun some thirty years ago, and we certainly have not found the proof (even the limited proof we have attained) easy to come by. Our tests have gone through some two dozen large-scale factor analyses, constant refinements and iterations, constant rethinking and re-orientation; there were many times when the whole enterprise seemed doomed to failure, and when it would have been easiest to throw in our hand. If that achievement of partial proof which is all we have succeeded in obtaining is 'easy', then God preserve us from having to do something really difficult! What Cattell is suggesting may be that *disproof* of an hypothesis by factor analysis is difficult or impossible, but that is not so. As Payne (1955) has shown, in his studies of the concept of *Spaltungsbegriff* put forward by Kretschmer as a central causal agent in his theory of schizothymia-cyclothymia, when the particular tests used by Kretschmer to define this concept are intercorrelated and factor analysed, there is no evidence at all of the existence of a factor corresponding to this concept. The experiment completely disproves the hypothesis, and there is no way in which it could be resurrected. Factor analysis can be used to test an hypothesis, and it can disprove that hypothesis. It does not differ in this respect from any other statistical technique.

Cattell has made many detailed criticisms of our method of carrying out factorial analyses, but these rest almost entirely on a misunderstanding of our intentions. Thus he complains that we tend to 'underfactor' our matrices of correlations, i.e. extract fewer factors than the (pretty arbitrary) statistical tests used for the purpose suggest may be significant. This would be reasonable criticism if our purpose were to discover traits inherent in a collection of randomly selected questions; it is not relevant to our endeavour to find support (or disproof!) for fairly precise hypotheses regarding the existence and orthogonality of a limited number of traits especially incorporated in the battery of questions. In the questionnaire whose construction we shall be discussing in this chapter, we tried to incorporate four major factors, namely P, E, N, and L (a dissimulation scale which also measures a conforming personality trait). Each item in the set of questions used was carefully selected to measure one or other of these four factors, and we could always have specified from the beginning where in the factor matrix the high loadings were expected to lie. The obvious method of testing such a set of hypotheses is clearly an analysis which extracts four factors, rotates them by some objective criterion (Promax in our case) to oblique simple structure, and allows us to see (1) whether each question has high and low loadings on the expected and predicted factors, and (2) whether the factors are reasonably orthogonal. Thus Cattell's criticism is irrelevant because it derives from his own methodology, which, as we have seen, is quite different from ours. In any case, we have shown elsewhere that when we follow Cattell's method, extract as large a number of factors as indicated by statistical tests, and then derive higher-order factors from these primaries, these correspond with great exactitude to factors extracted following our preferred method (H.J. Eysenck and S.B.G. Eysenck, 1969).

Many research workers, including Cattell & Guilford, lay much greater stress on the more elementary 'primary factors' which emerge first from a factor analysis, than on the more inclusive higher-order factors which occupy a more elevated position in the hierarchical structure produced by oblique simple structure. Our reasons for not following suit have been described in some detail elsewhere (H.J. Eysenck and S.B.G. Eysenck, 1969). We there draw the important distinction between T factors and C factors; the former are called *tautological*, because they essentially reproduce identical item content with change in wording. This kind of factor would not really advance our understanding; it would simply be a device to transform a categorical single-item response (Yes—No) into a scale having a number of graded responses. Its psychological contribution would be minimal. Consider typical questions relating to sociability: Do you like being with people? Have you many friends? Do you like talking to people? Do you like going to parties? Do you dislike being by yourself? These are all different ways of asking pretty much the same question, and while one might put forward a rather casuistic argument in the opposite direction, nevertheless high positive correlations between the questions seem a logical necessity. Primaries of this kind no doubt exist, and indeed one could take any trait-statement and, by rewording it slightly a number of times, obtain a factor to correspond to this hypothesized trait. Psychometrically this would be useful, by increasing the reliability of the measurement, but psychologically nothing very much would have been gained. Increases in reliability and the advantages of scaled over categorical responses are technically important, but we do not consider that such factors possess theoretical importance.

C factors are quite different; here we are dealing with heterogeneous content which could not be predicted on purely logical grounds to show positive correlations and constitute a single factor. Cattell is perhaps the only worker whose primary factors are *complex* in this sense; most others achieve complexity only at a higher level. This would certainly be true of our P, E, N and L factors; these are not tautological, but complex, and they correspond, not to true primaries, but to higher-order factors. Cattell's primaries thus are in quite a different position to those of most factor analysts; unfortunately they also suffer several disadvantages which in part arise from this very fact. As Eysenck (1971a) has shown, these factors are difficult if not impossible to replicate when analyses of Cattell items are carried out by other writers (e.g. Greif, 1970; H.J. Eysenck and S.B.G. Eysenck, 1969; Levonian, 1961a,b; Sells et al., 1968; Howarth and Browne, 1971; Timm, 1968). In the absence of such replication, these 16PF factors of Cattell's cannot be accepted as definitely proven. Also the reliabilities of the factors are quite low, and their intercorrelations quite high; as Eysenck (1972c) has shown, when corrected for attenuation, the intercorrelations between the primaries making up the group of extraversion or neuroticism (anxiety) factors which Cattell uses to define his higher-order factors are so high that they average around unity; thus in Cattell's own data (which were used to carry out these calculations) there is really no evidence for the independence of his primaries. Future work must show whether these objections are decisive; until then we must conclude that C factors are rare or entirely absent among primaries, and that psychological interest centres on higher-order factors, like P, E and N.

There are other criticisms which might be made of procedures which rely too much on factor-analytic theory and methods. Many of these have been enumerated by Pawlik (1973); some of them arise from properties of the mathematical model of factor analysis itself. For instance, the model is violated whenever the row vectors of X ($X = AF + A_u F_u$, where X is an $m \times n$ score matrix or data matrix in m variables and n subjects, A is the $m \times k$ factor pattern matrix in k common factors, and F denotes the $k \times n$ common factor score matrix; A_u is the $m \times m$ unique factor matrix, and F_u the $m \times n$ unique factor score matrix) cease to be linearly independent, as unique factor variance is thus shared by two or more variables. This often happens in personality research where algebraically derived variables are frequently included, such as sums or differences or ratios of scores already entered into the matrix. The model is also violated when, in spite of linear independence of the rows of X, unique variance components are correlated between variables; this happens when experimental errors are correlated. Quite different in kind is a criticism arising from the estimation of factors to be included in the rotation; Pawlik has shown that estimates of the minimal rank k of the correlation matrix by means of Guttman's criterion (which is very widely used) can be very wrong. He finds that the number of common factors is overestimated rather drastically in small-sample studies employing tests of low to medium reliability. Furthermore, this bias increases as the number of variables involved increases. These and many other objections should not lead one to a complete rejection of the factor-analytic method, but should lead one to a healthy distrust of analyses extracting a large number of common factors from single matrices, and lacking in external criteria (or a priori hypotheses) against which to evaluate the resulting factors. We believe that the hypothesis-generating role of factor analysis may easily lead to fantasy-generating, when not constrained by external criteria.

The hypothesis-testing function of factor analysis is of course also open to problems. The use of Procrustes-type methodologies in testing hypotheses may easily lead to erroneous notions of verification when in actual fact any set of data could under the circumstances have led to such 'verification' (Horn and Knapp, 1973). Another difficulty is that of frame hypotheses in such a way that they are in fact testable by factor-analytical methods. And of course the main problem (not unusual in social science, or even in science generally) is that of discovering hypotheses which are worthwhile testing. But these difficulties and problems are not insurmountable, and they are probably less serious than those enumerated in connection with the hypothesis-generating function of factor analysis.

Given that both these approaches to personality have problems which are quite different and separate, it would seem that if both approaches could be shown to lead to similar or identical solutions, then our faith in these solutions would be much strengthened. In the rest of this book we will be concerned with the hypothesis-testing method; to conclude this chapter we may perhaps look at the major outcomes of hypothesis-generating approaches in this field. What we would expect to find would be three major factors corresponding, if only roughly, to neuroticism-emotionality, extraversion-introversion, and psychoticism. We may begin by noting that even in the animal field there are analogues of these three factors which emerge from factor analyses of behavioural observations. Chamove, Eysenck and Harlow (1972) studied 168 juvenile macaques, using standard rating scales for behaviour in carefully controlled conditions; ratings were then inter-correlated and the correlation matrices factor analysed. The authors concluded that 'factors emerged, most strongly in the most stable condition, which were interpreted as affiliative, hostile and fearful. These factors were almost entirely independent and resembled the extraversion, psychoticism, and emotionality factors frequently found in humans' (p. 496). This finding may at first sight seem unexpected, but one may perhaps look at it from a logical point of view. In all these studies, whether dealing with men or with monkeys, we are concerned most of all with social behaviour (intraspecies), and such behaviour really only allows of three main reactions: we can actively socialize or not (extraversion-introversion), we can aggress and attack (psychoticism), or we can react with fear and try to run away (neuroticism-emotionality). If it is true that these three reactions exhaust the major possibilities inherent in social situations, then it is hardly to be wondered at that in fact these three factors should emerge in descriptive studies of social behaviour.

When we turn to work with humans, the material is so numerous that any detailed examination would be impossible. H.J. Eysenck and S.B.G. Eysenck (1969) have surveyed the available sources as far as E and N are concerned, and have shown that in nearly every single study using a wide-ranging set of tests and questions, these two factors (often with somewhat different names, but neverthe-less clearly recognizable) have emerged very clearly and strongly. The same authors also report independent experiments using items from the Cattell and Guilford scales respectively, specially selected by these authors as representing their various primary factors; these items were shown by analysis and factor comparison to give rise to E and N factors for all practical purposes identical with those found in the Eysenck Personality Inventory (EPI). There seems little doubt that these two factors form the backbone of higher-order factors in the human realm.

A very careful and thorough survey of the available literature has been undertaken by Royce (1973), who concludes that the data indicate 'a hierarchy with three second-order factors marked by a total of eleven first-order factors. Two of the second-order factors, extraversion-introversion and anxiety, are well known in the clinical and personality literature. . .' (p. 326). (Royce prefers the term 'anxiety', as used by Cattell, instead of neuroticism or emotionality, but makes it clear that the same factor as N is intended.) He goes on to say: 'Our third second-order factor, superego, represents a behavioural pattern of concern for the feelings of others, adherence to the moral codes of the individual's milieu, responsibility to others, feelings of a sense of duty, and a self-disciplined demeanor'. He specially refers to Cattell's demonstration and identification of this factor (Cattell *et al.*, 1970), which is clearly the obverse of the psychoticism factor we are here hypothesizing; all the traits characterizing the 'high superego' person are characteristically absent in the high P scorer, as we shall see.

The reader is referred for further details to Royce's carefully documented account, and to Cattell's voluminous writings; we only wish here to draw attention to the fact that although the two approaches mentioned are quite distinct in methodology and many other ways, nevertheless they agree very closely in the main conclusions reached. There are issues on which Cattell, Guilford and we differ, particularly in respect to the value and acceptability of primary factors; this disagreement is sometimes taken to cover wider areas. This clearly is not so; in respect to all the important substantive matters with which this book is concerned there is considerable if not perfect agreement. The work of Cattell in particular, unequalled in respect to statistical sophistication and width of coverage of tests and subjects, leads him to conclusions all of which we would accept, and most of which we have either replicated or anticipated. This state of affairs needs emphasizing because many critics point out the large amount of disagreement which is believed to exist among factor analysts. There are areas of disagreement, of course, as there are in any scientific discipline, but the amount of agreement is also quite large, and provides a solid basis for advance.

4

The construction of the P scale: Empirical

The early work with P was entirely on the basis of objective laboratory tests (Eysenck, 1952a, 1952b; S.B.G. Eysenck, 1956a; Eysenck, Granger and Brengelmann, 1957; Eysenck, 1955a); it was not thought that questionnaires could be used to much purpose with psychotic groups one of whose leading and indeed defining symptoms was precisely their lack of insight and self-knowledge. However, work with the MMPI suggested that this view might be mistaken, at least in part; the scales represented contrast the 'neurotic triad' with the 'psychotic triad' (Dahlstrom and Welsh, 1960), thus lending substance to our distinction between N and P, and a psychoticism concept is recognized (Butcher, 1969), although of course this is defined in terms of symptoms, and not, as in our case, in terms of personality traits. The actual description of the MMPI psychoticism variable is as follows: 'High PSY admits to a number of classic psychotic symptoms of a primarily paranoid nature. He admits to hallucinations, strange experiences, loss of control, and classic paranoid delusions of grandeur and persecution. He admits to feelings of unreality, daydreaming, and a sense that things are wrong, while feeling misunderstood by others' (Butcher, 1969, p. 146). This factor had reasonable alpha (internal consistency) coefficients in seven normal samples, ranging from .69 to .88; this suggests that high PSY scorers might have enough insight to admit to quite serious psychiatric symptoms. This does not necessarily imply that they would have enough insight to answer questions about their personality truthfully, but the possibility that they might cannot be ruled out altogether. PSY scores produced fairly clear differences between psychotics and neurotics, with schizophrenic, sociopathic and affective groups in the former category, and neurotic and personality disorder groups in the latter (p. 153). This grouping of sociopathic groups with schizophrenia and affective disorder (endogenous depression?), contrasted with the neurotic groups, is in good agreement with our genetic hypothesis.

On the other hand, the success of MMPI scales in differentiating neurotics from psychotics is not marked. Goldberg (1965) has reported on 861 MMPI profiles secured from seven hospitals and clinics throughout the USA; these were rated by twenty-nine clinical judges against a psychiatric diagnostic criterion. Also used were a large number of actuarial combinations of scale scores; these were then compared for efficiency with each other and with the judges' ratings. Success in predicting the criterion was small, in spite of the fact that the MMPI concentrates on symptoms of precisely the sort on which the psychiatric criterion diagnosis was based in the first place. The mean accuracy of the judges was expressed by a correlation coefficient of .28; that of the most valid actuarial combination by a coefficient of .39. Thus the percentage of the criterion variance predicted by the average judge was less than 10 per cent; that predicted by the best actuarial sign was

15 per cent. Much of the blame for this failure must of course rest with the unreliability of the criterion, which we have already discussed in the previous chapter; even so, the showing of the MMPI on its own ground is not impressive.*

There are of course other precursors of the P scale than the MMPI, all of them appearing much later than the original conceptualization of Psychoticism (Eysenck, 1952a). Cattell and Bolton (1969) derived their general factor of psychoticism chiefly from the MMPI scales of Depression, Hysteria, Paranoia and Schizophrenia, but later workers used scales of their own construction. Thus Sells *et al.* (1971) extracted several oblique factors bearing resemblance to different facets of P, such as his factors T6 (Agreeableness *vs.* Hostility), T7 (Relaxed Composure *vs.* Suspicious Excitability), T8 (Personal Relations) and T11 (Paranoid Sensitivity). Emphasis on hostility is more marked in the Comrey and Duffy (1968) second-order factor called Empathy-Hostility, which, in addition to these two scales, included Cattell's scales Protension, Sizothymia, and (with lower loadings) Dominance, Premsia, and Self-Sentiment. Other scales again lay stress directly on the concept of hostility (e.g. the Foulds scales), or its opposite, Cooperativeness (Guilford and Zimmerman, 1956). In a later section we shall provide evidence of intercorrelations between our scales and such other, apparently relevant scales as have been used to test one aspect or the other of the validity of the P scale. Forbes (1973) has presented a good review of antecedents of the P scale, and has carried out a large-scale factor analysis of many of the scales discussed, in an effort to discover their relationship to P; his work will be discussed in some detail in a later chapter.

Slightly encouraged by these studies in our belief that verbal measurement of P might not be impossible, we set about the task of formulating an explicit model of the typical P personality. This model was based on long continued experience with testing psychotic and neurotic patients in laboratory situations; clinical experience acquired during ward rounds, diagnostic conferences, and diagnostic testing of patients; and a detailed survey of the theoretical and experimental literature dealing with psychiatric disorders. The model was basically testable, in the sense that it predicted positive correlations between various traits hypothesized to form part of the P syndrome, but we were of course aware of certain difficulties which would inevitably arise in this connection. Certain traits might not be testable by means of questionnaire answers at all; e.g. insight (presumably somewhat lacking in high P scorers) could hardly be measured by asking subjects whether they had good or poor insight! Lack of insight, if present and at the same time not measurable, might affect responses to other questions in such a manner as to make the answers non-veridical, and thus make a proper testing of our hypotheses impossible. We tried to overcome some of these difficulties by elaborating a Lie scale (L scale) which in part at least might be used to measure a person's insight; this will be discussed in a later chapter. If our model might prove difficult to support empirically, it certainly fulfilled Popper's requirement that scientific theories should be *falsifiable*; our model seemed from the beginning eminently falsifiable—so

---

*Quite generally, such studies as have been done (Conklin, 1937; Karson and Freud, 1956; Lykken and Rose, 1963; Meehl, 1956; McMullen, 1967; Morris, 1947; Rubin, 1954; Winter and Stortroen, 1963) do not give the reader the impression that inventory items can discriminate very well between neurotic and psychotic groups, although they can discriminate between normal and abnormal (combined neurotic and psychotic) groups.

much so in fact that failure seemed almost inevitable at the beginning!

How, then, did we see our 'typical' high P scorer? We thought of him as cold, impersonal, hostile, lacking in sympathy, unfriendly, untrustful, odd, unemotional, unhelpful, antisocial, lacking in human feelings, inhumane, generally bloody-minded, lacking in insight, strange, with paranoid ideas that people were against him.* Given this model, we began writing P items (or adapting items from previous questionnaires, or occasionally taking items over without change) which would embody this model in the form of questions which would not have pathological content (MMPI questions are often rejected or ridiculed by normal subjects as obviously inapplicable, odd and 'mad'; we wanted to construct a questionnaire for normal people which would avoid this stigma). Once our first P questionnaire was completed, the later stages of construction fell into line with current psychometric procedures. P items were mixed in with items known to be good measures of E and N (and sometimes L), the resulting questionnaires administered to groups of normal subjects varying in size, but usually containing some two hundred men and two hundred women, and factor analyses carried out, separately for the two sexes. (We were impressed right from the beginning with the obvious sex differences which emerged in relation to P, and found it impossible to deal with this problem without keeping the calculations for the two sexes separate.) Items falling into the hypothetical P factor were retained for future work, items not loading on P were rejected, and new ones written; items loading on P and also on E or N were either rejected or re-written, and an improved version of the questionnaire produced and again tested in the same way. At various stages in this iterative process, psychotic, neurotic and criminal samples were tested, in order to make sure that external validation kept pace with the internal validation; had our emerging P scale failed to give high scores to psychotics and criminals, we would have been rather doubtful about the nature of our factor. Fortunately this problem did not arise; from the beginning our P scale did indicate that psychotics and criminals tended to score well above the normal level.

The P scale went through some twenty factor analyses on its way to publication, only some of which have been published in detail. No purpose would be served in publishing here all the results of all these analyses; they were useful to us in sharpening our understanding of the verbal reactions of our subjects to often quite minute changes in wording which would normally have seemed unimportant, and the ambiguities inherent in the wording of some questions. To the reader, however, this slow process on our side of gaining more insight into the structure of the factors involved would be tedious and uninformative; consequently we shall merely reprint some of the published Tables showing the factorial loadings of questions as they appeared at various stages of questionnaire construction, with comments on the deficiencies of the resulting scales. Our reasons for accepting or rejecting items were so complex that it would be difficult to objectify them, or to assign accurate weights to them; the only possible check on the value of our work must be the validation of the final product. Nevertheless a brief glimpse at some of the intervening stages may be of interest, and this is what we have attempted to do in this chapter. A later chapter will deal with the construction of the children's scale.

The total number of items originally written was much too large to even

---

*Given a personality as described above, the idea that 'people were against him' might not be paranoid at all, but a simple statement of fact!

consider the possibility of using them all in a factor analysis, particularly as items representing E and N had to be included in the analysis also, and consequently for our first series of studies the following method was adopted (H.J. Eysenck and S.B.G. Eysenck, 1968).

A member of the staff of the Department is associated with a commercial market research organization which holds weekly 'parties' to which random samples of the population are invited; they are shown films, given presents, take part in competitions, and answer questions regarding products and advertisements which are of interest to the firm concerned. We were allowed to introduce into this 'party' a short questionnaire of some twenty-four questions; the questions varied from week to week, but each questionnaire was answered by a group of some three hundred subjects who were a reasonably random sample of the total population. Each week we introduced six E questions and six N questions; we have a large stock of such questions with known factor loadings on E and N. We also introduced a dozen of our P questions, in order to test whether these were independent of E and N, and also whether they correlated together to form a separate factor. Each set of questions was then factor analysed by the principal components method, and three factors extracted; two of these were always clearly E and N, while the third was usually made up of several of the hypothetical P items. Some of these hypothetical items had no P loadings, others had high N loadings, or more rarely, high E loadings. Items having high P loadings and low E and N loadings were retained and included again on another occasion, together with a new batch of prospective P items; if they proved themselves again they were considered for our final scale. This process of selection was continued over a lengthy period of time, until we had accumulated a sufficient number of items to make possible the next stage of testing.

It would take too much space, and would not be of any great scientific interest, to reprint the outcome of all these preliminary studies. However, Table 3 brings together items having high P loadings and low E and N loadings. Column 1 gives the item number in Table 4, which prints in full the text of all the items used in our large-scale factor analysis; column 2 gives the number of the experimental session in which the responses were obtained for the analysis, the results of which are reported in this Table. Column 3 gives the loadings of the selected items for N, E and P, obtained on the first occasion that these items were used. Column 4 gives the loadings of the same items for N, E and P on the second occasion that each item was used, i.e. in conjunction with a quite different set of items than the first time. Not all the items were tried out a third time, and hence no figures are given for the third testing. It will be seen that there are quite a few rather high loadings on the

continues on page 52

TABLE 3   Items having high P and low E and N loadings

Number of question	Number of experiment	First occasion			Second occasion		
		N	E	P	N	E	P
18	01	−.06	.30	−.40			
29	01	−.09	.28	.48	.41	.07	.33
10	01	−.01	.23	−.58	−.04	.05	−.57
35	01	.10	.11	.24	.11	.26	.25

47	01	.00	.05	−.39	−.16	.06	−.48
58	01	.13	.01	.21	.02	.25	.55
	01	−.33	.07	.54			
19	02	−.03	.09	.60	.04	−.13	.39
30	02	−.06	−.15	.65	.15	−.36	.24
12	02	−.23	.11	.47	.06	.19	.04
36	02	.21	.03	.33	.40	.15	.21
59	02	.04	−.32	.57	.16	−.09	.64
20	03	.19	−.10	.55	.27	−.28	−.18
105	03	−.21	.16	.57	.04	−.00	−.54
38	03	.11	−.01	.66	−.06	−.12	−.16
13	03	−.02	.07	.18	.04	−.01	−.77
21	04	.07	.04	.64	.38	−.12	.24
3	04	.01	.00	.66	.37	.13	.49
15	04	−.23	.07	.44	−.09	.32	.45
39	04	.19	.11	.47	.31	.02	.20
52	04	.10	.04	−.33	−.01	.09	−.32
23	05	.11	.16	−.44	−.12	.36	−.24
4	05	.07	−.11	.40	.03	−.06	.61
16	05	.05	.22	.60	.23	.04	.31
40	05	.18	.06	.62	−.05	.12	.63
102	06	−.07	.18	−.33	−.48	−.04	.12
101	06	.02	.12	.54	.23	−.10	.25
104	06	.05	−.03	.28	.33	−.34	−.21
41	06	.08	−.16	.47	.22	−.26	.18
53	06	.29	.18	−.32	.09	.28	−.28
50	06	−.17	.00	.44	−.19	.10	.14
25	07	.29	−.02	.39	.26	.13	.44
7	07	−.01	.05	.66	−.02	.16	.71
32	07	−.10	.04	.71	.29	.02	.42
44	07	−.03	.04	.72	.11	−.11	.56
55	07	.15	.06	.44	.08	.28	.52
26	08	−.19	−.03	−.46	−.32	.03	−.63
8	08	.14	.24	.57	.25	.05	−.46
27	09	.01	.22	.66	.38	−.15	.27
9	09	.13	.11	.61	.07	−.04	.54
33	09	−.06	−.03	.70	−.09	−.06	.70
45	09	.12	.17	−.43	.07	−.01	−.66
56	09	.20	.17	.53	.14	−.04	.55
62	09	−.05	−.10	.62	−.12	.06	.69
70	10	−.08	.18	.64			
98	10	−.11	.09	−.48			
67	10	.15	.11	.48			
72	11	−.11	−.04	.38			
74	11	.10	.25	−.50			
77	11	.11	.01	.45			
80	11	.23	.20	.41			
82	11	−.04	−.24	.46			

TABLE 4   Final list of items for analysis

1. Are you more distant and reserved than most people?	Yes	No
2. Do you find it hard to get going some mornings?	Yes	No
3. Have you ever been afraid of losing your mind?	Yes	No
4. Do most things taste the same to you?	Yes	No
5. Can you get a party going?	Yes	No
6. Can you usually make up your mind easily?	Yes	No
7. Do you enjoy hurting people you love?	Yes	No
8. Do you often wonder why people do the things they do?	Yes	No
9. Do you find it hard to look people straight in the eye?	Yes	No
10. Are you generally in good health?	Yes	No
11. Do you do much day dreaming?	Yes	No
12. Do you agree that everything is turning out just like the Prophets of the Bible said it would?	Yes	No
13. Was your mother a good woman?	Yes	No
14. Would you consider yourself as efficient as most others?	Yes	No
15. Do you drink unusually much water?	Yes	No
16. Have you had more trouble than most?	Yes	No
17. Would you do almost anything for a dare?	Yes	No
18. Do you do many things that interest you?	Yes	No
19. Have you had an awful lot of bad luck?	Yes	No
20. Do you go to church about once a week?	Yes	No
21. Do you worry a lot about catching diseases?	Yes	No
22. Do you find it hard to keep your mind on what you are doing?	Yes	No
23. Did you love your mother?	Yes	No
24. Do you often feel fed up?	Yes	No
25. Do you get depressed in the mornings?	Yes	No
26. Would you enjoy hunting, fishing and shooting?	Yes	No
27. Are there several people who keep trying to avoid you?	Yes	No
28. Would you blame anyone for taking advantage of someone who lays himself open to it?	Yes	No
29. Is there someone who is responsible for most of your troubles?	Yes	No
30. Do you let your dreams warn or guide you?	Yes	No
31. Do you nearly always have a 'ready answer' when people talk to you?	Yes	No
32. Do people generally seem to take offence easily?	Yes	No
33. Would you take drugs which may have strange or dangerous effects?	Yes	No
34. Do you have thoughts too bad to talk about?	Yes	No
35. Do you believe that people are only honest for fear of being caught?	Yes	No
36. Do you often feel that you have been punished without cause?	Yes	No
37. Are you rather lively?	Yes	No
38. Do you believe in the second coming of Christ?	Yes	No
39. Do you seem clumsier than most people?	Yes	No
40. Do you have enemies who wish to harm you?	Yes	No
41. Would you refuse to play a game because you are no good at it?	Yes	No
42. Are you ever 'off your food'?	Yes	No
43. Are you full of energy at times?	Yes	No
44. Do your friendships break up easily without it being your fault?	Yes	No
45. Do you like to be busy most of the time?	Yes.	No
46. Does your mood often go up and down?	Yes	No

47. Was your father a good man?   Yes No
48. Do you like plenty of bustle and excitement around you?   Yes No
49. Do you ever keep on at a thing until others lose their patience with you?   Yes No
50. Would you say that you have never been in love?   Yes No
51. Do you like mixing with people?   Yes No
52. Is your weight more or less steady over the years?   Yes No
53. Have you had any peculiar or strange experiences?   Yes No
54. Do you sometimes feel you don't care what happens to you?   Yes No
55. Do people mean to say and do things to annoy you?   Yes No
56. Are you ever bothered by the idea that someone is reading your thoughts?   Yes No
57. Do you ever feel 'just miserable' for no good reason?   Yes No
58. Would you have been more successful if people had not put difficulties in your way?   Yes No
59. Do you feel sad most of the time?   Yes No
60. Would you call yourself happy-go-lucky?   Yes No
61. Are you often troubled about feelings of guilt?   Yes No
62. When you are in a crowded place like a bus do you worry about dangers of infection?   Yes No
63. Do you find it hard to show your feelings?   Yes No
64. Do you feel self-pity now and again?   Yes No
65. Can you usually let yourself go and enjoy yourself a lot at a gay party?   Yes No
66. Do you suffer from sleeplessness?   Yes No
67. Have people sometimes thought your ideas a bit odd?   Yes No
68. Would you call yourself tense or 'highly strung'?   Yes No
69. Do you like people around you?   Yes No
70. Do you quite enjoy doing things that are a little frightening?   Yes No
71. Do you worry a lot about your looks?   Yes No
72. Do you think you enjoy spicy foods more than your friends do?   Yes No
73. Has anyone ever tried to influence your mind?   Yes No
74. Are you always careful to make sure your doors are locked at night?   Yes No
75. Do you like practical jokes?   Yes No
76. Do you often feel very weak all over?   Yes No
77. Do you enjoy gossiping about people you know very well?   Yes No
78. Do you sometimes feel uneasy indoors?   Yes No
79. Do you normally prefer to be alone?   Yes No
80. Do people ever talk about you secretly?   Yes No
81. Do you feel as well now as ever you did?   Yes No
82. Have you always thought of yourself as different to others?   Yes No
83. Do you enjoy stretching and yawning?   Yes No
84. Do you like going out a lot?   Yes No
85. Do you believe in life after death?   Yes No
86. Does your voice change without you having a cold?   Yes No
87. Do you prefer to try new places to go on your holidays?   Yes No
88. Have you ever wished you were dead?   Yes No
89. Do you make friends easily with members of your own sex?   Yes No
90. Do you get depressed in the evenings?   Yes No
91. Do you usually work by fits and starts?   Yes No
92. Do you often rush even when you have a lot of time?   Yes No

table continues overleaf

93. Do you wake very early in the mornings and find it hard to get
back to sleep? Yes No
94. Would you call yourself talkative? Yes No
95. Did you love your father? Yes No
96. Do things sometimes seem as if they were not real? Yes No
97. When you were a child did you often like a rough and tumble
game? Yes No
98. Do you prefer loud to soft music? Yes No
99. Would it upset you a lot to see a child or animal suffer? Yes No
100. Do you like telling jokes or funny stories to your friends? Yes No
101. Do you often worry about whether you have locked your front
door? Yes No
102. Do you get as much sympathy from people as you need? Yes No
103. When you make new friends do you usually make the first move? Yes No
104. Do you mistrust people who are too friendly? Yes No
105. Are you most careful to do what you consider your duty at all
times? Yes No
106. Do you have trouble getting to sleep at bedtime? Yes No

factor prematurely and hopefully called 'P' and it is, of course, realized that it is quite possible that the factors so-called in each of the different experiments may in fact be quite independent factors having no relation to all the others. This is perhaps unlikely in view of the fact that most of the items retained high loadings when re-analysed in a different collection of items, but in any case this was of course only a preliminary exercise to find promising items for a larger and more inclusive analysis; no evidential value is attributed to the findings so far. All that can be claimed, perhaps, is that there do seem to exist sets of items which cohere together while having low loadings on N and E; whether or not these sets measure our hypothetical variable P must be decided on other grounds.

Our final list of items for analysis is given in Table 4. The items were administered to groups selected in the same way as before, in the same sequence, with instructions emphasizing speed, the necessity to answer every question, and the fact that there were no right or wrong answers. Subjects appeared to enjoy, or at least not to resent, the experience, and happily completed the inventory in between seeing their television shows and competing for prizes in various games. If the conditions under which the inventory was administered seem less than optimal, it should be remembered that we are dealing with a cross-section of the population, not with the very exceptional populations usually tested in this connection, i.e. sophomores. Conditions which might appear somewhat odd to university students are much more acceptable to ordinary people than would be the sterilized atmosphere of the psychological laboratory or clinic. Furthermore, the attitudes of students must be assumed to be far less naive than those of the 'guests' of the market research organization, put at their ease at considerable expense and not suspecting that their answers would be used in psychological experiments. Other groups of normals, as well as neurotics and psychotics, were also tested, under more usual conditions, but this chapter is concerned only with the results obtained from our 'market research' samples.

Eight hundred and ninety-four women and 550 men were tested in all, but of these a number failed to complete the questionnaire, so that the numbers forming part of the analysis were 821 women and 512 men. Table 3 gives the loadings of the three principal components factors extracted from the respective matrices of product-moment matrices and rotated to simple structure by Promax in the order N, E and P; again we have denoted the third factor 'P' somewhat prematurely, because complete proof of its nature is of course not yet obtainable; our main reason must be simple convenience of labelling, and if the reader rejects the interpretation of this factor as 'psychoticism' he may conveniently simply regard the letter 'P' as an indeterminate symbol. It is certainly notable that nearly all the items having high loadings on P are in fact items which in previous work with the MMPI and other inventories have successfully distinguished clinically diagnosed psychotics (of different types) from neurotics and normals; nevertheless, this may be taken only as suggestive, and certainly not as proof of the identity of this factor.

Coefficients of factor comparison (H.J. Eysenck and S.B.G. Eysenck, 1969) were calculated between sexes to determine the degree to which the factors in one sex were replicable in the other. The figures are all reasonably high: N = .960; E = .979; P = .948. The figure for the P factor is lower than those for either N or E, but the differences are trifling. We may conclude that similar if not identical factors can be derived in separate samples, distinguished by sex; it should be noted that it cannot be assumed without proof that sex does not influence factor identities— much evidence on this point is given in S.B.G. Eysenck and H.J. Eysenck (1968). The fact that sex does not seem to distort the factors extracted suggests that they have considerable stability from sample to sample.

The factors are not independent in either sample; the correlations for the women are: NE = .15; NP = .34; EP = −.05, and for the men: NE = .14; NP = .30; EP = −.13. Of these, the only correlation which is of any interest is that between N and P; in both sexes, there is an overlap between factors amounting to about 10 per cent. This is not only statistically significant, but sufficiently substantial to call for an explanation; it may be suggested that possibly the possession of high P by a person living in our culture pattern imposes a considerable stress on him which in turn results in higher strain. This higher strain, in turn, may lead to a slight increase in N scores; it is well known that N scores are responsive to strain in this fashion (H.J. Eysenck and S.B.G. Eysenck, 1968). This tentative explanation may of course not be the true one; the correlation states a problem which requires an experimental solution.

Cattell (1965) has opposed the type of analysis typified in the preceding section, calling it 'resolution into pseudo-second orders' which he also calls 'space-deformed'. 'When closely examined, the imitation, in loading pattern, of the true second orders by these pseudo-second orders is poor. This is because in one case the missing variance is a series of centroid factors, each a mixture of everything, while in the other it is the specific factor variance of the primaries, i.e. that part of the primaries which does not come into the second order common space.' H.J. Eysenck and S.B.G. Eysenck (1968) have shown that, in at least one case, Cattell's argument does not appear to be universally true; they actually compared by way of indices of factor similarity 'pseudo-second orders' and proper second-order factors extracted from the same matrix, and obtained very high indices indeed—so high that they suggested virtual identity of the E and N factors extracted. We cannot, therefore, agree with Cattell that 'pseudo-second-order factors' are of necessity inferior to 'proper second-order factors'; there are certain conditions when the two may be identical. We would suggest that the clue to this riddle lies in another sentence of Cattell's, taken from the same paper: 'The guesswork involved in deciding how many second orders exist before one has taken out the primaries, and the inelegance of seeking a solution in short, deformed space, combine to make this "pseudo-second-order" approach scientifically indefensible.' When what is involved is truly guesswork, then Cattell is undoubtedly right; remembering what we said in the section devoted to procedural aspects, we would agree that his objurgations apply to Thurstone's second case. They do not, however, apply to his first case, particularly when much theoretical and experimental work precedes the use of the factorial method. In the study by Eysenck and Eysenck referred to, dozens of previous analyses left very little doubt in our minds as to the number of (important) second-order factors to expect, or their nature; hence our 'guess' was perhaps a little more than a guess, and turned out to be correct. Similarly in the present case; we would argue that there are three main factors to be expected at the second-order level, and hence that we are justified in extracting and rotating three 'pseudo-second orders'. The analysis through primary to second-order factors to be reported in this section may help to illustrate our position. It should be said again that we do not wish to generalize our argument and state that Cattell's argument is erroneous under all circumstances; we would expect him to be right in the majority of cases, but we would be prepared to say that under special circumstances, involving Thurstone's first case, 'pseudo-second orders' and proper second orders may be virtually identical.

Twenty primary factors were extracted from the original matrices of correlations, and rotated by Promax, separately for men and women. These primary factors will not be given in detail here or discussed, as they are not relevant to our main point. From the intercorrelations of the primaries, seven second-order factors were extracted for each sex and again these will not be discussed. Finally, three third-order factors were extracted for both groups, and it is these factors which are to be compared with our 'pseudo-second order'. The criterion for ceasing to extract second and third factors was the usual one of extracting factors with latent roots of unity or above. To avoid subjectivity in these comparisons, indices of factor comparison (H.J. Eysenck and S.B.G. Eysenck, 1968) were calculated between the factors, for men and women separately. For the men, the indices were as follows: Neuroticism .98; Extraversion .99; Psychoticism .91. For the women they were: Neuroticism .99; Extraversion .97; Psychoticism .96. While these values differ from unity, they are sufficiently close to unity to give us confidence that our 'pseudos' are good enough approximations to the third-order factors to make their use permissible. For all practical purposes, it may be said that the choice between the two solutions is arbitrary when interest is in the higher-order factors; the simple three-factor solution is at a disadvantage, of course, when interest is in the primaries.

Cattell would argue, perhaps, that where there are differences between the two solutions the third-order factors are in principle preferable, because they give a more accurate picture of underlying reality. We are sceptical of this argument. 'Underlying reality' is a slippery concept, and we would find it difficult to suggest any practical way of testing such a statement. Further than that, however, we believe that the superiority of the third-order solution would be apparent only with perfect samples of infinite size. With the usually small and imperfect samples we work with, there is an inevitable chance error in the original correlations which is magnified when angles between successive higher-order factors are being determined; the hypothetical superiority of higher-order factors may in fact turn to inferiority through these cumulative and inevitable errors. We do not want to insist on the actual superiority of the original three-factor solution; we merely wish to state that we do not consider it as necessarily inferior to the third-order solution. Fortunately the argument is an academic one in the present case as the indices of factor similarity are so high as to suggest virtual identity.

The next published study (S.B.G. Eysenck and H.J. Eysenck, 1968) in our series was in some ways a replication and extension of the previous one; we attempted to construct a set of twenty items for the measurement of P, and assess the reliability of this scale.

The population tested consisted of 500 men and 500 women; these were contacted through employers, unions, personal approaches and in various other ways. No claims are made that these represent random samples, but they certainly range more widely than is customary in questionnaire research, which has concentrated almost exclusively on students. Students have been explicitly excluded from this sample, which will be designated NS (normal sample); two separate student samples were also tested, made up of 700 male and 700 female students.

Product-moment correlations were run for the male and female NS groups separately for the 106 questions included in the questionnaire; this list of questions has been given in Table 4. The matrices of correlations were then submitted to a principal components form of factor analysis, three factors were extracted, and rotated into oblique simple structure by means of Promax (Hendrickson and White, 1964). This solution will be called the 'three-factor solution'. As an alternative, twenty factors were extracted by principal components and rotated into simple structure by Promax; higher-order factors, seven for males and six for females, were then extracted, until at the third-order level the three factors of E, N and P appeared. This will be called the 'third-order solution'. The two solutions were sufficiently similar to give rise to high indices of factor similarity, although of course individual loadings may show dissimilarities. We shall concentrate on the three-factor solution as, for reasons given above, we consider it to be marginally superior on theoretical grounds.

In order to compare the results of this analysis with those of the previous one, indices of factor similarity were calculated (Eysenck and Eysenck, 1969). For all three factors in our present sample males and females show remarkable similarity: indices are .985 for N, .996 for E and .991 for P. When we compare the random sample (S.B.G. Eysenck and H.J. Eysenck, 1968) with the normal sample, results again show considerable similarities; the figures for the indices of factor similarity are given in Table 5. These figures indicate clearly that for both male and female samples the present groups give rise to factors which are very similar to those extracted from the random sample in the previous analysis. It seems, then, that replication is possible in the extraction and definition of P, as well as of N and E, and to this extent our study suggests confirmation of our hypothesis.

Upon consideration of the results of this and the previous analysis, twenty items were selected to represent the P factor, twenty items to represent the N factor, and twenty items to represent the E factor. Considerations present in our minds when selecting these items were as follows: (1) high loadings on the factor in question; (2) consistency of loadings over different samples and sexes; (3) low loadings on

TABLE 5 Indices of factor comparisons for male and female groups in random sample and normal sample

	RS_M vs. NS_M	RS_F vs. NS_F	RS_M vs. NS_F	RS_F vs. NS_M
N	.977	.997	.935	.980
E	.999	.992	.994	.984
P	.946	.992	.894	1.000

factors not being measured; (4) consistency of loading from three-factor solution to third-order solution; (5) known previous loadings in earlier analyses on different factors (cf. discussion in S.B.G. Eysenck and H.J. Eysenck, 1968). Table 6 shows the twenty items selected to measure factor P, together with the numbers of these items in the original 106-item questionnaire (to facilitate cross-checking with the previous analysis) and factor loadings for the three-factor solution on N, E and P, males and females separately. Consideration of the nature and wording of these twenty questions will clarify the notion of 'psychoticism' better than any verbal discussion could do at this stage. It should be noted, of course, that up to this stage the term 'psychoticism' implies an aspiration rather than a demonstrated relevance to psychotic behaviour.

The original study gives the twenty items respectively relevant to the N and E factors. There is little of special interest here, except perhaps to note the low P factor loadings of the items in both sets. This is of course a vital and indeed indispensable part of our theory, and its verification is of importance.

The factors as extracted are not of course necessarily orthogonal; the supreme virtue of the Promax type of rotation procedure is that it allows the factors to assume their natural positions relative to each other, rather than be forced into orthogonality, as would be the case with Varimax. Table 7 gives the correlations between the factors for this sample, as well as those for the random sample; it will be seen that again the P vs. N correlations are the only important ones, and that they are somewhat higher than in the RS group. It is not known why this should be so; possibly the absence of the young student groups from the NS groups may be responsible, although it is not clear why this should be so.

Reliabilities were estimated for the P scale by means of the generalized form of the Kuder-Richardson Formula 20 (Hoyt, 1941). These are given in Table 8 for the RS, the NS, and the student groups. Considering the shortness of the scale, these reliabilities, which centre around .75, are distinctly encouraging; they suggest that there is indeed some solid common core to these twenty items. It may be mentioned in this connection that in the case of neurotic and psychotic subjects reliabilities are as high and higher; for 310 psychotics our provisional figure is .78, while for 217 neurotics it is .76. These are of course consistency reliabilities, not repeat ones, but in our experience the latter tend to run at roughly the same level as the former for personality inventories of this kind. In any case, the former are perhaps more crucial for the theory underlying the construction of the P scale.

The results of this experiment need little discussion. It is clear that items can be found which (a) are theoretically relevant to the hypothesis of a 'psychoticism' factor, (b) cohere together factorially in a consistent manner, (c) show relative

TABLE 6   Loadings of twenty P items on N, E and P

	Three-factor solution					
	N		E		P	
	Males	Females	Males	Females	Males	Females
4. Do most things taste the same to you?	-.05	-.04	-.07	-.05	.37	.19
7. Do you enjoy hurting people you love?	.17	.27	.01	.03	.28	.03
10. Are you generally in good health?	.03	.08	.12	.12	-.42	-.47
13. Was your mother a good woman?	.03	-.16	.10	.03	-.37	-.02
16. Have you had more trouble than most?	.16	.12	.05	.07	.30	.29
19. Have you had an awful lot of bad luck?	.21	.01	.15	.07	.36	.49
21. Do you worry a lot about catching diseases?	.10	-.07	.10	.06	.39	.35
23. Did you love your mother?	-.02	-.24	.21	.08	-.25	-.00
27. Are there several people who keep trying to avoid you?	-.06	.08	.06	.03	.54	.35
29. Is there someone who is responsible for most of your troubles?	.28	.09	.06	-.04	.19	.44
30. Do you let your dreams warn or guide you?	-.08	.18	.02	-.00	.54	.24
32. Do people generally seem to take offence easily?	.13	-.02	.09	-.03	.40	.44
33. Would you take drugs which may have strange or dangerous effects?	.12	.30	-.03	.02	.19	-.07
40. Do you have enemies who wish to harm you?	.11	-.12	.07	.01	.46	.50
44. Do your friendships break up easily without it being your fault?	.11	.03	-.08	.05	.39	.44
47. Was your father a good man?	-.10	-.09	.06	.01	-.31	-.04
55. Do people mean to say and do things to annoy you?	.21	.11	.08	.14	.38	.40
58. Would you have been more successful if people had not put difficulties in your way?	.18	-.01	.03	.09	.26	.48
62. When you are in a crowded place like a bus do you worry about dangers of infection?	-.09	-.06	-.00	.03	.55	.20
99. Would it upset you a lot to see a child or animal suffer?	.01	.05	-.00	.11	-.30	.07

TABLE 7   Correlations among N, E and P factors

	RS		NS	
	Males	Females	Males	Females
N vs. E	−.14	.15	−.18	−.03
N vs. P	.30	.34	.45	.40
E vs. P	−.13	−.05	−.17	−.04
n	512	821	500	500

TABLE 8   Reliability of P scale for various groups tested

	Reliability
NS, males	.81
NS, females	.70
RS, males	.77
RS, females	.72
Students, males	.66
Students, females	.76

independence of N and E, (d) measure this factor P reliably in a normal population, (e) give similar results for males and females, and (f) produce repeatable patterns when different population samples are tested. All this is necessary but not sufficient to support our hypothesis; further work is clearly needed, particularly with respect to the answer patterns of abnormal (psychotic and neurotic) groups. However, as far as they go the data reported here are in line with our hypothesis, and support the notion of a psychoticism factor as one of the major dimensions of personality.

Our next study (S.B.G. Eysenck and H.J. Eysenck, 1969a) was concerned with the effects of age, sex and social class on P (as well as on E and N). Such knowledge as we possess on these factors is almost entirely restricted to E and N. Past work suggests that E decreases with age, is not strongly related to social class, and is higher in males than in females. N also decreases with age, is slightly higher in the lower social strata, and is higher in females than in males (S.B.G. Eysenck, 1960; H.J. Eysenck, 1956; S.B.G. Eysenck and H.J. Eysenck, 1964b; H.J. Eysenck, 1958). In the present study we use the sets of questions from the S.B.G. Eysenck and H.J. Eysenck (1968) paper to measure P, E and N; this inventory will be referred to as the PEN inventory.

With respect to P nothing is known, but we may form certain vague expectations based on the hypothesis that this factor will bear a similar relation to external factors as does clinically diagnosed psychosis. Thus it is known that the prevalence of schizophrenia is eight times higher in the lower social classes than in the upper; this suggests that there may be a negative correlation between P and social class (Hollingshead and Redlich, 1958). This expectation disregards the possibly direct relation between social class and manic-depressive disorder, for the simple reason that the schizophrenias are much more widespread than other functional psychotic disorders, and thus make up the larger part of a psychotic population. As regards sex, our expectation might be that males would show higher P scores than females; the evidence suggests that age-adjusted first-admission rates to public mental hospitals in the USA are some 20 per cent higher for men than for women (Kramer *et al.*, 1961). Age is difficult to prognosticate for; schizophrenia is often said to occur in the young, manic-depressive disorder in late middle age. It is thus barely possible that there might be a U-shaped relation between age and P, but this would depend on so many additional assumptions that even less confidence is felt in such a prediction than in those preceding it. All in all, the hypothetico-deductive method is more appropriate in studies where at least some well-documented knowledge already exists; in this field we are only just at the beginning of serious study of the incidence of P in normal populations, and extrapolations of the not very secure knowledge of correlates of psychotic behaviour in clinical groups cannot be a very safe guide to prediction.

We have already described the methods used to collect several thousand respondents for the PEN inventory. Several of the groups used constituted in fact close approximations to random samples of the population; these groups had been assembled by a market-research firm for other purposes. The remainder were collected in a relatively haphazard manner from a great variety of sources; this random type of selection does not make it likely that any strong source of specific selectivity would have crept in to vitiate our data. Subjects did not write their names, as it was thought that anonymity would be more likely to produce undissimulated answers, but they were asked to fill in their sex, age and occupation. Housewives and students were not made part of the main analysis as their social status could not be ascertained. All other respondents who gave classifiable data were graded according to the Field Manual, Part 2, 'Classification Definitions and Social Grading', of Research Services Ltd. This specifies five main groups: (1) upper middle class; (2) middle class; (3) lower middle class; (4) skilled working class; and (5) semi-skilled and unskilled working class. (A sixth group, referring to those at the lowest level of subsistence, was not included in our analysis.) We have in the above substituted numbers for the letter classification used by Research Services; this seems more suitable for our purposes, and does not of course make any difference to the results. For detailed discussion and definition of the grades used, the Manual should be consulted. In view of the relatively small number of respondents in class 1 this was combined with class 2, thus reducing the number of classes to four. The reliability and validity of the class score is probably not as high as might be desired, for obvious reasons; this factor would attenuate differences reported below, which might be much larger had a more valid score been available.

The results may be summarized as follows: (1) Age: young people are high on E, high on N and high on P; (2) Sex: males are high on E, high on P, and low on N; (3) Social class: middle-class people are low on E, low on N and low on P. None of these differences are very large, but they are all sufficiently marked to be statistically significant.

The social variables discussed so far may not be the only ones relevant to comparison between different groups; specific jobs may have characteristic personality patterns which cut across class lines (Eysenck, 1967). For this reason details have been given in the EPQ Manual of the mean P, E and N scores of groups of respondents having certain jobs or positions—nurses, firemen, teachers, etc. Also shown are two large groups of 700 male and 700 female students not included in our main analysis because they cannot be assigned a proper social status, and 327 housewives, also excluded for the same reason.

Students are rather high on N; both male and female students outrank all other groups in this respect (except the very small group of female apprentices). Considering their age they are very slightly introverted and below average on P, although not very much. Housewives are marginally higher on N and P than working women of roughly their own age; on E they do not differ. It is interesting that welfare workers of both sexes, as well as occupational therapists, have exceptionally low scores on P; butchers, bakers and factory workers have exceptionally high ones. Not too much must be read into these figures, of course, in particular because of the small size of some of the groups, but it is felt that this Table makes an interesting beginning for a dimensional study of personality correlates of different jobs and positions.

The results of this study tend on the whole to agree with previous work and with such anticipations as could reasonably be deduced from epidemiological psychiatric knowledge. They suggest that in making comparisons between experimental groups and standardization data for personality inventories, factors like sex, age and social class should be taken into account, and that standardization data should be given in much greater detail than is usually the case. It cannot of course be claimed that the data are representative of the population from which the sample was drawn; there are many subtle ways in which distortions could have come in to affect the overall picture. Nevertheless, the congruence between our present findings and results previously reported, and between different sections of our data, suggests that differences observed, although not large in absolute amount, are true differences. Furthermore, they are in line with common-sense observation and expectation; youth has always been the time of *Sturm und Drang*, and the high scores of our young sample on N, E and P is in line with this observation. Neither is the greater mental stability of the middle-class sample, as compared with the working-class sample, surprising in view of epidemiological evidence (Hoch and Zubin, 1961). The same applies to sex differences: the greater proportion of women neurotics and men psychotics has been noticed many times. These facts are of interest mainly in that they support the hypotheses concerning the nature of the factors labelled N and P respectively. It is to be hoped that further work will be carried on in this field to put on a safer footing the findings of this study.

The PEN has been used by several workers, but it suffers by having a significant correlation between N and P. An attempt was made to eliminate this correlation by changing several items, and the new scales were applied to 170 normal male and 192 normal female subjects, selected according to the criteria already discussed in relation to our previous sample (S.B.G. Eysenck and H.J. Eysenck, 1972).

The subjects were administered a 110-item questionnaire incorporating four types of items, believed on the basis of prior work and theoretical analysis to measure four different dimensions of personality. These four types of item consisted of N items, E items, P items, and in addition L (Lie scale) items forming a scale for the detection of dissimulation; Michaelis and Eysenck (1971) have shown that this scale, in addition to measuring dissimulation, may also be regarded as a personality scale for certain purposes, and under certain conditions. The items in the questionnaire were intercorrelated (product-moment) for men and women separately, and principal component factor analysis carried out; four factors were extracted and rotated by Promax. These four factors constitute the substantive result of our work; if we have been successful they should (1) correspond in their make up to the hypothetical factors P, E, N, and L, and (2) should be orthogonal—that is, uncorrelated with each other. Promax rotation allows the factors to be correlated—that is, it does not (like Varimax) impose constraints on them which force them into orthogonality; consequently, it is possible for the data to infirm our assumptions about orthogonality.

Results in the original paper are presented in the form of four Tables, giving the loadings of the most highly loading twenty items for each factor. Loadings are given separately for men and women, and in each case loadings are given for all four factors, to demonstrate not only that given items load highly on the factor they are supposed to measure, but also fail to load on the other three factors.

Table 9 lists the P items. It will be seen that these fall into line very well; the majority are items used in previous analyses, but there are several new items which show good loadings on P and low loadings on other factors.

Reliabilities and means for the resulting scales are given in Table 10, the reliabilities being calculated by Kuder-Richardson formula 20. It will be seen that, for the men, reliabilities for the scales are satisfactory, and that P is not significantly lower than E or L. For the women, the reliabilities are much the same as for the men, except for P, which is significantly lower. The reason for this would seem to be bound up with the large differences in mean scores between the sexes; men have much larger P scores than do women, a finding which replicates earlier results. Consistently low scores within a group are not compatible with a reasonably high reliability, and hence it seems likely that this is the explanation of the observed differences in reliability between the two samples. The other differences in mean scores between the sexes are also in the expected direction, and agree with previous findings. Women score significantly higher on N and on L; men are somewhat (though not significantly) higher on E.

Table 11 lists intercorrelations between factors, and also between the twenty-item scales. It will be seen that these are low throughout and mostly insignificant; a value of r of approximately .20 would be required for significance at the $p < .01$ level. The only consistent relationship which appears is the negative correlation between L and N; this is sufficiently low to suggest the almost complete absence of dissimulation (Michaelis and Eysenck, 1971). Altogether these figures suggest that we succeeded in our task of writing a set of items which would be reliable and orthogonal to existing factors.

The results given in this chapter preceded the analyses which resulted in the final version of the inventory, to be discussed in the next chapter. Most of the published material so far discussed dealt with the PEN, but another version rather widely used was the PI (Personality Inventory), consisting of a P scale slightly different from that contained in the PEN, and the N and E scales from Form A of the EPI. This scale will be referred to in later chapters, notably in connection with our work on delinquency; it is mentioned here for the sake of completeness. It is of course rather confusing that so many different versions of the P scale were used at different times, but these are practically interchangeable, and correlate very highly together, containing as they do largely identical items. The final version is slightly superior to earlier ones—higher reliability, greater independence of P from N and E,

continues on page 64

TABLE 9 Factor loadings of twenty items defining the psychoticism scale

	Males				Females			
	N	E	P	L	N	E	P	L
1. Do most things taste the same to you?	.11	.07	.33	.22	.09	.12	.18	.15
2. Would it upset you a lot to see a child or an animal suffer?	.25	-.10	-.52	.12	.31	.14	-.12	.04
3. Do you think that marriage is old-fashioned and should be done away with?	-.08	-.05	.47	-.05	.01	-.03	.45	.01
4. Do you love your mother?	.08	.21	-.43	.14	-.17	.14	.04	.01
5. Do you enjoy hurting people you love?	.10	-.10	.48	-.18	.10	.07	.29	-.12
6. Can you easily understand the way people feel when they tell you their troubles?	.09	.12	-.31	.23	.12	.16	-.41	.17
7. Would you like to think that other people are afraid of you?	.08	.05	.42	-.07	.02	.15	.46	-.11
8. Would you take drugs which may have strange or dangerous effects?	.18	.08	.36	-.16	.14	.22	.26	-.12
9. Do you enjoy practical jokes that can sometimes really hurt people?	.00	.17	.24	-.05	-.18	.03	.26	-.11
10. Is your mother a good person?	.04	.23	-.58	.08	-.13	.07	-.03	.04
11. Have you always been known as a loner?	.18	-.36	.23	.12	.01	-.30	.40	.10
12. Do your friendships break up easily without it being your fault?	.20	-.15	.30	.03	-.11	-.03	.32	.12
13. Would you feel very sorry for an animal caught in a trap?	.17	-.02	-.42	.07	.25	.18	-.28	-.05
14. Are you always specially careful with other people's things?	.03	-.02	-.45	.34	.03	-.24	-.24	.19
15. When you are in a crowd, do you worry about catching germs?	.15	-.06	.25	.17	.20	.07	.30	.14

16. Do you try not to be rude to people?	.11	−.09	−.36	.22	.06	−.16	−.31	−.06
17. Do you sometimes get cross?	.16	.03	−.46	−.28	.15	.04	−.21	−.12
18. Have you ever told a lie?	.03	−.02	−.56	−.20	−.07	.03	.04	−.21
19. Do good manners and cleanliness matter much to you?	.06	−.03	−.37	.40	.14	.02	−.38	.04
20. Did you mind filling in this questionnaire?	−.11	.04	.32	−.13	.08	−.09	.18	−.01

TABLE 10 Reliability, means and standard deviations for twenty-item scales of P, E, N and L for men and women

	Reliabilities		*Means and SDs*	
	Males	Females	Males	Females
P	.74	.57	2.74±2.72	1.57±1.70
E	.79	.78	12.67±4.12	12.43±3.96
N	.84	.82	9.59±4.71	12.31±4.31
L	.78	.74	6.74±3.88	7.84±3.76

TABLE 11 Intercorrelations between factors and between scales

	Intercorrelations between factors					
	NE	NL	NP	EL	EP	LP
Males	−.03	−.14	.03	−.16	−.01	.04
Females	−.06	−.21	.19	−.08	.03	−.07
	Intercorrelations between scales					
Males	−.01	−.16	−.01	−.19	−.08	−.10
Females	−.14	−.18	.12	−.08	−.05	−.07

better distribution of scores (more normal)—but in essence what has been established with the use of earlier scales would almost certainly be true of the final P scale also.

5

The construction of the P scale: The final version

The final version of the EPQ is described in considerable detail in the Manual of the EPQ (Eysenck and Eysenck, 1975); most of the data here given are taken from that publication. However, accumulation of data has continued beyond the point where the Manual was written, and consequently we have on occasion given means, standard deviations and other statistics based on larger samples than those referred to in the Manual. Our collection of samples has been much simplified by our finding (to be discussed presently) that social class has relatively little influence on scores on the scales used; age and sex are clearly much more important, as well as being much easier to ascertain. The relative lack of importance of social class makes the construction of reasonable samples much easier, and if our claim be accepted that class is of marginal influence only, then our samples may be regarded as reasonably representative. Even so, we have always tried to include members of all social classes: details are given in the Manual. We do not claim to have used truly random or representative samples, but we have avoided the frequent error of test makers of using students as representatives of the non-psychiatric population; the great majority of our subjects are in fact not students, but wage earners, housewives, and other 'normal' groups.

The final version of the Adult EPQ is given below. The items are of course largely identical with those used in previous versions, i.e. the PEN and the PI, but a determined effort has been made to select the best items, rewrite items which were considered promising, and introduce new items only where there was good reason to think that they would round out the existing factor structure. It may prove interesting to the reader to check our factor loadings for each item used in previous studies against the factor loadings of the same item as obtained in previous analyses; this is a more convincing argument for factor immutability than statistical estimates of standard errors, or other similar manipulations of data from a single application. Of equal interest, of course, is the comparison of data from the male and female samples; we have looked for consistency in this comparison before accepting items into our final questionnaire.

The EPQ (Adult)

1.	Do you have many different hobbies?	E
2.	Do you stop to think things over before doing anything?	—P
3.	Does your mood often go up and down?	N
4.	Have you ever taken the praise for something you knew someone else had really done?	—L
5.	Are you a talkative person?	E

6.	Would being in debt worry you?	—P
7.	Do you ever feel 'just miserable' for no reason?	N
8.	Were you ever greedy by helping yourself to more than your share of anything?	—L
9.	Do you lock up your house carefully at night?	—P
10.	Are you rather lively?	E
11.	Would it upset you a lot to see a child or an animal suffer?	—P
12.	Do you often worry about things you should not have done or said?	N
13.	If you say you will do something, do you always keep your promise no matter how inconvenient it might be?	L
14.	Can you usually let yourself go and enjoy yourself at a lively party?	E
15.	Are you an irritable person?	N
16.	Have you ever blamed someone for doing something you knew was really your fault?	—L
17.	Do you enjoy meeting new people?	E
18.	Do you believe insurance schemes are a good idea?	—P
19.	Are your feelings easily hurt?	N
20.	Are *all* your habits good and desirable ones?	L
21.	Do you tend to keep in the background on social occasions?	—E
22.	Would you take drugs which may have strange or dangerous effects?	P
23.	Do you often feel 'fed-up'?	N
24.	Have you ever taken anything (even a pin or button) that belonged to someone else?	—L
25.	Do you like going out a lot?	E
26.	Do you enjoy hurting people you love?	P
27.	Are you often troubled about feelings of guilt?	N
28.	Do you sometimes talk about things you know nothing about?	—L
29.	Do you prefer reading to meeting people?	—E
30.	Do you have enemies who want to harm you?	P
31.	Would you call yourself a nervous person?	N
32.	Do you have many friends?	E
33.	Do you enjoy practical jokes that can sometimes really hurt people?	P
34.	Are you a worrier?	N
35.	As a child did you do as you were told immediately and without grumbling?	L
36.	Would you call yourself happy-go-lucky?	E
37.	Do good manners and cleanliness matter much to you?	—P
38.	Do you worry about awful things that might happen?	N
39.	Have you ever broken or lost something belonging to someone else?	—L
40.	Do you usually take the initiative in making new friends?	E
41.	Would you call yourself tense or 'highly-strung'?	N
42.	Are you mostly quiet when you are with other people?	—E
43.	Do you think marriage is old-fashioned and should be done away with?	P

44.	Do you sometimes boast a little?	−L
45.	Can you easily get some life into a rather dull party?	E
46.	Do people who drive carefully annoy you?	P
47.	Do you worry about your health?	N
48.	Have you ever said anything bad or nasty about anyone?	−L
49.	Do you like telling jokes and funny stories to your friends?	E
50.	Do most things taste the same to you?	P
51.	As a child were you ever cheeky to your parents?	−L
52.	Do you like mixing with people?	E
53.	Does it worry you if you know there are mistakes in your work?	−P
54.	Do you suffer from sleeplessness?	N
55.	Do you always wash before a meal?	L
56.	Do you nearly always have a 'ready answer' when people talk to you?	E
57.	Do you like to arrive at appointments in plenty of time?	−P
58.	Have you often felt listless and tired for no reason?	N
59.	Have you ever cheated at a game?	−L
60.	Do you like doing things in which you have to act quickly?	E
61.	Is (or was) your mother a good woman?	−P
62.	Do you often feel life is very dull?	N
63.	Have you ever taken advantage of someone?	−L
64.	Do you often take on more activities than you have time for?	E
65.	Are there several people who keep trying to avoid you?	P
66.	Do you worry a lot about your looks?	N
67.	Do you think people spend too much time safeguarding their future with savings and insurances?	P
68.	Have you ever wished that you were dead?	N
69.	Would you dodge paying taxes if you were sure you could never be found out?	−L
70.	Can you get a party going?	E
71.	Do you try not to be rude to people?	−P
72.	Do you worry too long after an embarrassing experience?	N
73.	Have you ever insisted on having your own way?	−L
74.	When you catch a train do you often arrive at the last minute?	P
75.	Do you suffer from 'nerves'?	N
76.	Do your friendships break up easily without it being your fault?	P
77.	Do you often feel lonely?	N
78.	Do you always practise what you preach?	L
79.	Do you sometimes like teasing animals?	P
80.	Are you easily hurt when people find fault with you or the work you do?	N
81.	Have you ever been late for an appointment or work?	−L
82.	Do you like plenty of bustle and excitement around you?	E
83.	Would you like other people to be afraid of you?	P
84.	Are you sometimes bubbling over with energy and sometimes very sluggish?	N
85.	Do you sometimes put off until tomorrow what you ought to do today?	−L

continues overleaf

86.	Do other people think of you as being very lively?	E
87.	Do people tell you a lot of lies?	P
88.	Are you touchy about some things?	N
89.	Are you always willing to admit it when you have made a mistake?	L
90.	Would you feel very sorry for an animal caught in a trap?	−P

Table 12 shows the loadings of the original 101 items on four factors extracted and rotated into oblique simple structure, using the same methods of extraction and rotation as before. Also given are the letters indicating the scales in which the items appear in the scoring key; a stroke indicates that the item is not scored. The population on which the analysis was carried out consisted of 1,796 males and 2,565 females; this is an unusually large number, but we believe that many factor analyses reach inconclusive results because of insufficient numbers of subjects. Comparison with previous analyses, on smaller numbers of subjects, and using somewhat different sets of items, indicated that by and large items have retained their loadings with considerable accuracy; this is reassuring. Table 13 shows the intercorrelations between the factors; it will be seen that these are rather low, with the exception (not unexpected) of L, which correlates negatively with P and N, as usual. These correlations are sufficiently low to indicate that the respondents filled in the questionnaires with a minimum of dissimulation. There is a slight correlation (negative) between E and N, too slight to matter substantively, and an even slighter one between P and N (positive). All in all, the factors are as near orthogonal as could have been hoped. Table 14 shows the intercorrelations between the scales; these are quite similar to those between the factors.

TABLE 12 Loadings of 101 items on four factors

	Males n = 1,796				Females n = 2,565				
	P	E	N	L	P	E	N	L	
1.	−.02	.31	.05	.05	−.02	.25	−.01	−.00	E
2.	−.29	−.00	.03	.03	−.27	−.11	.01	.05	P
3.	.08	.10	.52	−.02	.10	.10	.52	−.10	N
4.	.07	.07	.08	−.38	.04	.06	.04	−.41	L
5.	−.02	.52	.03	−.05	−.02	.59	.08	.01	E
6.	−.37	−.02	.24	.08	−.36	−.03	.15	.08	P
7.	.11	−.05	.47	−.11	.02	−.02	.44	−.19	N
8.	−.02	.05	.00	−.54	−.02	.02	.02	−.54	L
9.	−.31	.07	.12	.14	−.22	.01	.21	.19	P
10.	−.08	.65	.07	.02	.02	.66	.01	.07	E
11.	−.39	.10	.07	−.10	−.25	.11	.11	.01	P
12.	−.25	.05	.51	−.04	−.25	.05	.46	−.05	N
13.	−.16	.04	−.07	.34	−.11	.04	−.03	.44	L
14.	.11	.21	−.08	−.11	.16	.13	−.11	−.12	—
15.	−.01	.57	−.01	.01	−.05	.56	.01	−.04	E

16.	.10	−.10	.37	−.03	.13	−.06	.39	−.15	N
17.	.06	.04	.18	−.38	.02	.02	.12	−.42	L
18.	−.18	.53	−.02	−.02	−.14	.51	−.05	−.07	E
19.	−.37	.09	.03	−.09	−.39	.07	.03	−.09	P
20.	−.14	−.10	.51	−.03	−.10	−.02	.51	.05	N
21.	.10	.14	−.01	.44	.13	.03	.00	.47	L
22.	.03	−.59	.13	.05	−.00	−.61	.11	.04	E
23.	.36	−.01	.00	−.08	.37	−.03	−.03	−.12	P
24.	.15	−.03	.55	−.02	.12	−.04	.54	−.10	N
25.	−.08	−.07	−.06	−.54	−.02	−.08	−.09	−.52	L
26.	.01	.54	.02	−.09	−.04	.51	.08	−.10	E
27.	.36	−.01	.18	.03	.27	−.02	.08	−.06	P
28.	−.10	.09	.53	.02	−.05	.05	.54	−.09	N
29.	−.01	.11	.13	−.40	.03	.13	.04	−.39	L
30.	.10	−.50	.01	.07	.18	−.50	.04	.09	E
31.	.35	.14	.20	.05	.36	.05	.17	.06	P
32.	−.06	−.16	.52	.06	.05	−.11	.56	.15	N
33.	−.26	.12	.14	.37	−.13	.19	.09	.39	−
34.	−.11	.52	−.08	−.06	−.21	.47	−.02	−.03	E
35.	.41	.13	.08	−.01	.28	.06	.04	−.06	P
36.	−.23	−.12	.61	−.01	−.16	−.03	.66	.06	N
37.	.04	−.00	.07	.41	.06	−.05	.01	.38	L
38.	.18	.38	−.09	.16	.22	.40	−.15	.14	E
39.	−.40	.16	.15	.15	−.34	.12	.16	.14	P
40.	−.11	.06	.54	.09	−.04	.03	.57	.07	N
41.	−.03	.05	.01	−.39	−.03	−.01	−.06	−.42	L
42.	−.00	.58	−.00	.10	.02	.57	.06	.10	E
43.	−.19	.13	.04	.06	−.09	.11	.07	.15	−
44.	.04	−.06	.49	.19	.15	−.03	.53	.20	N
45.	.29	.12	.04	−.26	.28	.09	−.01	−.27	−
46.	.06	−.54	.12	.12	.07	−.57	.10	.09	E
47.	.43	.05	.03	.07	.37	.02	.02	.01	P
48.	−.10	.01	.42	−.29	−.08	.03	.35	−.34	−
49.	−.11	.18	.08	−.42	−.04	.18	.09	−.43	L
50.	.12	.63	.04	.23	.21	.61	.06	.22	E
51.	.32	.03	.09	−.03	.26	.06	.04	−.10	P
52.	−.08	.18	.37	.08	.02	.09	.48	.11	N
53.	−.12	.01	.02	−.53	−.13	−.02	.06	−.51	L
54.	−.04	.37	.04	−.17	.02	.36	.04	−.14	E
55.	.25	−.01	.14	.22	.24	−.04	.06	.16	P
56.	.05	−.02	.42	−.20	−.01	−.01	.33	−.31	−
57.	−.04	.08	−.05	−.40	.00	.09	−.03	−.36	L
58.	−.17	.59	−.05	−.06	−.22	.55	−.02	−.10	E
59.	−.40	−.03	.18	.03	−.31	.01	.27	.12	P
60.	.18	.01	.30	.04	.17	−.01	.34	.13	N
61.	−.11	.15	.09	.37	−.08	.11	.08	.34	L
62.	.09	.23	−.04	.09	.11	.37	−.02	.17	E
63.	−.27	.05	.06	.13	−.23	.02	.11	.15	P
64.	.08	.00	.44	−.04	.05	.02	.51	−.02	N

table continues overleaf

65.	.06	.12	.03	−.48	.07	.03	−.06	−.47	L
66.	.02	.34	−.10	−.02	.16	.33	−.13	.04	E
67.	−.24	.08	.03	−.03	−.18	.14	−.01	.01	P
68.	.24	−.08	.41	.06	.26	−.08	.40	−.01	N
69.	.13	.13	.06	−.50	.10	.07	.05	−.52	L
70.	.02	.24	.06	−.14	.02	.26	.07	−.08	E
71.	.32	.07	.24	.07	.33	.01	.19	.01	P
72.	−.05	.19	.37	−.09	−.02	.13	.38	−.12	N
73.	−.20	.05	.05	.35	−.16	.05	.00	.35	−
74.	.40	.02	.02	.07	.41	.06	−.02	.03	P
75.	.24	−.04	.33	−.05	.18	−.03	.32	−.11	N
76.	.20	.02	.04	−.27	.16	.04	−.00	−.29	L
77.	.11	.67	−.02	.17	.16	.60	−.01	.13	E
78.	−.36	−.00	.04	.06	−.29	.02	−.01	.06	P
79.	−.18	−.17	.51	−.03	−.22	−.09	.51	−.00	N
80.	−.00	.08	−.02	−.34	−.06	.08	.06	−.31	L
81.	.27	.02	−.01	−.19	.18	.06	−.04	−.20	P
82.	−.03	−.08	.53	.05	.05	−.04	.56	.16	N
83.	.18	.03	.10	−.38	.14	−.03	.11	−.38	−
84.	.05	−.23	.13	.18	.03	−.18	.11	.23	−
85.	.23	−.05	.28	.14	.28	−.00	.22	.06	P
86	.18	−.08	.52	.07	.26	−.11	.45	.02	N
87.	−.00	.09	−.01	.49	.07	.05	−.04	.52	L
88.	.23	.04	.08	−.15	.13	.01	.01	−.15	P
89.	−.16	−.10	.50	−.05	−.15	−.03	.46	.04	N
90.	.13	.29	.04	−.08	.22	.23	−.01	−.15	−
91.	−.04	−.03	−.08	−.38	−.00	−.03	−.05	−.38	L
92.	.04	.52	.04	−.10	.01	.55	.07	−.06	E
93.	.32	.07	.19	.00	.31	−.02	.10	.01	P
94.	.07	.12	.39	−.11	.03	.16	.40	−.16	N
95.	−.08	−.13	.05	−.46	−.07	−.04	−.02	−.40	L
96.	.03	.63	.07	.11	.05	.68	.06	.11	E
97.	.27	.10	.27	.11	.32	.06	.22	.09	P
98.	−.13	.07	.39	−.16	−.02	.01	.38	−.16	N
99.	−.12	.08	−.01	.41	−.02	.17	−.02	.43	L
100.	−.30	.05	.05	−.04	−.21	.04	.02	−.05	P
101.	.26	−.03	−.04	−.03	.16	−.01	.02	.05	−

TABLE 13 Intercorrelations of P, E, N and L factors

	PE	PN	PL	EN	EL	NL
Males	.04	.11	−.23	−.10	−.09	−.15
Females	.05	.09	−.19	−.21	−.07	−.15

TABLE 14 Intercorrelations between scales for 500 men and 500 women. Asterisks denote statistical significance at $p < .01$ level

	P	E	N	L	
P	–	.06	.12**	−.23**	
E	.07	–	−.16**	−.10	MALES
N	.07	−.14**	–	−.04	
L	−.19**	−.09	−.15**	–	

FEMALES

Scored forms are available for 1,796 male and 2,565 female subjects, and it may be of interest to consider the distributions of the scores. The reason for this interest is simply that these provide an *ad aculos* demonstration of the observed form of distribution; it would be quite wrong to consider the shape of the observed distributions as being necessarily indicative of the 'true' distribution of the underlying trait. The observed distribution of scores depends on such factors as choice of items, the percentage endorsement of the particular items chosen, their intercorrelation, and many other such factors which might not be replicated in another scale made up of different items. Ideally, of course, one would select items in such a way that normality of distribution could be obtained, but this is less important than the other criteria we have had in mind for the selection of items, and consequently we have not used score distribution in considering items for inclusion. Several of the distributions, notably those for P, deviate markedly from normality, being positively or negatively skewed. There would be little point in providing a more accurate statistical description of the shape of the curves in terms of higher moments, and we have not done so.

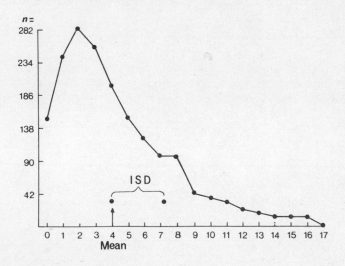

Figure 14 Distribution of male P scores

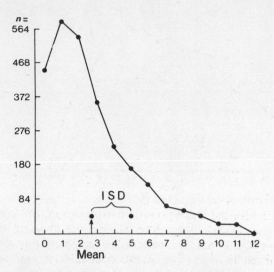

Figure 15   Distribution of female P scores

Figures 14 and 15 show the distributions for P, for males and females respectively. Both show the same kind of skewness, the females more markedly than the males. This is of course due to the higher mean score of the males; means and standard deviations have been indicated in the graphs. Because of the differences in total number of male and female subjects, and in the different number of steps on the abscissa for the different scales, the units on the ordinate in the various graphs are not identical; this does not importantly affect the overall shape of the curves, but does make detailed comparison difficult. Such comparisons would serve little purpose, and would add little to what can be gleaned from the means and standard deviations provided.

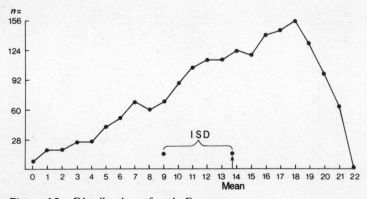

Figure 16   Distribution of male E scores

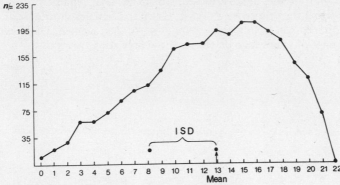

Figure 17 Distribution of female E scores

Figures 16 and 17, which give the distributions for extraversion, are somewhat closer to normal, but are also skewed, although in the opposite direction to P. In other words, few people are high P, but many are high E, comparatively speaking, and defining these traits entirely in terms of our questionnaire. Males, as usual, have a higher mean, and consequently show a more skewed distribution.

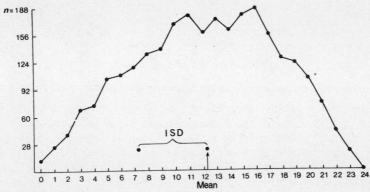

Figure 18 Distribution of male N scores

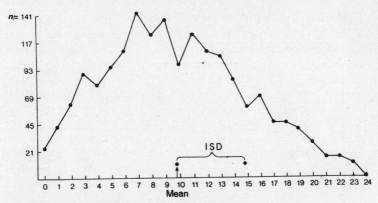

Figure 19 Distribution of female N scores

Figures 18 and 19 give the distributions of males and females for N; these are much more normal than those for P and E. Males and females show a slight skew in opposite directions, men having a lower mean score than women. The distributions span a wider range of scores than do those of the preceding two traits.

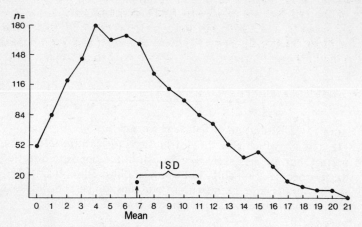

Figure 20   Distribution of male L scores

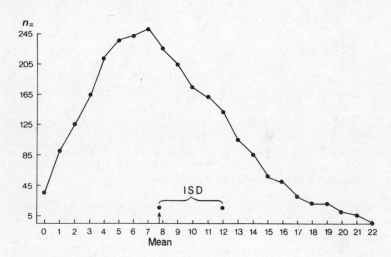

Figure 21   Distribution of female L scores

Figures 20 and 21 again show a slight skew, more notably so for the men than the women; this is due to the higher scores of the women. These, like the other scores, could of course easily be transformed into a semblance of normality by suitable transformations, but there seemed to be little point in doing so. As we shall see in connection with the work on genetic factors, where normality of distribution is important, transformations did succeed in making the results simpler and easier to deal with.

We next turn to the question of the reliability of the scales. Table 15 gives results for various groups tested and retested with an interval of one month, a time interval long enough for subjects to have forgotten their original replies, but not long enough for any serious personality changes to have occurred. The results are quite favourable, with reliabilities mostly lying in the .80 to .90 region. The reliabilities in the last line are of course the most trustworthy, being based on a sample of 257 subjects, and having age and sex effects removed; these values range from .78 (for P) to .89 (for E). From the point of view of test-retest reliability, we may say that the EPQ is not inferior to any other published personality test.

TABLE 15   Test-retest reliabilities, one month intervening

MALES		n	P	E	N	L
1.	Dental Students	80	.83	.89	.87	.90
2.	Polytechnic Students	23	.80	.89	.92	.79
3.	Social Workers	16	.79	.92	.91	.76
4.	University Students	17	.76	.89	.90	.90
	TOTAL	136	.83	.90	.89	.86
FEMALES						
1.	Dental Students	31	.80	.88	.80	.87
2.	Polytechnic Students	8	.78	.96	.89	.87
3.	Social Workers	44	.86	.93	.86	.84
4.	University Students	38	.51	.80	.74	.61
	TOTAL	121	.71	.87	.80	.86
Grand Total, with effects of Sex and Age removed		257	.78	.89	.86	.84

Consistency reliabilities (also sometimes known as alpha coefficients) are an indication of the degree to which the questions in the scale cover a given area. Such reliabilities should not be too low (if they are, clearly the scale is too heterogeneous to measure any particular concept satisfactorily), but it would be a mistake to look for very high values either. If reliabilities are very high, this suggests that the area covered is too restricted; in terms of a terminology introduced by us some time ago (H.J. Eysenck and S.B.G. Eysenck, 1969) we would be dealing with the tautological item content. It is always possible to achieve very high reliabilities by simply using questions which are merely variants on a single theme; this must be avoided if the resulting factors and scales are to have any general meaning.

Table 16 gives alpha coefficients for males and females separately; we have used two groups of subjects—the one a normal, fairly random sample of the population, the other a sample of criminals tested in prison. The coefficients observed are satisfactory, being neither too high nor too low; most are above .80, with only P scale reliabilities falling below this value. We may conclude that for higher-order factors of personality, these reliabilities are adequate, and not inferior to those observed for other tests measuring similar factors.

TABLE 16   Internal consistency reliabilities

	MALES		FEMALES	
	Normal Group	Prisoners	Normal Group	Prisoners
P	.74	.71	.68	.77
E	.85	.84	.84	.86
N	.84	.84	.85	.88
L	.81	.82	.79	.86
Number in Sample	500	934	500	71

Standardization data on 2,312 men and 3,262 women are given in the Manual, separately for age and sex; the detailed figures will not be presented here again, but it may be of some interest to look at some of the age, sex and class regressions in diagrammatic form. We shall begin by looking at age. Figure 22 shows the decrease in P score with age; this is clearly much more marked for males than for females,

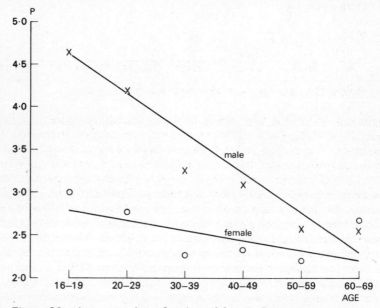

Figure 22   Age regression of male and female P scores

due no doubt to the much higher initial scores for the men. Both decline and interaction effects are statistically highly significant; in the discussions of different regressions that follow, we will not repeat this observation, nor will we present the details of the analyses. (With such large groups any effect that is visually clear is *eo ipso* very significant statistically, and although the calculations have been made, it would be a task of supererogation to present all the figures. Details are given in the Manual. Figure 23 shows the age effects on E; here too there is a clear decline, which again is more marked for men than for women. Indeed, the usual superiority of men appears to be found only in the below-forty groups; above that age, women appear more extraverted. This cross-over effect has probably not been found before because most work has been done with students, or in any case with younger age groups.

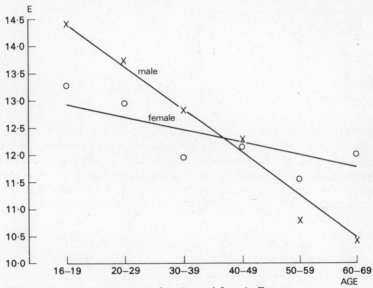

Figure 23   Age regression of male and female E scores

Figure 24 shows the age effects on N; N too declines, perhaps rather less precipitately than P and E, and here males and females run parallel, for all intents and purposes. The decline is not large, but nevertheless quite definite. Figure 25 shows the age effect on L; this is clearly the most marked of all. Again both sexes run pretty well parallel, and for both there is a strong increase in L; the score almost doubles between adolescence and old age. There can be no doubt about the importance of age for the measurement of personality; all four scales reveal significant effects, whether we use the term 'significant' in the statistical or in the common-sense meaning. Older people are less extraverted, less neurotic, less high on P, but much more orthodox (if we may interpret high L scores in this manner). It seems clear that questionnaires should always be accompanied by age norms, as otherwise scores become somewhat meaningless. The same is clearly true of separate sex norms; while the scores of men and women overlap extensively, they are nevertheless unquestionably different, and must be kept separate.

We must next turn to social class. For the purpose of the analysis, subjects were assigned to one of five groups: (1) upper middle class; (2) middle class; (3) lower middle class; (4) skilled working class; and (5) semi-skilled and unskilled working class. Analysis in combination of age, sex and class trends showed no age X sex class interaction effects, so that it became possible to analyse these two variables in

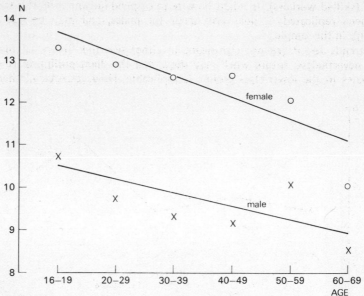

Figure 24 Age regression of male and female N scores

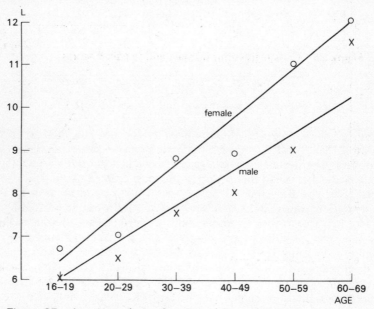

Figure 25 Age regressions of male and female L scores

isolation. (See Manual for details.) In the analysis of class effects, E and N show no effect, for either sex. Results for P and L are graphed in Figures 26 and 27. The statistical analysis shows that for L there is a highly significant linear trend, for both sexes; the lower-class groups have higher L scores. For females, there is also a somewhat inconvenient significant cubic trend, indicated by the high scores for

78

group 4 (skilled workers). It might be wise to suspend judgment on this trend until it has been replicated; it does not occur for males, and may be due to some peculiarity in the sample.

The trends for P are not significant in either sex, but Figure 26 may be of interest nevertheless; future work may show that the slight pulling-apart of males and females in the lower-class groups is replicable. However, overall there seems

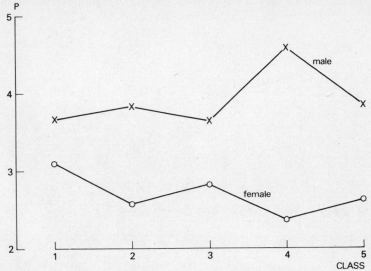

Figure 26   Class regressions of male and female P scores

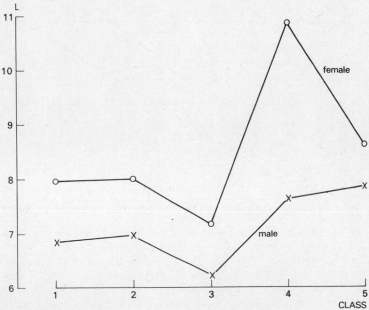

Figure 27   Class regression of male and female L scores

little doubt that class differences are slight or non-existent for P, E and N, and that as far as L is concerned we can best deal with this at present by postulating a one-point increase in score for the working-class as compared with the middle-class groups. Unlike age and sex, therefore, class does not need to be taken into account too seriously in constructing norms. In the Manual we have given separate norms for many different professions; this information is of interest to users of the scale, but it is not included here as it is irrelevant to the main purposes of this book.

6

The construction of the Junior P scale

The personality dimensions of E and N are measurable in the child population as well as in the adult population (H.J. Eysenck and S.B.G. Eysenck, 1969), and the Junior EPI has taken its place beside the Adult EPI for just that purpose. In this chapter, we shall survey the evidence regarding the possibility of measuring P in child populations, discuss the construction of the Junior EPQ, and furnish evidence on the age and sex correlates of P in young children. Our first reported study (S.B.G. Eysenck and H.J. Eysenck, 1969b) suggested that our anticipation of being able to measure P in children was not entirely erroneous.

A special printed inventory was constructed which contained the items making up the N, E and L questions of the Junior EPI (S.B.G. Eysenck, 1965a,b); in addition, it contained thirty-five potential P items. These P items were specially written for the purpose of this study; they were based on our experience with adult items in the factorial studies already cited. A few items were added to the re-written adult items on the basis of special suggestions given by experts in the field, particularly Dr S. Rachman. The direction of scoring will be intuitively evident in each case; there is never any doubt about the 'abnormal' answer to each question. The whole questionnaire is reproduced below so that our discussion of the items can be related to the actual inventory used.

The Junior PEN

1.	Do you like plenty of excitement going on around you?	YES	NO
2.	Do you often need kind friends to cheer you up?	YES	NO
3.	Do most things taste the same to you?	YES	NO
4.	Do you nearly always have a quick answer when people talk to you?	YES	NO
5.	Do you sometimes get cross?	YES	NO
6.	Do you enjoy hurting people you like?	YES	NO
7.	Are you moody?	YES	NO
8.	Would you rather be alone instead of meeting other children?	YES	NO
9.	Are you usually very unlucky?	YES	NO
10.	Do ideas run through your head so that you cannot sleep?	YES	NO
11.	Are other children's feelings much more easily hurt than yours?	YES	NO
12.	Do you always do as you are told at once?	YES	NO
13.	Do you like practical jokes?	YES	NO
14.	Do you always seem to be in trouble at home?	YES	NO
15.	Do you ever feel 'just miserable' for no good reason?	YES	NO
16.	Are you rather lively?	YES	NO

17.	Do you hate very strong peppermints?	YES	NO
18.	Have you ever broken any rules at school?	YES	NO
19.	Do you sometimes like teasing animals?	YES	NO
20.	Do lots of things annoy you?	YES	NO
21.	Do you like doing things where you have to act quickly?	YES	NO
22.	Are there many children at school who won't play with you?	YES	NO
23.	Do you worry about awful things that might happen?	YES	NO
24.	Can you always keep every secret?	YES	NO
25.	Do you very often just sit and do nothing?	YES	NO
26.	Can you get a party going?	YES	NO
27.	Do you get thumping in your heart?	YES	NO
28.	Do you feel sad most of the time?	YES	NO
29.	When you make new friends do you usually make the first move?	YES	NO
30.	Have you ever told a lie?	YES	NO
31.	Would it upset you a lot to see a dog that has just been run over?	YES	NO
32.	Are you easily hurt when people find fault with you or the work you do?	YES	NO
33.	Do you like telling jokes or funny stories to your friends?	YES	NO
34.	Even if it were very dangerous, would you still like to go to the moon in a rocket?	YES	NO
35.	Do you often feel tired for no good reason?	YES	NO
36.	Do you always finish your homework before you play?	YES	NO
37.	Is there anyone special who has it in for you?	YES	NO
38.	Are you usually happy and cheerful?	YES	NO
39.	Are you touchy about some things?	YES	NO
40.	When you are in a crowded place like a bus, do you worry about catching illnesses from people?	YES	NO
41.	Do you like mixing with other children?	YES	NO
42.	Do you say your prayers every night?	YES	NO
43.	Do you like to be busy most of the time?	YES	NO
44.	Do you have 'dizzy turns'?	YES	NO
45.	Are you in more trouble at school than most children?	YES	NO
46.	Do you like playing pranks on others?	YES	NO
47.	Do you often feel fed-up?	YES	NO
48.	When people are friendly, do you wonder whether they really mean it?	YES	NO
49.	Do you sometimes boast a little?	YES	NO
50.	Do you usually feel fine?	YES	NO
51.	Are you mostly quiet when you are with others?	YES	NO
52.	Do you sometimes get so restless that you cannot sit in a chair long?	YES	NO
53.	Do you worry a lot about catching illnesses?	YES	NO
54.	Do you often make up your mind to do things suddenly?	YES	NO
55.	Are you always quiet in class, even when the teacher is out of the room?	YES	NO
56.	Do children often mean to say and do things to make you cross?	YES	NO

57.	Do you have many frightening dreams?	YES	NO
58.	Can you usually let yourself go and enjoy yourself at a gay party?	YES	NO
59.	Would you do dangerous things for a dare?	YES	NO
60.	Are your feelings rather easily hurt?	YES	NO
61.	Are you often punished without any reason?	YES	NO
62.	Have you ever said anything bad or nasty about anyone?	YES	NO
63.	Would you call yourself happy-go-lucky?	YES	NO
64.	Would it bother you if you knew your home front door was unlocked at night?	YES	NO
65.	Do you worry for a long while if you feel you have made a fool of yourself?	YES	NO
66.	Do you often like a rough and tumble game?	YES	NO
67.	Do your friends stop playing with you, even when it is not your fault?	YES	NO
68.	Do you always eat everything you are given at meals?	YES	NO
69.	Would you like to go to the moon on your own?	YES	NO
70.	Do you find it very hard to take no for an answer?	YES	NO
71.	Do you like going out a lot?	YES	NO
72.	Do you like chocolate biscuits better than ginger ones?	YES	NO
73.	Do you sometimes feel life is just not worth living?	YES	NO
74.	Would you feel very sorry for an animal caught in a trap?	YES	NO
75.	Have you ever been cheeky to your parents?	YES	NO
76.	Do other people think of you as being very lively?	YES	NO
77.	Do you like strong tasting medicines?	YES	NO
78.	Does your mind ever wander off when you are doing a job?	YES	NO
79.	Would you rather sit and watch than play at parties?	YES	NO
80.	Could you do much better at tests if you were not hurried?	YES	NO
81.	Do you find it hard to get to sleep at nights because you are worrying about things?	YES	NO
82.	Do people tell you a lot of lies?	YES	NO
83.	Do you usually feel fairly sure you can do the things you have to?	YES	NO
84.	Do you often feel lonely?	YES	NO
85.	Are most children really bullies?	YES	NO
86.	Are you shy of speaking first when you meet new people?	YES	NO
87.	Do you often make up your mind when it is too late?	YES	NO
88.	Do you often get in a muddle?	YES	NO
89.	When children shout at you do you shout back?	YES	NO
90.	Do you sometimes feel specially cheerful and at other times sad without any good reason?	YES	NO
91.	Do you like wandering off on your own, without telling anyone?	YES	NO
92.	Do you find it hard to really enjoy yourself at a lively party?	YES	NO
93.	Do other children pick on you?	YES	NO
94.	Do you often get into trouble because you do things without thinking first?	YES	NO
95.	Do you like doing things that are a bit frightening?	YES	NO

A sample comprising 236 girls and 250 boys was tested, all of them members of a comprehensive school in the North of England. They varied in age from 11 to 15, roughly in equal numbers, with just one or two younger children included; the age of two boys was unknown. The inventory was given by their teachers as part of their school work, and does not seem to have aroused any undue apprehension or comment; children seem to take questionnaires very much as a matter of course. This sample is not, of course, a random one, but it does give a fair grouping of dull, average and bright children and, in any case, such selection as may have taken place unwittingly is not likely to have had the effect of artificially creating a factor where otherwise there would not be one.

Principal component analyses were carried out on the product-moment intercorrelations between the N, E and P items for the girls and boys separately; because of limitations on numbers of items simultaneously analysed, the L items had to be excluded. Three factors were extracted, and rotated into oblique simple structure by means of the Hendrickson and White (1964) Promax formula. Cattell has criticized this method of extracting what he calls 'pseudo-second-order factors' (Cattell, 1965), but H.J. Eysenck and S.B.G. Eysenck (1969) have demonstrated that such 'pseudo' second-order factors are virtually identical with 'genuine' second-order factors under conditions similar to those obtaining in the present analysis. Our main reason for not going through the routine of extracting primary factors first and then going on to higher-order factors was that in view of the small numbers of items in each of the main three superfactors, no very compelling primaries could have been expected; consequently, the method adopted seemed preferable.

The three factors extracted from the matrices of intercorrelations for the boys and girls seemed to be fairly clearly identifiable as N, E and P, in that order; the latent roots of the three factors were 7.34, 4.62 and 3.18 for the boys and 8.35, 4.51 and 3.02 for the girls. The intercorrelations between the factors were .06 and .04 (E vs. P), −.02 and .15 (N vs. P), and −.22 and −.31 (E vs. N)—demonstrating the virtual independence of P from both N and E. It is not clear why in this sample E and N should appear to be correlated; previous studies on much larger numbers of children have usually shown them to be quite uncorrelated (S.B.G. Eysenck, 1965a). However that may be, our interest in this book is, of course, in the P factor and its relations with E and N, and it is interesting to note that the positive and significant correlation between P and N which was found with adults is not found with children; an explanation of this difference is not obvious. However, it has often been pointed out that factor correlations are very dependent on precise qualities of the sample in question and several repetitions of the present study will, no doubt, be required before we can say with certainty just what the precise relationships between our factors are, and on what features of the sample they may depend.

Table 17 shows the loadings of the N items on N, E and P, for the boys and girls separately. It will be seen that in almost every case the N loadings are high, and the E and P loadings low; the one exception is item 94 (Do you often get into trouble because you do things without thinking first?) which has rather high loadings on P as well as on N.

Table 18 shows the loadings of the E items on N, E and P, for the boys and girls separately. Here again, E items are high in almost every case, but there are a few exceptions to this rule. Item 13 has loadings on P as well as on E (Do you like

TABLE 17 Factor loadings of N items on N, E and P factors

N Items	N	Boys E	P	N	Girls E	P
2	.28	.17	−.03	.35	.12	−.11
7	.34	.05	−.02	.31	−.11	.17
10	.34	.02	−.05	.48	.15	−.03
15	.48	.02	.00	.43	−.00	.03
20	.34	−.02	−.13	.37	−.20	.09
23	.48	.01	−.07	.59	.12	−.09
27	.39	.24	.01	.25	.03	.11
32	.50	.04	−.27	.49	−.05	−.19
35	.47	−.08	.13	.47	−.03	−.13
39	.42	.08	−.14	.42	.11	−.15
44	.44	−.03	−.03	.42	−.05	.08
47	.50	−.06	.19	.31	−.12	−.07
52	.24	.20	.06	.35	.15	.06
57	.41	−.05	.00	.27	−.05	.15
60	.49	−.09	−.30	.57	.07	−.17
65	.40	−.06	−.22	.41	−.02	−.17
70	.36	.21	−.05	.32	−.06	.08
73	.46	.01	.18	.50	.03	.06
78	.31	−.01	.25	.40	.17	.02
81	.57	.04	−.14	.57	.13	−.14
84	.59	.01	−.05	.41	−.28	−.07
87	.31	−.07	.36	.40	.05	−.03
90	.40	.11	−.03	.52	.05	−.11
94	.35	.14	.45	.47	.09	.25

practical jokes?) and so has 46 (Do you like playing pranks on others?); these are obviously much alike. Item 66 (Do you often like a rough and tumble game?) and item 89 (When children shout at you do you shout back?) seem to be definitely P rather than E items, on the showing of this analysis, and their presence in the original E scale might be questioned. We will return to this point again.

Table 19 lists the remaining items, i.e. those written with the specific intention of tapping the P variable. Success in finding genuine P items seems to have been partial; there are several good items (high P loading for both boys and girls, low N and E loadings). Items 6, 19, 45, 59 and 91 are examples of such items. Others measure N as much as P; examples are items 14, 25 and 61. There is a general tendency for hypothetical P items to load on this factor and by including such items as 66 and 89 it seems likely that a reasonable factor score might be obtained.

We may summarize our results by saying that for both boys and girls three factors similar to the hypothesized N, E and P have emerged, though not without some unexpected changes of items from one factor to another. These changes do not alter the interpretation of these factors, except in small detail, but they are of interest in test construction. It should perhaps be added that the change from a

TABLE 18 Factor loadings of E items on N, E and P factors

E Items	Boys N	Boys E	Boys P	Girls N	Girls E	Girls P
1	.11	.46	.16	.17	.38	.14
4	−.12	.28	−.18	−.16	.26	.16
8	−.06	−.48	−.04	−.15	−.69	−.01
13	−.04	.29	.32	.00	.21	.37
16	−.05	.52	.01	.05	.37	.02
21	−.02	.28	−.21	−.26	.19	.22
26	.05	.68	−.21	−.17	.43	.17
29	.13	.30	−.20	−.07	.20	−.08
33	.09	.49	.12	−.03	.11	.16
38	−.02	.34	.03	.04	.52	−.00
41	.04	.58	.05	.16	.58	.05
46	−.12	.20	.39	.05	.25	.55
51	−.00	−.42	−.16	.07	−.25	−.23
54	.02	.22	.11	.24	.26	.02
58	.06	.65	−.13	−.06	.60	.01
63	−.17	.29	.18	−.23	.31	.29
66	−.13	.19	.36	.14	.20	.35
71	.22	.60	.09	.26	.53	.10
76	.07	.56	−.07	.07	.52	.23
79	−.02	−.59	−.08	−.13	−.64	.05
83	−.16	.16	−.25	−.16	.21	.00
86	.22	−.38	.05	.26	−.19	−.11
89	−.06	−.01	.45	.11	.05	.31
92	.17	−.51	.09	.08	−.65	.07

two-factor structure makes some re-evaluations of this kind practically inevitable, even though their precise nature could not have been foreseen. It seemed desirable to use the information gained by the factor analysis in order to construct new N, E and P scales and discover their internal reliabilities. For this purpose, eighteen items were chosen for each scale, on the basis of their high loadings on the factor they were intended to measure and of their low loadings on the other scales. Using the generalized form of the Kuder-Richardson formula 20 (Hoyt, 1941), reliabilities were then calculated for the sets of eighteen items; these will be called alpha coefficients. Also calculated in each case were the correlations of each item with the total set of items for that factor minus the particular item, alpha for the total set of items minus the item in question, and alpha for the total set minus the coefficient just described; this last figure tells us whether any particular item increases or decreases the total reliability of the sub-set in questions as compared with the full set of eighteen items. The overall coefficients of reliability are:

N: .8070
E: .7741
P: .6799

TABLE 19 Factor loadings of P items on N, E and P factors

P Items	Boys N	Boys E	Boys P	Girls N	Girls E	Girls P
3	−.10	−.08	.12	.12	.00	−.07
6	.10	.04	.34	−.22	−.24	.38
9	.35	−.10	.07	.20	−.08	.03
11	−.10	.21	.17	−.11	.05	.17
14	.36	.07	.26	.32	−.18	.25
17	.05	−.11	−.05	.24	−.04	−.13
19	−.02	.03	.47	.06	.03	.24
22	.28	−.22	.01	.11	−.54	.00
25	.42	.03	.26	.39	−.20	.12
28	.36	−.28	−.19	.10	−.47	.10
31	.29	.18	−.31	.16	.16	−.26
34	.02	.18	−.03	−.10	.06	.41
37	.33	.13	.01	.21	−.13	.31
40	.16	−.04	.03	.26	−.01	−.13
43	−.19	.19	−.22	.00	.11	−.04
45	.05	.08	.37	−.05	−.09	.33
48	.25	.03	.05	.28	−.02	−.03
50	−.33	.22	.11	−.05	.58	−.15
53	.22	−.08	.05	.29	−.04	.00
56	.32	−.13	.22	.33	−.23	.06
59	.10	.16	.25	.02	.08	.53
61	.27	.03	.18	.32	−.05	.25
64	.20	.04	−.19	.05	.09	−.29
67	.38	−.09	−.11	.36	−.22	−.04
69	−.03	−.02	−.00	−.17	−.22	.41
72	.02	−.05	−.11	.14	.13	−.11
74	.20	.19	−.41	.15	.11	−.13
77	.00	−.03	−.17	−.06	−.15	.31
80	.14	.15	−.17	.06	−.03	−.07
82	.30	−.07	.19	.33	−.19	.09
85	.16	−.06	−.00	.06	.44	.20
88	.40	.01	.36	.45	.15	.11
91	.07	−.14	.20	.28	−.14	.30
93	.40	−.25	−.16	.30	−.30	.16
95	.00	.18	.18	.03	.17	.46

The E and N factors as they emerge from our analysis do not seem to necessitate any changes in the descriptive or theoretical properties of these two factors; in view of the large number of analyses preceding the present one to which the items included had been subjected, any marked change would indeed have been surprising. It is with the P scale in particular, however, that we are here concerned, and questions may be asked about the psychological content of this scale and the theoretical nature of this factor. In trying to answer these questions it is inevitable that we must enter upon rather speculative areas and rely on the apparent meaning of the items defining this factor most clearly. Future work must clarify our conclusions and either support or disconfirm them.

Looking at the questions loading on P and trying to interpret the psychological traits underlying the answers, we find the following nine sets of descriptive epithets as characteristic of high P scorers:

1. Solitary; not caring for other people. (6,91)
2. Troublesome; not fitting in. (45)
3. Cruel; inhumane. (31,74)
4. Lack of feeling; insensitive. (6,19)
5. Sensation-seeking; 'arousal jag'. (69,95)
6. Hostile to others; aggressive. (66,89)
7. Liking for odd, unusual things. (69,91)
8. Disregard for danger; foolhardy. (34,59,64)
9. Making fools of other people; upsetting them. (13,46)

What emerges from these admittedly subjective interpretations of questionnaire responses is a fairly congruent picture of an odd, isolated, troublesome child; glacial and lacking in human feelings for his fellow-beings and for animals; aggressive and hostile, even to near-and-dear ones; trying to make up for lack of feeling by indulging in sensation-seeking 'arousal jags' without thinking of the dangers involved. Can we say that this picture represents the essence of what psychotics are like? The question obviously cannot be answered in any reasonable manner. Psychiatrists differ too much among themselves as to the descriptive pattern of psychotic behaviour, or even as to the existence of 'psychosis' as a unitary concept, to make their opinions a useful check on validity. Furthermore, psychiatrists are more concerned with clinical symptoms, usually of great severity, while we are here dealing with the personality patterns of school children all of whom (with few possible exceptions) are classed as normal, in the sense of not being patients at some psychiatric clinic. All one can say at this moment is that many psychotics do seem to show some such pattern of traits and behavioural characteristics underlying the more florid and clinically more noticeable set of symptoms which leads to their certification, or at least brings them into contact with a psychiatrist. Any further claims, such as that this factor may in some sense predispose persons with high scores towards psychotic breakdown, require detailed investigation by way of follow-up studies; in the absence of such studies no such claims would be admissible at the moment. The only point which is relevant is that diagnosed adult psychotics do in fact give answers to similar questions in the adult psychoticism inventory which suggests a very similar pattern to that described above; so do criminals. The precise meaning of these findings cannot at present be assessed with any real accuracy.

One point may be of interest in connection with these findings. H.J. Eysenck and S.B.G. Eysenck (1969) have shown that the trait of 'sociability', which is usually thought of as a univocal factor, breaks in two when items employed in the usual sociability scales are intercorrelated and factor analysed. The analysis suggested that introverts are unsociable because they do not care much for other people, although they are quite able to behave in a suitable sociable manner should they care to do so; it is not lack of ability but lack of desire which leads them to prefer a somewhat withdrawn type of existence. Neurotics, however, (i.e. people with high N scores) are actually afraid of social contacts and worried about their success in such contacts; this fear prevents them from making as many contacts as they would like, although they are not as unmotivated to mix with people as are the introverts. People scoring high on P also seem to be unsociable, but for reasons which are different from those suggested as accounting for the behaviour of the high N and the low E scorers. High P scorers actually seem to hate and dislike other people, even those close to them; they do not seem to fear them, nor to be indifferent to them. Thus the behaviour pattern of 'lack of sociability' is by no means a simple one; as one might have suspected (because of the central importance in our lives of other people) attitudes towards people in general are highly complex and interrelate with at least three major personality dimensions. Hence a simple rating of 'sociable' or 'unsociable' is clearly quite insufficient; what one needs to know is rather the particular form a person's interaction with others takes—whether it is one of indifference, fear or hate.

Having established that there did in fact exist the possibility of constructing a P scale for children, we next set about improving the scale, extending it, and applying it to large samples of boys and girls of different ages, in order to discover the age limits within which the scale could with advantage be applied. The revised scale has been published elsewhere (Eysenck, Eastings and Eysenck, 1971). This scale, labelled the Junior Personality Inventory (Junior PI), also incorporates a special Lie scale. It was applied to over three thousand children during school hours; 1,876 of these were boys and 1,557 were girls. The ages of the children involved and the number of each age and sex group are shown in Table 20. Also given in the Table are the main results of the study, i.e. the reliabilities (alpha coefficients) of the four scales used, the means and standard deviations of the children's scores on these scales, and the intercorrelations between the scales.

As can be seen from the Table, the L scale is clearly the most satisfactory at all ages as far as reliability is concerned; this exceeds .8 even at the seven-year-old level, and never sinks much below it. E and N do not reach a satisfactory level until the age of 9 or 10, with E somewhat unsatisfactory for the girls even up to the age of 12, and N rather more satisfactory for the girls almost from the beginning. These differences may be due to the fact that the L scale has more items than the other scales, making it more reliable, and to the fact that girls, as we have always found in our work, are less extraverted and more emotional than boys. The P scale is clearly somewhat less satisfactory than the other scales, with reliabilities seldom exceeding .6; reliabilities seem more satisfactory for the boys than for the girls, perhaps because of the higher scores for the boys. The reliabilities of the scales are, of course, a mirror of inter-item similarity; they should not be taken to throw any light on the validity of the scales. Cattell and Tsujioka (1964) have discussed the problems involved in this relation and have concluded that a two-item scale could have zero reliability and yet be perfectly valid, i.e. correlate unity with a particular criterion. Nevertheless, it seemed desirable in future revisions to lengthen and improve the reliability of the P scale, and possibly the E scale, in so far as the younger age groups are concerned. Even as they stand, however, we believe that the scales could be used with advantage for experimental work with groups of children; individual testing for clinical purposes appears to be premature.

The means, as already mentioned, show that boys have much higher scores on P than do girls; this agrees with similar findings in relation to adults, where men score

TABLE 20 Standardization data for the Junior PI

| | | Reliability coefficients | | | | Means and Standard Deviations | | | | | | | | Intercorrelations between scales | | | | | |
| | | | | | | P | | E | | N | | L | | | | | | | |
Age	n	P	E	N	L	M	SD	M	SD	M	SD	M	SD	PE	PN	PL	EN	EL	NL
Boys																			
7	134	.521	.526	.698	.826	7.996	2.654	14.056	2.804	10.840	3.746	14.728	4.600	−.065	.057	−.542	−.383	.302	−.312
8	195	.559	.513	.664	.793	7.710	2.686	14.503	2.694	11.320	3.529	13.577	4.413	.006	−.065	−.326	−.064	.185	−.240
9	203	.634	.580	.766	.797	8.027	2.892	14.441	2.888	11.170	4.187	11.310	4.489	.196	−.088	−.243	−.168	−.004	−.311
10	154	.535	.759	.757	.808	7.438	2.600	14.692	3.572	12.546	3.969	9.484	4.382	.464	−.264	−.197	−.402	.022	−.207
11	181	.610	.614	.782	.851	8.019	2.880	14.536	2.954	11.914	4.193	9.044	4.931	.271	−.091	−.331	−.254	−.015	−.269
12	253	.597	.720	.788	.778	8.233	2.816	15.026	3.293	10.844	4.334	8.213	4.083	.264	−.095	−.467	−.299	−.096	−.098
13	308	.622	.768	.794	.778	7.893	2.903	15.046	3.525	11.719	4.272	7.911	4.038	.320	−.132	−.386	−.158	−.169	−.056
14	285	.591	.763	.799	.784	8.242	2.818	15.277	3.471	10.135	4.350	7.130	4.020	.219·	−.069	−.326	−.134	−.128	−.197
15	163	.570	.771	.785	.745	8.347	2.765	15.426	3.439	10.472	4.172	6.696	3.627	.396	−.010	−.313	−.223	−.150	−.249
	1,876																		
Girls																			
7	150	.460	.495	.738	.796	4.483	2.209	13.750	2.668	10.153	3.865	17.710	3.656	.024	−.000	−.313	−.124	−.011	−.241
8	182	.463	.584	.776	.843	4.376	2.192	13.846	2.909	12.558	4.090	15.404	4.520	.092	.132	−.389	−.126	.178	−.473
9	177	.495	.584	.742	.786	4.986	2.277	14.531	2.824	12.444	3.897	14.404	4.040	.313	−.030	−.149	−.208	.113	−.342
10	132	.555	.650	.800	.821	5.231	2.422	15.072	2.906	12.561	4.312	11.508	4.357	.261	−.210	−.022	−.264	.050	−.074
11	215	.503	.611	.783	.819	4.691	2.292	14.679	2.789	11.909	4.195	11.774	4.417	.264	−.086	−.319	−.279	−.047	−.319
12	223	.575	.682	.810	.806	5.195	2.498	14.899	3.014	12.516	4.344	9.926	4.263	.279	−.123	−.309	−.234	−.030	−.226
13	218	.573	.755	.810	.788	5.998	2.560	15.156	3.337	12.764	4.252	9.858	4.045	.289	.067	−.476	−.222	−.111	−.253
14	177	.566	.750	.792	.722	5.853	2.559	15.288	3.308	13.133	4.045	9.782	3.569	.329	.056	−.239	−.072	−.182	−.405
15	83	.585	.852	.832	.820	5.590	2.614	14.843	4.211	12.964	4.342	8.940	4.279	.352	−.131	−.329	−.208	.021	−.248
	1,557																		

more highly than women (S.B.G. Eysenck and H.J. Eysenck, 1969a). E and N also fall in line with previous work, with boys more extraverted and less emotional (S.B.G. Eysenck, 1965a). On the L scale, girls have higher scores; this was already found to be so in the original work of Hartshorne and May (1928), who left it open whether girls were more prone to lying, or actually were better behaved! In regard to age, P scores tend to rise, as do E scores. N scores do not seem to vary with age. The results are in line with previous work (S.B.G. Eysenck, 1965b).

The inter-scale correlations show that P and N, the two 'pathological' scales, are virtually uncorrelated; this adds support to the two-dimensional view expressed above, as opposed to the Freudian unidimensional hypothesis. E, however, is not entirely uncorrelated with P and N; it correlates positively with P, at a level that is not far short of .3, and negatively with N, at a rather low level. These correlations are somewhat higher than might be desirable, but they indicate that the overlap between scales amounts to less than 10 per cent of the variance; nevertheless, efforts should be made, by suitable item selection, to reduce this overlap to zero.

The L scale shows the usual and expected negative correlation between the two 'pathological' scores. Children who score high on the Lie scale tend to have lower scores on the P scale (−.3) and on the N scale (−.2). This would seem to justify the use of the L scale either to exclude high L scorers (on the grounds that they are falsifying their scores), or to correct, by regression formula, the obtained P and N scores. It seemed possible to improve the scales used by factor analysis, and consequently the data for all the age and sex groups separately were correlated and factor analysed. It would be impossible to reprint here all the Tables which report the results of this work; suffice it to say that we have based the final version of the JEPQ on these analyses. Our main concern was: (1) to obtain items having high loadings on one and only one of the four scales; (2) to obtain scales which would have reasonable reliability; (3) to obtain scales reasonably orthogonal to each other; (4) to obtain scales having reasonable test-retest reliability. The former three demands can be tested against the data from our study, and much effort was expended in trying to obtain the optimum set of questions, over both sexes and all age groups. The final JEPQ is given below; against each item we have indicated which of the four scales it measures. A minus sign indicates that the 'no' answer is scored positively for that trait and that question. There are a few buffer items included in the questionnaire; it was thought undesirable to take these out from the questionnaire that was used to furnish us with the factor-analytic information of which the composition of the scales depended originally.

Table 21 gives the means and standard deviations for boys and girls separately and for nine age groups in each case. There are no obvious age trends for P, although there appears a somewhat U-shaped quadratic trend for both boys and girls, with the ten- and eleven-year-olds having the lowest scores; this trend is significant statistically. The differences are probably not large enough to cause concern in comparing children of different ages. Boys clearly have higher scores

The Junior EPQ

1. Do you like plenty of excitement going on around you? E
2. Are you moody? N
3. Do you enjoy hurting people you like? P
4. Were you ever greedy by helping yourself to more than your share of anything? −L

5. Do you nearly always have a quick answer when people talk to you?   E
6. Do you very easily feel bored?   N
7. Would you enjoy practical jokes that could sometimes really hurt people?   P
8. Do you always do as you are told at once?   L
9. Would you rather be alone instead of meeting other children?   −E
10. Do ideas run through your head so that you cannot sleep?   N
11. Have you ever broken any rules at school?   −L
12. Would you like other children to be afraid of you?   P
13. Are you rather lively?   E
14. Do lots of things annoy you?   N
15. Would you enjoy cutting up animals in Science class?   P
16. Did you ever take anything (even a pin or button) that belonged to someone else?   −L
17. Have you got lots of friends?   E
18. Do you ever feel 'just miserable' for no good reason?   N
19. Do you sometimes like teasing animals?   P
20. Did you ever pretend you did not hear when someone was calling you?   −L
21. Would you like to explore an old haunted castle?   E
22. Do you often feel life is very dull?   N
23. Do you seem to get into more quarrels and scraps than most children?   P
24. Do you always finish your homework before you play?   L
25. Do you like doing things where you have to act quickly?   E
26. Do you worry about awful things that might happen?   N
27. When you hear children using bad language do you try to stop them?   L
28. Can you get a party going?   E
29. Are you easily hurt when people find things wrong with you or the work you do?   N
30. Would it upset you a lot to see a dog that has just been run over?   −P
31. Do you always say you are sorry when you have been rude?   L
32. Is there someone who is trying to get their own back for what they think you did to them?   P
33. Do you think water ski-ing would be fun?   E
34. Do you often feel tired for no reason?   N
35. Do you rather enjoy teasing other children?   P
36. Are you always quiet when older people are talking?   L
37. When you make new friends do you usually make the first move   E
38. Are you touchy about some things?   N
39. Do you seem to get into a lot of fights?   P
40. Have you ever said anything bad or nasty about anyone?   −L
41. Do you like telling jokes or funny stories to your friends?   E
42. Are you in more trouble at school than most children?   P
43. Do you generally pick up papers and rubbish others throw on the classroom floor?   L
44. Have you many different hobbies and interests?   E

45.	Are your feelings rather easily hurt?	N
46.	Do you like playing pranks on others?	P
47.	Do you always wash before a meal?	L
48.	Would you rather sit and watch than play at parties?	—E
49.	Do you often feel fed-up?	N
50.	Is it sometimes rather fun to watch a gang tease or bully a small child?	P
51.	Are you always quiet in class, even when the teacher is out of the room?	L
52.	Do you like doing things that are a bit frightening?	E
53.	Do you sometimes get so restless that you cannot sit still in a chair for long?	N
54.	Would you like to go to the moon on your own?	P
55.	At prayers or assembly, do you always sing when the others are singing?	L
56.	Do you like mixing with other children?	E
57.	Are your parents far too strict with you?	P
58.	Would you like parachute jumping?	E
59.	Do you worry for a long while if you feel you have made a fool of yourself?	N
60.	Do you always eat everything you are given at meals?	L
61.	Can you let yourself go and enjoy yourself a lot at a lively party?	E
62.	Do you sometimes feel life is just not worth living?	N
63.	Would you feel very sorry for an animal caught in a trap?	—P
64.	Have you ever been cheeky to your parents?	—L
65.	Do you often make up your mind to do things suddenly?	E
66.	Does your mind often wander off when you are doing some work?	N
67.	Do you enjoy diving or jumping into the sea or a pool?	E
68.	Do you find it hard to get to sleep at night because you are worrying about things?	N
69.	Did you ever write or scribble in a school or library book?	—L
70.	Do other people think of you as being very lively?	E
71.	Do you often feel lonely?	N
72.	Are you always specially careful with other people's things?	—P
73.	Do you always share all the sweets you have?	L
74.	Do you like going out a lot?	E
75.	Have you ever cheated at a game?	—L
76.	Do you find it hard to really enjoy yourself at a lively party?	—E
77.	Do you sometimes feel specially cheerful and at other times sad without any good reason?	N
78.	Do you throw waste paper on the floor when there is no waste paper basket handy?	—L
79.	Would you call yourself happy-go-lucky?	E
80.	Do you often need kind friends to cheer you up?	N
81.	Would you like to drive or ride on a fast motor bike?	E

TABLE 21   Standardization data for the Junior EPQ

		P		E		N		L		
	Age	M	SD	M	SD	M	SD	M	SD	n
	7	4.41	2.59	17.73	3.08	9.91	4.03	14.18	4.17	137
	8	4.62	2.92	18.20	3.59	10.48	3.91	12.76	4.38	200
	9	4.23	2.70	18.04	3.25	10.70	4.66	11.14	5.10	193
	10	3.82	2.92	18.21	3.26	10.00	4.61	9.53	4.59	156
Boys	11	3.81	2.82	18.46	3.50	10.32	5.02	8.32	4.47	220
	12	4.70	3.23	18.53	3.73	10.59	5.12	6.83	4.01	226
	13	4.69	2.98	18.99	3.94	9.94	4.91	5.77	3.76	228
	14	5.19	3.26	19.15	3.88	10.18	5.02	4.54	3.39	243
	15	4.87	3.25	18.95	3.91	9.75	4.86	4.81	3.36	148
	7	2.69	2.39	16.12	3.08	10.44	4.32	15.53	3.73	140
	8	2.32	2.14	16.89	3.37	11.05	4.41	15.08	3.87	195
	9	1.89	1.94	16.57	3.65	11.05	4.81	15.23	5.02	202
	10	1.95	1.86	17.62	3.40	11.30	4.63	11.87	4.66	120
Girls	11	1.95	1.64	17.56	3.75	11.61	4.92	10.56	4.37	209
	12	2.27	1.94	18.21	3.65	11.69	4.92	8.31	4.20	235
	13	2.54	2.34	18.65	3.49	11.46	4.89	6.44	3.83	211
	14	3.02	2.59	19.10	3.59	12.55	4.85	6.13	3.87	206
	15	2.75	2.25	18.64	3.59	12.12	4.69	6.33	3.80	118

than do girls. Age trends for the other scales are much more marked and deserve careful attention.

Figure 28 shows the age trends for N. Clearly, boys show no change with age; the regression line is straight and flat. Girls, however, show a distinct upward slope, with an increase in N score of over 20 per cent as we move from the age of 7 to that of 15. It seems likely that this change is due to hormonal changes accompanying puberty, but there is of course no direct evidence for such an hypothesis. E (Figure 29) shows an increase for boys and girls, with the girls having a steeper slope, but starting out rather lower down, and reaching the boys' level at the age of 13 or so. L (Figure 30) shows the most marked age trend we have ever seen, with both boys and girls running parallel, and girls throughout having higher scores. With increasing age, L drops from 15 at age 7 to 5 at age 15, i.e. a drop of more than a point a year. Clearly, children's scores must be compared with standardization data derived from groups of the same sex and age.

The JEPQ has been administered to thousands of children of all ages and much of the detailed information concerning it has been given in the Manual of the test (S.B.G. Eysenck and H.J. Eysenck, 1975) and elsewhere (S.B.G. Eysenck and H.J. Eysenck, 1973a). Some of these data will here be repeated, to round off the description of the inventory, and the relation of scores to age and sex. First, let us consider the test-retest reliabilities of the test scales. Table 22 gives one-month retest reliabilities for older children. Those of the E, N and L scales are all within

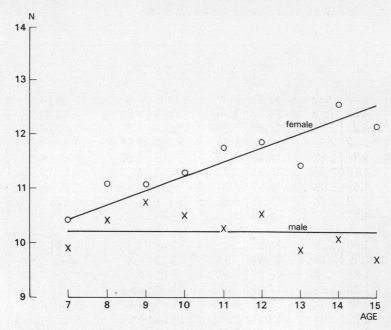

Figure 28   Age regression for children: N scale

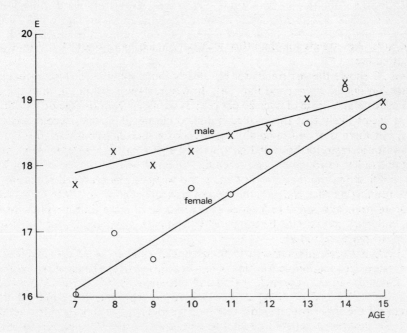

Figure 29   Age regression for children: E scale

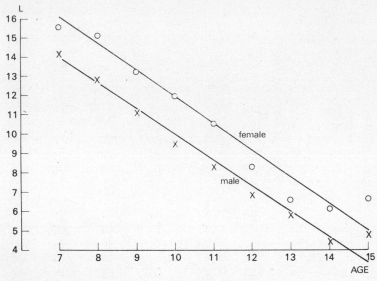

Figure 30 Age regression for children: L scale

the .7 to .9 range; those for P are a little below the .7 value. Table 23 reports retest reliabilities for younger as well as older children, with an interval between test and retest of six months, thus giving time for some genuine changes to take place in the personality of the children. It is clear that for the younger children (7, 8 and 9 years of age) reliabilities are rather low. From the age of 10 onwards, reliabilities are usually above .6, and frequently above .7 (leaving out unusually small sample groups); values for P tend to be lower for girls, but not for boys, compared with the other scales. This may be due to lower scores being obtained by girls, as compared with boys.

TABLE 22 Junior EPQ: test-retest reliabilities, one month intervening

	Age	n	P	E	N	L
	12	58	.69	.83	.71	.59
	13	84	.69	.75	.74	.79
Boys	14	48	.69	.77	.81	.79
	TOTAL	190	.69	.78	.75	.75
	11	32	.78	.84	.64	.78
	12	83	.69	.79	.79	.82
Girls	13	125	.56	.69	.77	.89
	14	101	.55	.86	.82	.89
	TOTAL	341	.61	.78	.79	.88

TABLE 23   Junior EPQ: test-retest reliabilities, six months intervening

	Age	*n*	P	E	N	L
	7	84	.38	.34	.34	.62
	8	104	.50	.53	.34	.67
	9	86	.39	.53	.74	.75
	10	116	.67	.57	.71	.67
Boys	11	194	.62	.60	.75	.72
	12	198	.72	.60	.70	.59
	13	200	.63	.67	.72	.65
	14	189	.76	.74	.66	.70
	15	48	.77	.33	.77	.79
	7	88	.52	.44	.51	.65
	8	82	.43	.55	.40	.62
	9	100	.70	.54	.56	.76
	10	102	.47	.73	.74	.74
Girls	11	184	.48	.60	.55	.73
	12	198	.51	.74	.71	.72
	13	176	.66	.76	.74	.66
	14	176	.63	.78	.69	.75
	15	28	.33	.82	.77	.83

TABLE 24   Junior EPQ: internal consistency reliabilities

	Age	*n*	P	E	N	L
	7	137	.64	.57	.75	.82
	8	200	.70	.71	.73	.82
	9	193	.65	.64	.82	.87
	10	156	.73	.66	.81	.83
Boys	11	220	.69	.72	.85	.83
	12	226	.74	.76	.86	.80
	13	228	.69	.81	.85	.79
	14	243	.73	.80	.86	.77
	15	148	.74	.80	.85	.75
	7	140	.66	.54	.80	.81
	8	195	.64	.64	.80	.81
	9	202	.62	.71	.84	.89
	10	120	.57	.69	.82	.85
Girls	11	209	.43	.75	.85	.83
	12	235	.55	.75	.85	.82
	13	211	.67	.74	.85	.80
	14	206	.70	.77	.86	.81
	15	118	.61	.75	.84	.79

Consistency reliabilities (alpha coefficients) are given in Table 24. These are encouragingly high, even for the younger groups. Figures for N and L, in particular, are strikingly high for such short scales and, if anything, superior to similar values for adults; P and E have lower reliabilities, but these are still acceptable.

Intercorrelations between the scales are given in Table 25. It will be seen that these follow the pattern of adult figures, but that the correlations between the L scale and the N and P scales are very much higher; this may be due to the fact that the L-scale scores for children (particularly young children) are extremely high. It is not known whether this suggests that young children dissimulate more than older ones, or that they are simply more naive, more conformist and less able to introspect.

TABLE 25 Junior EPQ: intercorrelations between scales

	Age	n	PE	PN	PL	EN	EL	NL
	7	137	−.08	.22	−.48	−.09	.16	−.39
	8	200	.17	.30	−.43	−.02	.03	−.28
	9	193	.04	.23	−.48	−.20	.08	−.39
	10	156	.06	.20	−.43	−.13	−.09	−.30
Boys	11	220	.03	.13	−.34	−.26	−.00	−.31
	12	226	.07	.26	−.46	−.26	−.06	−.10
	13	228	.07	.18	−.37	−.25	−.24	−.18
	14	243	−.00	.18	−.40	−.13	−.09	−.10
	15	148	−.02	.11	−.33	−.15	−.17	−.22
	7	140	.01	.31	−.53	.00	.08	−.36
	8	195	.00	.24	−.33	−.13	.07	−.31
	9	202	−.06	.36	−.44	−.22	.12	−.45
	10	120	.09	.23	−.36	−.14	−.16	−.29
Girls	11	209	.02	.24	−.35	−.07	−.05	−.30
	12	235	−.04	.06	−.24	−.26	−.00	−.27
	13	211	.08	.11	−.37	−.21	−.19	−.18
	14	206	.18	.19	−.35	−.19	−.11	−.26
	15	118	.20	.17	−.27	−.26	−.27	−.19

The children's scale has not received as much empirical support as regards validity as has the adult scale. The main source of confidence in its meaningfulness rests on the psychometric data given in this chapter, the content similarity to the adult scale, and research (described in a later chapter) on antisocial behaviour. It was hypothesized that the Junior scale should show evidence of the same kind of relation between personality and antisocial conduct as has the adult scale, and as we shall see, this prediction was in fact verified. Apart from these studies on the correlation between P and antisocial conduct, there are one or two suggestive experiments which give tentative support to the interpretation of the children's P factor as psychoticism.

The first of these studies reports aesthetic preference judgments of children from 9 to 13, both male and female, using specially selected items from the Maitland Graves (1946) Design Judgment Test (Eysenck, 1972d). Factorial analysis of ratings made by the children disclosed a general factor of aesthetic sensitivity, and comparative studies with large groups of adults (both artists and non-artists) seemed to confirm this interpretation. P, E, N and L scales were applied to the children and while the latter three scales disclosed little of interest in relation to aesthetic sensitivity, the P scale had many negative loadings (in particular for the girls) with aesthetic sensitivity at the various ages (separate analyses were done for the four age and the two sex groups). Eysenck concluded 'tentatively that the cold, impersonal, aggressive, unemotional individual that emerges from the items of the questionnaire has little aesthetic sensitivity' (p.7). To put it another way, the high-scoring P child tends to disagree with the aesthetic judgments made by the average peer group of which he is a member; he is 'odd', 'unusual' in his preferences, compared to the normal child. This is perhaps what one would have expected to find. It is interesting to note that Frith and Nias (1974), working with a specially constructed set of designs (stimuli were generated by computer and consisted of a matrix of squares, half of which were black and half white) and with eighty-eight College of Education students, who were asked to rate the designs on a seven-point scale, found that high scorers on psychoticism preferred 'uncertain' designs that were disliked by the group as a whole. This study will be described in more detail later on; it is mentioned here as proof that similar results are obtained in aesthetic preference judgments regardless of whether adult or child high P scorers are being used.

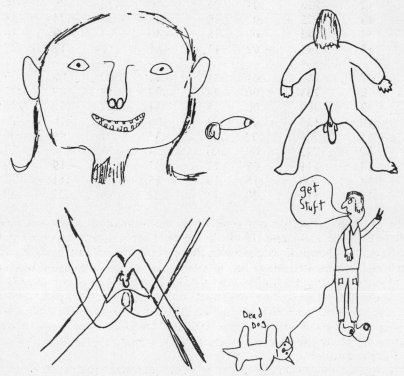

Figure 31   Examples of drawings which were rated as moderately or very bizarre (from Hodgson and Rundall, to appear)

In the other study mentioned, Hodgson and Rundall (1976) asked seventy boys aged 11 and 12 to draw a person; the drawings were then rated by three persons on a qualitative scale and also for being 'bizarre' (defined as peculiar, possibly suggesting a disturbed personality). Inter-rater reliabilities were high and of the same order as those reported by Eysenck, Russell and Eysenck (1970) for quality and reasonably high (above .7 on the average) for bizarreness ($r = .35$). Figure 31 gives some examples of bizarre drawings as judged by the raters. This study is of interest because it links up our concept of P directly with the well-known studies of schizophrenic artists; these too have usually been characterized by some quality of 'bizarreness' which is difficult to define, but usually easy to recognize. Not too much should be claimed for this study, of course, as far as validation of the concept of P is concerned; nevertheless, the results are certainly in the expected direction.

7

Psychoticism and psychosis

Having discussed at some length the construction of the P scale and its psychometric properties, we must next turn to its validation. This is, of course, like all problems of validation, a complex matter, but we may perhaps start with the simplest (or at least apparently simplest) deduction from the hypothesis elaborated in our first chapter and state that psychotics and criminals should have elevated P scores. The case of criminals will be dealt with in the next chapter; in this chapter, we shall deal with the question of the various psychotic groups tested and their P scores, as related to various control groups. We shall start with the simplest manner of carrying out such a comparison, namely the presentation of mean scores and standard deviations for various male and female groups who underwent the test. These scores are given in Table 26, which is taken from the Manual. The term 'Psychotics' in the Table means largely schizophrenics, both outpatients and inpatients (there were no significant differences between these two groups, or the various subgroups of schizophrenia). Endogenous depressives have been kept separate from schizophrenics because they showed significant differences in P score; this point will be discussed presently.

TABLE 26 Abnormal groups: means and standard deviations

MALES	n	Age	P	E	N	L
Psychotics	104	35.1	5.66±4.02	10.67±5.22	13.39±6.06	9.62±5.12
Neurotics	216	34.7	4.19±2.96	9.42±5.37	16.56±4.64	8.01±4.60
Endogenous Depressives	58	43.6	4.10±2.82	9.98±5.44	15.92±5.48	9.72±4.61
Prisoners	1,023	25.9	5.72±3.56	13.62±4.69	13.13±5.23	6.78±4.29
Drug Addicts	8	27.2	6.94±5.75	8.88±6.98	17.88±3.94	8.62±3.20
Personality Disorders	56	30.6	5.78±3.44	10.09±6.31	15.71±4.74	7.06±4.45
Sex Problems	23	35.7	4.87±3.24	11.91±5.53	12.43±6.05	7.07±4.05
Alcoholics	14	33.9	5.93±2.16	9.79±5.13	19.64±2.13	4.14±3.37
Normal Comparison	2,312	27.5	3.78±3.09	13.19±4.91	9.83±5.18	6.80±4.14

table continues overleaf

FEMALES	n	Age	P	E	N	L
Psychotics	72	39.3	4.08±3.19	10.58±4.66	14.56±5.23	11.59±5.14
Neurotics	332	34.9	3.25±2.71	9.46±5.43	17.88±3.94	9.58±4.51
Endogenous Depressives	68	43.7	3.48±2.47	10.24±5.76	16.54±4.36	12.01±4.04
Prisoners	71	27.1	6.41±4.07	12.32±5.19	14.60±5.58	9.01±4.89
Drug Addicts	4	32.5	6.25±3.20	9.25±4.86	20.00±1.15	3.25±2.50
Personality Disorders	75	31.0	5.75±3.51	10.19±5.99	18.35±4.64	7.17±4.30
Sex Problems	25	30.6	3.58±3.16	9.96±4.27	16.32±4.18	9.44±4.59
Alcoholics	5	44.0	5.50±3.39	10.50±4.56	18.50±2.50	8.80±2.02
Normal Comparison	3,262	27.0	2.63±2.36	12.60±4.83	12.74±5.20	7.73±4.18

It will be seen that psychotics and prisoners, as predicted, have the highest P scores; those of drug addicts, personality disorders, individuals with sex problems and alcoholics are also elevated. Endogenous depressives have P scores which, while higher than normal, are well below the other groups mentioned. All psychiatric groups (but not the prisoners) are markedly introverted. Psychiatric groups and criminals have elevated N scores, in particular the neurotics and the personality disorders. Psychiatric groups show elevated L scores, but prisoners do not; this suggests that, had they not dissimulated, psychotics and neurotics would have had even higher P and N scores than are actually found. An analysis of groups with high and low L scores respectively supports this view. The results given in Table 27 are very much as expected. It will be seen that the P scores of all groups are much higher when L scores are less than or equal to 7; E scores do not seem to be much affected; N scores are also much higher, except perhaps for the neurotics themselves! The numbers in the subgroups are not very large and not too much should be read into the figures, but they do illustrate the point that L scores must be taken into account in interpreting the P and N scores of individuals and groups.

Intercorrelations between scales for the various abnormal groups are given in Table 28; these are on the whole comparable with those for normal groups. Correlations between L, on the one hand, and P and N on the other, are much higher for the psychotic groups and the neurotics and prisoners than for the normals; this is not unexpected on the basis of previous results. Also higher than for normals are the correlations in these groups between E and N; this too has been observed previously on several occasions. While the general pattern of intercorrelations is therefore much the same for normals and abnormals, the trends observed are much more clearly brought out in the abnormal sample.

It should be noted, in relation to these Tables as well as in relation to later work, to be reported presently, that diagnostic criteria in relation to depression are too diverse to permit of any reasonable decision regarding its being part of the general psychoticism group or not. The continuing controversy in psychiatry about the

TABLE 27 Abnormal group means, separated according to high or low L scores

Lie score greater than seven

MALES		Age		P		E		N		L	
	n	M	SD	M	SD	M	SD	M	SD	M	SD
Psychotics	40	36.70	14.02	5.66	4.44	11.52	5.09	12.28	6.11	11.86	3.27
Neurotics	82	37.63	12.00	3.28	2.27	9.10	5.08	16.34	5.21	11.92	3.14
Endogenous Depressives	30	47.67	12.40	3.65	3.24	9.43	5.60	15.93	5.72	12.63	2.66
FEMALES											
Psychotics	30	36.50	11.58	3.82	3.53	11.53	4.16	13.03	5.00	13.17	3.39
Neurotics	168	36.96	12.02	2.83	2.65	8.80	5.48	17.87	3.88	12.37	3.34
Endogenous Depressives	49	45.26	13.18	3.48	2.64	11.19	5.70	16.39	4.20	13.42	3.04

Lie score less than or equal to seven

MALES											
Psychotics	29	30.00	11.17	6.29	3.84	9.71	5.36	16.07	5.51	4.24	2.28
Neurotics	103	30.39	9.99	5.01	3.28	9.52	5.72	17.16	4.04	4.48	2.10
Endogenous Depressives	14	33.57	13.53	5.04	2.26	9.82	5.90	18.64	4.25	4.89	2.11
FEMALES											
Psychotics	12	31.25	10.41	6.33	2.80	9.12	6.68	16.92	5.63	4.17	1.99
Neurotics	98	30.46	11.50	4.34	2.76	9.81	5.39	18.15	3.99	4.90	1.89
Endogenous Depressives	9	33.44	10.78	3.44	1.96	5.94	3.66	17.06	4.82	5.44	2.08

TABLE 28 Intercorrelations between scales: abnormal groups

MALES	n	PE	PN	PL	EN	EL	NL
Psychotics	104	.19	.11	−.21	−.12	.11	−.53
Neurotics	216	.03	.16	−.33	−.27	−.00	−.16
Endogenous Depressives	58	−.03	.22	−.14	−.42	−.15	−.12
Prisoners	934	−.08	.04	−.28	−.24	−.07	−.18
FEMALES							
Psychotics	72	−.00	.06	−.42	−.40	.04	−.38
Neurotics	332	−.04	.13	−.29	−.34	−.05	−.17
Endogenous Depressives	68	.06	.07	−.04	−.20	.20	−.13
Prisoners	71	−.09	.14	−.53	.00	.00	−.32

existence or otherwise of clearly differentiated neurotic and psychotic depressive states (Eysenck, 1970c) has caused some psychiatrists to try and diagnose endogenous depression by reference to psychotic symptoms, while others have made the diagnosis in terms of more severe, as opposed to less severe, depressive symptoms. In this way, the diagnostic criteria used by psychiatrists make it inevitable that our group of 'endogenous depressives' should not be purely made up of psychotic individuals, but would include a fair proportion of neurotic patients with severe depression. For reasons given elsewhere (Eysenck, 1970c), we believe that the distinction between psychotic and neurotic depression is justified, and that consequently our group of endogenous depressives must be regarded as a poor sample, adulterated by the inclusion of many neurotic patients. This point should be kept in mind in interpreting these and later findings.

The fact that psychotics—both schizophrenics and endogenous depressives (even given the divergent habits of diagnosing the latter)— have much higher L scores than other groups may not necessarily indicate conscious dissimulation; it may be indicative of a certain defensiveness, or even of a particular personality. We shall discuss the interpretation of the L scale in a later chapter, but we may note here that from the point of view of differentiating psychiatric groups, it is clearly not sufficient to look at scores on individual scales; we should look at combinations of scores.

In addition to these results, using the EPQ, there are a few studies in which previous versions of the P, E, N and L scales have been used. The first of these studies (Davis, 1974) to be discussed does not add much of value, largely because the population tested had IQs so low that one must seriously question their ability to understand the questions properly. The mean IQ in this group of 103 'testable male patients who were admitted to a Special Hospital for abnormal offenders' was only 80, and apparently the IQ correlated very significantly with P ($r = -.44$), suggesting that perhaps the least intelligent subjects could not properly understand or evaluate the questions. Davis used the Eysenck-Withers Personality Inventory (S.B.G. Eysenck, 1966) as a measure of N, E and L; this inventory was specially constructed for use with mentally subnormal groups. Its use constitutes an admission that special wording of questions is required to make personality inventories usable for this group, and the failure to reword the P items in a similar manner to make them more readily intelligible makes interpretation of the results difficult. The low reliability found for the P scale in this group (.61) confirms this criticism. Davis carried out a factor analysis, but oddly enough only worked with three factors; clearly four are demanded by the theory and have always in the past been found. With only three factors extracted, it is clearly impossible to achieve a solution with P, E, N and L emerging as separate factors, and in Davis's solution N and P emerge with high loadings on the same factor. Davis suggests that this is due to the fact that P is merely another measure of emotionality; it seems more likely that his finding is entirely due to his failure to extract the proper number of factors. Davis compared fourteen patients diagnosed as psychotics and fourteen controls on the P scale (or rather a novel scale constructed by himself, its items derived from early versions of the P scale) and found the psychotics only insignificantly higher than the controls; in view of what has been said about his study, this hardly constitutes a disproof of the hypothesis that P is related to psychosis. This conclusion is further strengthened when it is realized that the 'controls' seem to have contained mainly psychopaths and criminals, who according to our hypothesis would also score high on P.

Of much greater interest is a study by McPherson *et al.* (1974) in which they compared 77 psychotics, 35 neurotics and 112 normal controls on the EPQ, using a scoring system slightly differing from that finally adopted. The small numbers of patients used became even smaller in making various comparisons because not all patients were included in certain tests; this seriously affects statistical significance levels. Both P and N correlated significantly with L (−.33 and −.38 respectively); this suggests a considerable amount of dissimulation. Test-retest correlations were available for fifty-seven psychotic patients; these were satisfactory, amounting to P = .73, E = .69, N = .85 and L = .84. In the psychotic group, older patients had lower P scores ($r = −.23$); there was also a just non-significant correlation with the synonyms test ($r = −.20$). The mean P scores of the forty-two male and the thirty-five female psychotics were respectively 5.55 (SD 4.04) and 4.31 (SD 2.89); because of the small numbers this is not significant statistically, but is in line with our general finding of higher male scores. Chronicity was uncorrelated with P, but L did show a positive correlation of .36 with total time in hospital.

Psychotics, excluding depressives (who as in our own work had the lowest P scores of all psychotic groups), had a mean P score of 5.25; neurotics of 4.69 and normals of 4.54. On N, the scores were 12.89, 17.00 and 9.34. On the L scale, scores were 12.57, 10.23 and 5.73. The mean P score of the psychotics is larger, but not significantly so, than that of the neurotics; this is in part due to the small number of neurotics and in part to the failure of the authors to correct for the very high L scores of the psychotics. As we have pointed out in connection with earlier studies, P scores cannot be interpreted in isolation from L scores. On the whole, these findings are not unlike those discussed in relation to our own work on previous pages.

Of greater interest than this replication is the attempt by McPherson *et al.* to relate P to psychiatric status within the psychotic group. Ratings were made on sixty patients of affective flattening, incongruous affect, negative thought disorder and positive thought disorder: 'For all four signs, those patients showing the sign had the higher P-scale scores. In the case of affective flattening. . .and positive thought disorder. . .the differences were significant. No significant differences, or systematic trends, were found on the E, N or L scales.' Twenty-seven schizophrenic patients were administered a symptom questionnaire and divided into three groups: those who admitted to no delusions; those who admitted only to 'integrated' delusions (persecution, grandeur, self-denigration); and those who admitted to 'non-integrated' delusions. The three groups did not differ in age or Synonyms scores, but they did differ very significantly on P with means of 2.63, 4.38 and 6.82 ($p<.01$). Thus the more clearly defined the psychotic illness, in its symptomatology, the higher the P scores; this agrees well with the results of the Verma and Eysenck study to be discussed next. So does the correlation between social withdrawal and Extraversion ($r = −.23$), which just falls short of significance. On the whole, and given the small number of cases in this study, it is reassuring to note that most of the Verma and Eysenck findings are replicated.

Another demonstration of the fact that the presence of classical schizophrenic symptoms is positively correlated with P comes from a small-scale study by Slade (1975), who tested a normal control group, a schizophrenic group showing auditory hallucinations, and a matched schizophrenic group without hallucinations. P scores for the normals averaged 2.8; for the non-hallucinated psychotics, 4.8; and for the hallucinated psychotics, 7.2. The groups did not differ significantly on E or N, but did differ significantly from each other on P. Thus clearly the presence of auditory hallucinations is correlated with P and even non-hallucinated psychotics can be differentiated from normal controls, although their P scores are significantly below those of hallucinated psychotics.

Verma and Eysenck (1973) attempted to test the hypothesis that, within a psychotic sample of patients, P would correlate with severity of psychosis. In other words, they postulated that the personality variable P, which is defined in terms excluding psychotic symptoms, would nevertheless be correlated, within a psychotic population, with the number and severity of symptoms displayed by the patient. This is not a necessary deduction from the general theory, but it seems a likely one and certainly one worth testing. The sample for this study consisted of 153 patients, 85 women and 68 men, admitted for short-term psychiatric treatment. The patients were diagnosed as psychotic and the likelihood of organic involvement in their illness was ruled out by the psychiatrist concerned. Their age range was kept between twenty years and fifty years in order to avoid the preponderance of age-linked influences such as emotional stress and sensitivity in adolescence and melancholia of the late fifties. Intellectually, the subjects were not subnormal. This was checked from the results of their intelligence tests, where available, and by reports from the psychiatric social workers about their educational levels and work experience, etc., where intelligence scores were not available.

This study was conducted within the first two weeks of the patient's admission into hospital, before drug-therapy, electro-convulsive therapy, institutional care or other therapeutic measures could exert significant influences on them. Each case was studied individually, and measures, described in detail later, were applied in the following order with intervals between them as the time and condition required:

(a) Interview and rating on the Inpatient Multidimensional Psychiatric Scale (IMPS);
(b) Cognitive tests;
(c) Psychoticism, Extraversion and Neuroticism Inventory (PEN Inventory);
(d) Hostility and Direction of Hostility Questionnaire (HDHQ);
(e) Motor test.

(a) Interview and rating—IMPS
The Inpatient Multidimensional Psychiatric Scale (IMPS), developed by Lorr, Klett, McNair and Lasky (1963), has certain advantages of theoretical construction, factorial stability and validity over all other rating scales, and appears to have been carefully prepared, keeping in view the limitations and shortcomings of these various devices. It describes behaviour manifestations and symptom-complexes under ten relatively independent categories. The syndromes postulated are as follows:

A. *Excitation* (EXT). The defining characteristics are excess and acceleration of speech and motor activity. Mood level and self-esteem are high. Restraint in expression of emotion and feeling is lacking.
B. *Hostile-Belligerence* (HOS). Manifest and verbal hostility, expressions of

resentment and an attitude of suspicion of others' intentions are characteristics of the syndrome.

C. Paranoid Projection (PAR). This is defined by morbid beliefs that attribute hostility, persecution and even a controlling influence to others.

D. Grandiose Expansiveness (GRN). This includes delusions of grandeur, an attribute to self-importance, and at times a conviction of having a divine mission.

E. Perceptual Distortion (PCP). This is characterized by hallucinations that threaten, accuse, demand or extol.

F. Anxious Intropunitiveness (INP). This syndrome is marked by anxiety, fears, lowered mood level and self-depreciation; guilt, remorse and self-blame for real or imagined faults are equally important.

G. Retardation and Apathy (RTD). This shows slowed and reduced motor activity, ideation and speech. Apathy and disinterest are also characteristics.

H. Disorientation (DIS). This represents disorientation of time, place and person.

I. Motor Disturbance (MTR). Rigid, bizarre postures, grimacing and repetitive movements are the main behaviours.

J. Conceptual Disorganization (CNP). Irrelevant, incoherent and rambling speech as well as neologisms and stereotyped use of words, etc., characterize the syndrome.

Detailed cues to identify these behaviour manifestations and rateable verbalizations concerning current feelings, thoughts and beliefs are available with the scale. The emphasis is on the measurement of currently discernible behaviour, feeling and attitude, and is therefore restricted to the observation within the interview situation only. The Disorientation rating and the Conceptual Disorganization scales of the IMPS were not used in this study, as disorientated patients could not be of much help in supplying information, could not fill in questionnaires properly, and could not do the tests.

An independent rating on the IMPS was obtained from the ward sister or charge-nurse on each patient. This rating was, of course, on the ward behaviour of the patients, while the psychologist's rating was based on interview behaviour and it was not anticipated that agreement would be very high. It seemed desirable to have both types of behaviour rated independently.

(b) Cognitive tests

1. Intelligence.

Cognitive tests used in this research were selected from the Wechsler Adult Intelligence Scale. The two sub-scales, Similarities and Picture Completion, one each from the Verbal and Performance Scales, were employed in this investigation.

2. Mental Control

Mental control is one of the first things to be assessed when a patient is admitted to hospital for psychiatric treatment. The slowing down of thinking, loss of mental shift, rigidity and tendency towards perseveration are associated with the severity of mental disorder. In this study, mental control was assessed on the items taken from a standardized memory scale of Wechsler (1945). This consists of three sub-items: (i) counting backwards from 20 to 1; (ii) repeating the alphabet quickly; (iii) counting by threes.

(c) PEN Inventory

The scale was administered individually and was readministered to most subjects after six to eight weeks.

(d) Hostility and direction of hostility

The Hostility and Direction of Hostility Questionnaire (HDHQ) was designed by Caine, Foulds and Hope (1967) with a view to measuring the manifestation of hostility or punitiveness. Items used in this questionnaire were culled from the MMPI and five sub-scales were devised. The questionnaire yields a general hostility score and a direction of hostility score, either of extrapunitiveness or intropunitiveness. The five sub-scales are grouped as follows: Acting Out Hostility (AH), Criticism of Others (CO) and Delusional Hostility (DH) constitute the extrapunitive scale; and Self-criticism (SC) and Delusional Guilt (G) form the intropunitive scale. The direction of hostility is worked out as (2SC+G)–(AH+CO+DH): the sum of intropunitive tests, counting Self-criticism twice over, less the sum of the extrapunitive tests.

In the framework of postulated personality theory, attempts have been made by Foulds and his colleagues to show that the first component of General Hostility is more concerned with psychotics than with neurotics or normals. The second component of Direction of Hostility seems to suggest that paranoids are at the extreme end of extrapunitiveness and melancholics at the other end of intropunitiveness. The non-paranoid schizophrenics come in-between.

(e) Motor test

In the present study, an experiment was designed to find the level of psychomotor performance of the psychotic patients under ordinary conditions as well as under conditions of stress. The task selected for performance was very simple and did not involve any specific ability or skill. The subject had to cancel every third number of a cancellation sheet which contained numbers printed in random order. In the psychomotor performance the speech of the subject was also included, the subject being required to call out every number he cancelled.

The task was set to be performed under two conditions—once under stress, once without stress. The stress was introduced by giving the subject special instructions to work as quickly as possible and to call out the cancelled number correctly every time. Furthermore, he was also instructed that there would be a time signal given to him at regular intervals of thirty seconds to warn him of the time. The time for the actual performance was kept constant for both stressful and stress-free conditions, that is two minutes percondition. The presentation of the condition was in A B B A design.

Condition A stands for the performance of the task under normal conditions without stress;

Condition B stands for the condition with stress.

A rest pause of equal duration was introduced at the end of each condition in order to dissipate the fatigue effect.

A practice trial of fifteen seconds was given to each subject before the actual experiment commenced.

At the end of the experiment, a discrepancy score was worked out by taking the difference between the numbers of digits cancelled under the two different conditions.

The main results of the study are reported in Table 29, which gives means and standard deviations for the various tests and ratings, for men and women separately, and also the correlations of the P scale with each of the other tests and ratings.* The mean P scores of our sample may be compared with our standardization data; in the present sample, the means are very near 5, which is slightly (but not significantly) larger than our means obtained from 156 male psychotics (4.83, SD 3.28) and 154 females (4.92, SD 3.64) (standardization sample). The E scores of the present sample are slightly elevated, significantly so in the case of the females (10.04, SD 4.58; 10.26, SD 4.44). On N our present sample is definitely higher (9.64, SD 4.90; 9.46, SD 5.13). The differences, though significant, are small; they may stem from the fact that our sample had to be selected by exclusion of patients unable to carry out the motor and cognitive tests. For the Lie scale, there are no norms making a direct comparison possible, as our previous samples of psychotics had been tested with a form of the PEN which did not include the L scale. However, the obtained values lie distinctly above those recorded from normal (non-psychiatric) samples, which average around 4.7 (SD 2.8) and also above those recorded from out-patient neurotics, which average around 5.1 (SD 3.0); the differences between the psychotics in this sample and the normal and neurotic groups tested are statistically significant. When we compare our psychotics with normal groups on P, E and N, we find, as expected, that they are much higher on P (normal males have a mean P score of 2.5, SD 2.7, and females one of 1.97, SD 2.1). On N, too, the psychotics are notably higher than normals, having means of 7.3, SD 4.4 (males) and 8.6, SD 4.3 (females). On E, the psychotics are significantly lower, normals scoring 12.7, SD 4.1 (males) and 12.4, SD 3.7 (females). Neurotic in- and out-patients score higher on N than do our psychotics, with scores roughly two points above. Our sample emerges from all these comparisons as equal in P to previously studied psychotic groups, and definitely superior to normal or out-patient neurotics; in-patient neurotics are somewhat below psychotics on P, but not very much (mean value of P = 4.6, SD 3.1). The only group to equal psychotics on P is prisoners (S.B.G. Eysenck and H.J. Eysenck, 1970b); their mean P score is 4.81 for the men and 5.69 for the women.

Scores on the various tests, questionnaires and ratings were intercorrelated by means of the product-moment formula, leaving out only the 'Disorientation' and 'Conceptual Disorganization' items on the IMPS for reasons of lack of variance. Correlations were established separately for men and women and the resulting matrices were separately factor-analysed by means of Principal Components; the resulting factors were rotated through Promax to oblique simple structure

---

*As noted in the description of the experiment, the ratings made by the psychologist and the psychiatric nurse were not strictly comparable, the material on which these ratings were based being so very different. It is nevertheless of interest to see to what extent these ratings correlate; these correlations are, of course, not reliabilities in the usual sense and must be expected to be much lower than would be usual—or tolerable—for ordinary reliabilities. The correlations were calculated for men and women separately and are given below for the scales used: Excitation: .32, .50; Hostile belligerence: .23, .21; Paranoid projection: .28, .43; Grandiose expansiveness: .51, .11; Perceptual distortion: .39, .15; Motor disturbance: .01, .13. Some of these figures are so low as to suggest that there was little the two raters had in common (e.g. motor disturbance), but in most cases the correlations suggest that, in spite of the quite different ways of acquiring information, the information ultimately acquired was not too dissimilar (e.g. excitation or anxious intropunitiveness). It is clear that there is not so much redundancy in the data as to make the use of both sets not worth while.

TABLE 29 Means and standard deviations of male and female samples; correlations with P score; and factor loadings of combined sample. Asterisks denote level of significance.

Item No.		Males (68) Mean	SD	Females (85) Mean	SD	Correlations with P Males	Females	Second-order factors 1	2	3	4	Super-factors 1	2
1.	Age	31.72	8.15	34.22	8.28	-.08	-.20	-.52	-.20	.08	-.11	-.02	-.30
2.	Similarities — Cognitive tests	9.31	2.35	8.98	2.52	-.06	-.25*	.20	.59	-.14	.25	-.31	-.14
3.	Picture completion	7.99	1.81	6.80	2.30	-.33**	-.15	.14	.66	.06	.11	.31	-.14
4.	Mental control	6.57	2.21	6.82	1.95	-.25*	-.38**	.13	.62	-.15	.04	-.48	-.04
5.	P — PEN Inventory	4.88	3.85	5.07	3.35	—	-.04	.37	-.40	.25	.19	.69	.20
6.	E	10.10	4.75	11.06	4.27	-.15	-.04	-.18	.11	-.05	.23	-.03	-.31
7.	N	10.84	5.19	10.64	5.06	.66**	.53**	.77	-.04	-.08	-.04	.30	.61
8.	L	5.60	3.42	6.84	3.37	-.26*	-.17	-.69	-.37	-.08	-.14	-.10	-.32
9.	Hostility — Foulds Inventory	22.99	9.96	21.58	8.89	.74**	.65**	.59	-.19	.27	.06	.56	.40
10.	Direction of H	1.54	8.58	4.74	7.80	-.25*	-.24*	.44	.19	-.22	-.26	-.32	.52
11.	Urge to act out H	5.37	2.90	5.55	2.72	.51**	.49**	.41	-.05	.21	.15	.41	.18
12.	Criticism of others	5.69	3.04	5.55	2.82	.61**	.56**	.17	-.19	.32	.12	.51	.02
13.	Projected delusion H	2.72	2.50	2.45	2.25	.77**	.58**	.15	-.39	.13	.13	.62	.06
14.	Self-criticism	6.04	2.93	6.01	2.75	.33**	.25*	.73	.01	.02	-.13	.16	.64
15.	Guilt	3.16	2.17	2.86	1.86	.52**	.47**	.71	-.09	.15	-.09	.34	.60
16.	Excitement — IMPS (Psychologist)	8.37	11.84	7.44	12.08	-.13	.04	-.09	.19	.00	.28	.01	-.31
17.	Hostile belligerence	9.59	13.88	10.67	14.03	.09	.26**	.24	-.02	-.10	.29	.18	.02
18.	Paranoid projection	13.32	11.27	8.82	9.68	.35**	.23**	.03	.04	.72	-.16	.45	-.04
19.	Grandiose expansiveness	3.65	6.12	2.15	6.34	-.08	.15	.12	.18	.54	-.22	-.20	.08
20.	Perceptual distortion	7.93	9.37	4.72	6.97	.40**	.14	-.05	-.30	.58	-.36	.43	.15
21.	Anxious intro punitiveness	25.59	16.68	26.93	17.43	.01	-.03	.53	.12	-.20	-.25	-.23	.59
22.	Retardation and apathy	6.15	8.73	5.81	7.89	.07	-.05	.35	-.37	-.34	-.12	.03	.51
23.	Motor disturbance	4.37	6.38	3.75	4.40	-.10	.00	-.31	-.20	-.35	.22	.10	.22
24.	Excitement — IMPS (Psychiatric Worker)	10.12	15.90	15.58	19.69	.05	.16	.08	.20	.04	.72	.34	-.48
25.	Hostile belligerence	8.50	12.26	11.29	16.51	.28*	.24*	.18	-.01	-.02	.63	.42	-.28
26.	Paranoid projection	9.87	13.31	9.66	14.38	.16	.19	-.12	-.02	.59	.04	.46	-.25
27.	Grandiose expansiveness	4.00	8.43	3.27	7.22	-.20	-.04	-.16	.24	.53	.24	.34	-.47
28.	Perceptual distortion	4.34	8.10	4.06	9.05	.04	.28**	-.07	-.06	.53	.09	.53	-.11
29.	Anxious intro punitiveness	18.84	15.03	22.08	15.75	.00	.07	.29	-.03	-.09	.06	.07	.21
30.	Retardation and apathy	7.82	10.95	10.69	13.49	.01	.23*	.13	-.30	-.10	-.11	.10	.27
31.	Motor disturbance	5.01	9.83	7.88	9.18	.08	.30**	.06	-.18	.33	.23	.54	-.14
32.	Motor test—Normal (A) — Motor test	168.16	44.47	163.90	35.90	-.03	-.31**	.12	.44	-.15	-.12	-.46	-.10
33.	Motor test—Timed (B)	179.38	49.18	179.26	90.32	-.04	-.24*	.00	.41	.05	-.13	-.32	-.02
34.	Motor test—A-B	11.22	12.80	16.94	15.36	-.07	-.14	.26	.27	.21	-.54	-.25	.45

positions, ten factors being extracted. (The number of factors to be rotated was determined by reference to the number of eigenvalues in excess of unity.) Higher-order factors were extracted and rotated according to the Promax formula. We will discuss here, first of all, the primary factors emerging from this process.

The first factor to appear may be identified rather confidently as one of psychoticism; it is defined primarily by questionnaire scores, but also has loadings on ratings and cognitive tests. Taking men first, we find that this factor has loadings on P (.72), Hostility (.90), Criticism of others (.89), Projected delusion (paranoid) hostility (.88), Urge to act out hostility (.71), Guilt (−.54), Direction of hostility (−.47), and on Hostile belligerence (.47), second IMPS rating. All these items have loadings of above .40; loadings with lower values are N (.39), Self-criticism (.29) and the cognitive tests: Similarities (−.20); Picture completion (−.25), and Mental control (−.12). For the women, the following loadings are worthy of note: P (.62), N (.74), L (−.48); Hostility (.99), Urge to act out hostility (.75), Criticism of others (.91), Projected delusion (paranoid) hostility (.66), Self-criticism (.55) and Guilt (.67).

The male and female factors are clearly similar, although the number of high loadings is larger on the male factor. The correlations between the component scales of the Hostility inventory are responsible for the fact that these have higher loadings than P on this factor. It is interesting that some rating and performance scores have been incorporated in this factor, although these contribute mainly to other primaries concerned with ratings and performance, respectively; one might have expected relations between different 'measures' factors to have emerged rather by way of inter-factor correlations. These will be discussed later.

Factor 2 is clearly an extraversion factor, with E having a loading of .70 for the males. Other high loaders are Direction of hostility (−.81), Self-criticism (−.72), Guilt (−.65), all on the Foulds scales; N (−.50) on the PEN; and the following on the IMPS: Excitement (.44), Anxious intropunitiveness (−.67), Retardation (−.58), all on the psychologist's ratings; and Anxious intropunitiveness (−.78), and Retardation (−.84), on the psychiatric nurse's rating. For the women, the loading on E is even higher (.99), with Direction of hostility (−.31), Urge to act out (.35), and Self-criticism (−.32) loadings from the Foulds scales. Expansiveness (.56) in the psychologist's ratings had a high loading, with only three rather small loadings from the psychiatric nurse: Excitement (.23), Hostile belligerence (.27), and Expansiveness (.23). Age has a negative loading for the women (−.58); it has often been documented that people get more introverted with age. Why no such correlation is found among the males is not clear.

Factor 3 is a P rating factor, just as factor 1 is a P self-rating factor. There are three items with moderate loadings from the psychologist: Paranoid projection (.32), Perceptual distortion (.28), and Hostile belligerence (.23); there are four items with rather higher loadings from the psychiatric worker: Paranoid projection (.95), Expansiveness (.36), Perceptual distortion (.93), and Motor Disturbance (.73). There is also a loading of −.39 on Mental control. For the women there is no such loading on Mental control. They load on the Foulds scale of Acting out hostility (−.34) and the Hostile belligerence (.35) and Paranoid projection (.35) ratings by the psychologist. Again, loadings are higher for the ratings of the psychiatric nurse: Hostile belligerence (.68), Paranoid projection (.80), Expansiveness (.35), Perceptual distortion (.80), and Anxious intropunitiveness (.41). For both men and women, therefore, emphasis in this factor is on paranoid projection and perceptual disturbance and motor disturbance, with just a smattering of hostility.

Rated hostility comes out more clearly in factor 4. High loadings appear on Hostile belligerence (.78) and Retardation (−.29), as rated by the psychologist, and Excitation (.48) and Hostile belligerence (.41) as rated by the psychiatric nurse. For the women, loadings are on Excitation (.90) and Hostile belligerence (.64) in the psychologist's ratings, and Excitation (.48), Anxious intropunitiveness (−.41) and Retardation (−.32) in the psychiatric nurse's ratings.

Factor 5 is a test factor, with loadings on the cognitive tests. For the men, these are as follows: Similarities (.40), Picture completion (.73), and Mental control (.48); there are negative loadings on P (−.33) and Perceptual distortion (−.69). For the women, the factor loadings are on Similarities (.79), Picture completion (.84), Mental control (.52) and the two parts of the Motor Test: Part A (.87), Part B (.63). Here P only has a loading of −.19 and Perceptual distortion one of −.16. There is some evidence here of a relation between cognitive tests, on the one hand, and ratings and self-ratings on the other, but it is not very strong; again, we would expect such relations to emerge more clearly in the intercorrelations between factors.

Factor 6 is an Age factor, with loadings near unity for this variable and otherwise only much lower loadings; this is of little interest. Factor 7, for both sexes, related to the L scale, but the loadings are so confused and contradictory that it is not possible to make any psychological sense of this factor. Factor 8 appears to be concerned mainly with the two scores of the Motor Test. For the males, these load .93 and 1.01, with the (A−B) score loading .65. Mental control also loads (.45) and so do ratings for Excitation (.41) and Hostile belligerence (.29), as rated by the psychologist. For the women, these two scores (A and B) were taken up in factor 5; factor 8 for them only contains the (A−B) score, with a loading of .87. This factor is best regarded as a doublet and/or an artifact. The remaining factors are either doublets, e.g. for the males and the two ratings of Expansiveness (.86 and .67), or else are uninterpretable. We thus emerge with five clearly interpretable factors, similar for both sexes, and of some psychological interest, plus a sixth factor (age) which is equally clear but of little interest. We must next turn to the relations between the factors.

In view of the fact that the differences in scores were relatively small between sexes and that similar factors emerged at the primary level for both sexes,* it seems advisable to combine sexes for the higher-order factor analysis in order to have a sufficiently large sample. The analysis outlined above for the sexes separately was therefore repeated on the combined sample and second-order factors calculated; four factors emerged and their loadings are given in Table 29. Factor 1 loads mainly on the hostility scales of the Foulds inventory, on N and P, negatively on L, and on some of the rating scales, notably anxious intropunitiveness, retarded and apathetic, and motor disturbance; there is also a high negative loading on age, suggesting that this configuration appears more frequently in the younger patients. The highest loading on the Foulds scales is on self-criticism, followed by guilt; direction of

*Few of the means showed significant differences between the sexes. Picture Completion and the psychologist's rating on Paranoid projection were the only comparisons significant beyond the .01 level; the L scale of the PEN, the psychologist's rating on Perceptual distortion and the (A−B) score on the Motor Test reached significance at the 5 per cent level. On the whole and bearing in mind that out of thirty-four comparisons one or two would have reached the 5 per cent of significance by chance, these results suggest substantial similarity between the sexes.

hostility is thus mainly inwards (intropunitiveness). Factor 2 loads highly on the various tests used (similarities, picture completion, mental control and the motor test), with negative loadings primarily on P and on some of the ratings and Foulds scales. Factor 3 has loadings mainly on the ratings, particularly paranoid projection, grandiose expansiveness, and perceptual distortion; P and some of the Foulds scales are also represented, but not so prominently. Factor 4 is largely an artifact, having high loadings just on two ratings, hostile and belligerent. The first three factors might with advantage be regarded as 'instrument' factors, loadings on the Foulds scales (factor 1), the objective tests (factor 2), or the ratings (factor 3). It is interesting that on all factors P has a reasonable loading, suggesting that all three do in fact measure different aspects of P; this is also suggested by the fact that on each factor items from different 'instruments' do have sizeable loadings. In addition, the factors are positively correlated, with an average in the twenties. This suggests the extraction of third-order factors (super-factors); two of these were found in the analysis, and their loadings are given in Table 29.

The first factor is clearly a P factor; P has the highest loading, and the factor transcends 'instruments', having loadings on objective tests (items 2, 3 and 4, 32, 33), Foulds inventory scores (items 9, 11, 12, and 13), and ratings (items 18, 20, 24, 25, 26, 27, 28). Age has no loading on this factor. Factor 2 discriminates the outgoing, extraverted, extrapunitive type of psychotic from the inward-looking, introverted, intropunitive type. There are negative loadings on E, excitation, hostile belligerence, grandiose expansiveness, and positive loadings on N, inward direction of hostility, self-criticism, guilt, anxious intropunitiveness, and retardation and apathy. These results suggest that within the psychotic field extraverted and introverted behaviour patterns may be distinguished with a considerable degree of clarity, and thus reinforce the findings of Armstrong *et al.* (1967); and of Venables and Wing (1962). The former concluded, from an examination of the Maudsley Personality Inventory (MPI) scores of schizophrenic patients, that 'these results raise the possibility that a significant degree of what is included within the process-reactive frame of reference may be considered a function of extraversion-introversion' (p.69). Our results suggest that some even broader grouping is possible, embracing not only schizophrenics, but also other types of psychotics.

In order to look at individual cases, and also at clusterings of diagnostic units, factor scores were calculated for all patients, on the two super-factors. These were plotted in two-dimensional space, but inspection did not reveal any very clear pattern, except that depressive disorders seemed to be particularly prominent in the extravert-high P quadrant, paranoid disorders in the extravert-low P quadrant, and schizophrenics in the introvert-medium P part of the space. In order to put this causal observation on a more quantitative basis, patients were grouped into four groups—schizophrenics, paranoids, affectives, and unclassified; numbers in these categories were fifty-one, thirty-two, sixty and nine respectively. Means and variances were then calculated for these groups, and differences were tested on both factors for the first three groups; the fourth group of unclassifieds was too small to make statistical treatment worth while, and in any case they fell very near the central point of the plot. Our impression about the relative positions of the other groups was borne out; all the differences related to factor 1 (P) were significant, the difference between paranoids and affectives being the most significant ($p < .001$). None of the differences on factor 2 were significant statistically, although the difference between schizophrenics and the other two groups is more likely than not to be replicated on repetition of the experiment. None of these results, however, can be taken to have any very fundamental meaning in view of the degree of selection that has preceded our experiment; eliminating the most severely ill cases, who would not have been able to do the test at all, may have meant removing an unduly large proportion of high-P schizophrenics, leaving the less seriously ill. The data are reported for the sake of completeness, but no far-reaching conclusions can be based on them. Table 30 gives the means and standard deviations of the four groups.

As mentioned in the description of the experimental design, the great majority of patients were re-tested with the PEN inventory after six to eight weeks; sixty-one men and seventy-two women were in fact retested. The results of the test and retest comparison are given in Table 31; part 1 gives the test-retest correlations, and part 2 gives the means for the first and second tests and the statistical significance of the observed differences.

TABLE 30 Means and standard deviations of four abnormal groups

	Factor 1 (P)	Factor 2 (introv.)
Schizophrenics	−.1126 ± 1.0240	.1867 ± .9375
Paranoids	−.6343 ± 1.0474	−.0935 ± .1947
Affectives	−.4275 ± .8627	−.1426 ± 1.2346
Unclassified	.0439 ± .8793	−.1439 ± 1.3491

TABLE 31 Test-retest correlations. Asterisks denote level of significance

	Males	Females	Combined
P	.49	.55	.53
E	.63	.73	.68
N	.60	.85	.63
L	.71	.75	.73

Means

	M_1	M_2	F_1	F_2	C_1	C_2
P	4.62	3.11**	5.31	3.71***	4.99	3.44***
E	9.97	10.70	11.00	11.21	10.53	10.98
N	10.67	9.41*	11.22	10.01*	10.97	9.74**
L	5.61	5.92	6.81	6.56	6.26	6.26

Asterisks denote level of significance of correlated t-tests at the .05, .01 and .001 levels (one, two and three asterisks respectively)

It will be seen that the test-retest correlations are quite high, with the exception of P; considering the mental state of the patients, and the exceptionally rapid changes taking place in their behaviour during this period, these values indicate some degree of stability. As regards the changes in the means, there is obviously no change in E and L, and only a relatively slight change towards lower N; there are, however, marked changes in the P scores in the direction of lower degrees of psychoticism. It seems likely that it is this marked change that is responsible for the low retest reliability of the P score; it is unlikely that such rapid changes affect every individual equally, and hence there would result a change in rank order, producing equally lowered retest correlations and greater change in means. The fact that the retest correlations are still quite substantial suggests that the P score might with advantage be used as a predictive test, low scores predicting better chances of improvement in the patients' clinical condition. The study under review by itself is, of course, not in a position to establish this important point.

Our results may best be discussed in the context of the theory of arousal, which has often been applied, although in contradictory ways, to psychotic behaviour generally and schizophrenic behaviour specifically. Mednick (1958) has postulated that schizophrenia represents a learned response to unbearable anxiety or arousal; this arousal develops within the individual as a result of hyperreactivity to external stimuli. (The connection between arousal and hyperreactivity has been experimentally documented in normal subjects by Eysenck, 1967b.) Arieti (1956) and many other theorists of widely differing background have published statements broadly along the same lines. Others have given an entirely different account, ascribing schizophrenic reactions to sluggish autonomic reactivity (Gellhorn, 1953). When skin resistance is used to measure arousal, widely varying results have been reported. Ax *et al.* (1961), Williams (1953) and Zahn (1964, 1968) report higher then normal tonic levels; Crooks and McNulty (1966), S.B.G. Eysenck (1956b), Goldstein (1965), Howe (1958) and Venables (1964) report lower than normal tonic levels. De Vault (1955), Paintal (1951) and Ray (1963) fail to find any significant differences either way. Fenz and Velner (1970) report 'the conclusion that, depending on the psychological measures used, the selection of *S*s, and the experimental situation, schizophrenics fall anywhere along the continuum of arousal, although in most cases toward the high or low ends of the continuum'. Reviews of the literature bear this out; Lynn (1963) concluded from his review of the Russian literature that there are two types of schizophrenia: a majority group characterized by low sympathetic tone and reactivity, and a minority group with usually high sympathetic tone and reactivity. Gellhorn (1967), in a later study, also reported schizophrenic patients of high and low sympathetic reactivity. Thayer and Silber (1971) argued that tonic arousal level would be a basic parameter influencing psychophysiological responsiveness to discrete stimuli; they found that this was true both in a normal and in a schizophrenic group of subjects, with psychiatric status itself a negligible factor.

These results agree well with Eysenck's proposal that the arousal syndrome is associated with the extraversion-introversion dimension (Eysenck, 1967b); if P is independent of E, then we would expect, as we seem to find, that both high-arousal and low-arousal subjects are to be found among patients diagnosed as psychotics. This notion does of course break with a cherished psychiatric belief, dating back to before Jung, that introversion and schizophrenia have some special affinity. The work of Page (1934), and particularly the follow-up studies of Michael, Morris and

Soroker (1957), have given no support to this view, which in any case was not based on empirical data. The results of this study bear out the hypothesis that it is possible to divide psychotic populations by reference to differences in extraversion-introversion, just as it is possible to divide normal or neurotic populations in this manner, and that this division coincides with important behavioural differences.

This discussion of arousal as a possible factor in psychotic reactions is merely intended to raise the problem; a more extended review of the evidence will be presented in chapter 9.

The results of the various studies reported and quoted in this chapter are not unfavourable to the general hypothesis that the P scale measures something appropriately called 'psychoticism'. We find that psychotics do indeed score highly on this scale, higher than normals and also higher than neurotics; the differentiation from neurotics becomes somewhat clearer when the very high L scores of psychotics are corrected for, and when possibly wrongly diagnosed endogenous depressive patients are not included in the psychotic sample. Within the psychotic group as a whole, there is an increase in P with increases in the severity of the symptoms defining the psychosis; the greater the severity of the psychosis, the higher the P scale score. This is shown in ratings, in self-ratings, and in objective performance tests. Psychotics also have much lower N scores than do neurotics; this is another important way of distinguishing the two diagnostic groups. For practical purposes it is clearly best to use a combination of all the scales in order to classify a given person; this is made very clear by the results of our discriminant function study. However, as noted before, such classification into a psychiatric system of diagnostic labels is not a very useful endeavour in our view; we are concerned much more with a dimensional analysis of the joint normal and abnormal fields. For this purpose, clearly the P scale forms an essential part.

Studies correlating directly P and N scores with diagnoses of psychosis and neurosis have certain drawbacks which should be mentioned, additional to the lack of diagnostic reliability already discussed. One obvious difficulty is the fact that psychotics tend to have high L scores; this automatically depresses their P scores, making comparisons with other groups awkward. Another is the fact that many neurotics may also have a high P component, or psychotics a high N component, which does not find expression in the diagnosis. For these reasons, and also in order to obtain a more meaningful comparison between the symptom-oriented psychiatric diagnosis and the personality-oriented questionnaire approach, the following experiment was carried out. We selected seven psychiatric status groups (normals, criminals, schizophrenics, personality disorders, anxiety states or dysthymics, reactive depressives, and endogenous depressives); each group contained sixty-three males and sixty-three females. The ages of the members of these groups ranged from 25 to 35 years, with the exception of the endogenous depressives whose mean age was just in excess of 40. The cases were taken from our files, in random order; this means that the psychiatric disorders came from different hospitals, were diagnosed by different psychiatrists using different approaches and systems, and were as heterogeneous as possible. These conditions are the inverse of optimal for obtaining positive results in the study in question; they were purposely chosen in order to test the viability of our theories against the worst possible criterion.

The data were analysed by discriminant function analysis, treating the males and females as independent samples. This type of analysis combines scores from all the scales used in such a way as to give the maximum discrimination between groups;

this forms the first component. Later components are extracted on the same principle, but with the proviso that they must be orthogonal to the first component, i.e. independent of it. Three significant components were extracted from the data for both sexes. Figures 32 and 33 show the results, for males and females respectively. The first two components only have been plotted; the third component was a rather minor one, putting together the prisoner and the personality disorder groups; it may be interpreted as an 'antisocial' factor.

PSYCHIATRIC ABNORMALITY

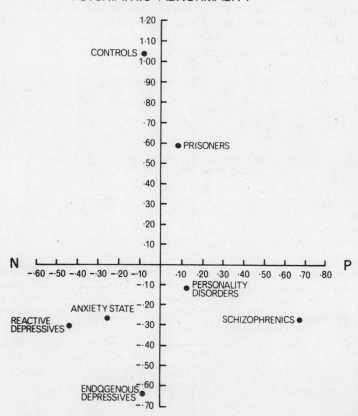

Figure 32   Position of seven psychiatric groups on two main discriminant function variates: Males

The first two components are clearly in line with our general set of hypotheses. The first component has at one extreme the controls, at the other the psychiatric groups; prisoners are intermediate. This is clearly a psychiatric abnormality component; it is interesting that for the females the prisoners are quite closely linked with the schizophrenic group, which is not true for the males. This agrees with our finding that female prisoners had P scores in excess even of male prisoners, although generally females have lower P scores than males. Prison psychiatrists have always found female prisoners much more disturbed psychiatrically than male ones. This finding therefore agrees well with experience and previous results.

117

The second component contrasts the neurotic disorders (dysthymia and reactive depression) with the psychotic ones (schizophrenia and endogenous depression), with personality disorders rather closer to the latter. This is in good agreement with Lewis's (1974) statement that such personalities 'fall mid-way between normality and psychosis' (p.133). It is interesting to note that even with the very adulterated diagnosis for the two types of depression used by the psychiatrists taking part in this study, nevertheless reactive depression, for both males and females, fell on the same side as dysthymia, and endogenous depression on the same side as schizophrenia.

PSYCHIATRIC ABNORMALITY

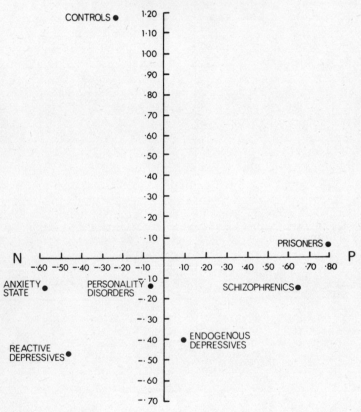

Figure 33 Position of seven psychiatric groups on two main discriminant function variates: Females

The outcome of this study, therefore, is quite clear-cut, in spite of the much less than optimal conditions of its execution. The study is not to be regarded, as we have insisted before, as in any sense a validation of the questionnaire or the idea of dimensional analysis; we cannot regard the psychiatric diagnostic categories as a suitable criterion. What the study does show is that there are intelligible relationships between the two systems, such that *categorical* terms in the psychiatric system can be translated into positions within the *dimensional* framework of the psychological system. This is an important finding; unless there were such a relationship, it would clearly be unjustifiable to use terms like 'neuroticism' and 'psychoticism' in relation to purely psychological dimensions. The psychiatric nomenclature can only be justified by empirical demonstrations such as those offered in this chapter.

8

Psychoticism, criminality and antisocial behaviour

H.J. Eysenck (1970e) has developed a theory of antisocial behaviour based on learning theory principles and related to personality; according to this theory, extraverts should indulge in antisocial behaviour more frequently than introverts, on the basis of their hypothesized lesser conditionability (H.J. Eysenck, 1967b), which in turn is due to lower cortical arousal. The general theory maintains that conditioning is at the basis of the development of socialized behaviour and 'conscience', so that people who condition poorly would be disadvantaged in acquiring those conditioned socialized responses which go to make up our non-delinquent behaviour. Neuroticism, in this account, acts as an amplifying device, by virtue of its drive properties; it multiplies in Hullian fashion with the habits at the top of the habit hierarchy to produce behaviour. We shall not here be concerned with the details of this theory, or the empirical evidence for and against it; nor will we emphasize here certain obvious points, such as the fact that environmental influences clearly interact with the probably largely genetic 'conditionability' of the organism. It will also be obvious that there are considerable difficulties in translating the concept of 'antisocial behaviour', for which the theory was constructed, into some other, more observable and quantifiable one, such as criminal behaviour, or the even more remote one of 'being a prisoner in one of Her Majesty's prisons'. We are here concerned, rather, with the fact that while the formula Criminal Behaviour = E $\times$ N may cover some cases of psychopathy and criminality, it clearly does not cover all, and the additional fact that, as was disclosed in our discussion of the genetic basis of psychoticism, there appears to be considerable excess of psychopathy and criminality in the biological relatives of schizophrenic individuals. This suggested the hypothesis that criminals and other people indulging in antisocial activities would be characterized by high P scores in a significant number of cases, and it is with the documentation relevant to this hypothesis that this chapter is concerned.

In the first experiment conducted to test our hypothesis, we used the PI, an early version of our final scale, the construction of which has been described in a previous chapter. We actually carried out factor analyses of the intercorrelations between the items separately for the prisoners and for our control group A (to be described presently) in order to make certain that the structure found in the normal population would also apply in prison. It is conceivable that the structure which obtains in the population as a whole might very well not be identical with that found in distinct sub-groups, such as prisoners, or inmates of mental hospitals, etc. To simply use the scores of scales validated in the normal population, in order to compare random samples of the normal population with samples of some specific sub-population, is not admissible unless it can be shown that the structure on which the scales are based is similar for the two groups. Unless this is done, the meaning of the scale scores can be dramatically different, thus making comparison hazardous. Details given in our first paper (S.B.G. Eysenck and H.J. Eysenck, 1970b) suggest that the structure produced by factor analysis is remarkably similar for controls and prisoners, thus obviating this difficulty.

One control group (Group A) consists of 532 male non-prisoners (and presumably largely non-criminals, although proof for this assertion would be difficult to furnish) who were selected in the course of an investigation of the relation between personality and sport in children; adults used here were the parents of the children employed in the investigation and constitute a reasonably random sample of the population, with the upper-class and upper-middle-class membership significantly curtailed (no public school boys took part in the study, and no grammar school children). In the absence of more detailed information regarding the social status of the prisoners, it is impossible to say that the two samples were exactly matched on this variable, but certainly both samples were predominantly working-class. The control group can be regarded as approximating a random sample, but with an under-representation of upper-class and upper-middle-class persons and, of course, a non-representation of unmarried persons. The two samples are far from perfectly matched, particularly in age; control group A has a mean age of 44.6 years.

A second control group (Group B) consisted of 423 university students, with a mean age similar to that of the criminals. A third control group (Group C) consisted of 185 industrial apprentices, aged 17.9 years; these were tested at their place of employment and constituted a low-drive group (Eysenck, 1964). None of these three control groups is ideal for our purpose; indeed, it seems unlikely that ideal groups exist, particularly when not very much is known about the exact nature of the criminal sample in question. Group A is representative of the general population, but all its members are married and are considerably older than the experimental group; there is good agreement on social class, however, between the groups. Group B is a good match for age, but intelligence and education are obviously higher than for the criminals, and so probably is social class. Group C is younger than the experimental group, entirely working-class and unmarried; it differs most from Group A in these particulars. It seems likely that having three such control groups, none individually very satisfactory, would throw more light on the hypotheses under investigation than would any amalgamation of the groups. Previous work with similar groups has suggested that students are somewhat high on N, as compared with other samples of similar age and that apprentices are somewhat high on E. Quite generally, N, E and P seem to decline with age, and to be lower in the upper social classes. With these limited items of information in our possession, we may now consider the results of our study.

Table 32 gives the correlations between the P, E and N factors for prisoners and controls (Group A) separately. The patterns of correlations are not dissimilar and none depart too far from zero, although in control group A the correlation between P and N is higher than has been found in other groups. Among the mothers (i.e. the wives of the fathers constituting the control group) the correlation between P and N was .18; among two student groups (male and female) it was .19 and .09; and in two random sample groups (male and female) it was .08 and .12. It thus seems that a slight positive correlation exists between the P and N factors of our inventory, but this does not, of course, mean that scales could not be constructed which would give zero correlation. For practical purposes, the observed correlations are in any case of no great importance. Correlations between scales are given in Table 33, where again there is a slight positive correlation between P and N which could be eliminated by further item substitution.

TABLE 32 Intercorrelations between P, E and N factors for prisoners and controls (Group A)

	Prisoners	Controls
P *vs.* N	.04	.34
P *vs.* E	.05	.07
E *vs.* N	−.11	.07

TABLE 33 Intercorrelations between P, E and N scales (24 items) for prisoners and controls

	Prisoners	Controls Group A	Group B	Group C
P *vs.* N	.30	.26	.16	.11
P *vs.* E	.09	.14	.08	.15
E *vs.* N	.02	.08	−.17	.03

The reliabilities (homogeneity coefficients) for the three scales are shown in Table 34 for prisoners and controls (Group A) separately. For P and N the coefficients are almost identical, but for E the prisoners have a much lower coefficient; this may be due to the possibility that certain questions in the E scale (particularly those relating to sociability) may produce different interpretations and answers in prisoners than in normal controls, due to the process of incarceration. However that may be, the lowered reliability of this scale in the prisoner population must inevitably make the discovery of significant differences from the normal control group more difficult.

TABLE 34 Reliability coefficients of P, E and N scales for prisoners and controls (24-item scales)

	Prisoners	Controls Group A	Group C
P	.60	.59	.57
E	.67	.78	.74
N	.81	.81	.78

Table 35 lists the mean scores of the control groups and the criminal group on P, E and N; also given are the standard deviations for both groups. It will be obvious that there are, as anticipated, important differences between the various control groups; students are the highest on N, apprentices on E. Nevertheless, overall results are very much as predicted. As far as P is concerned, prisoners have far and away the highest score; they exceed the mean of the other groups by about one whole SD. As far as E is concerned, prisoners have higher scores than Group A, slightly higher scores than Group B, and lower scores than Group C; it will be remembered that Group C was composed of significantly younger members than the prisoner group, and that these industrial apprentices have always come out exceptionally extraverted in previous studies. As far as N is concerned, prisoners have the highest scores, but Group B (students) runs them a close second; again it will be remembered that students have always been characterized by unusually high N scores. (For the 24-item version of the scales, the students actually surpass the prisoners with respect to N scores.)

TABLE 35   Scores of prisoners and three control groups for P, E and N, on 18- and 24-item scales

Group	n	P		E		N		
		M	SD	M	SD	M	SD	
Prisoners	603	4.44	2.60	10.61	3.04	8.70	4.08	
A. Married men	534	1.66	2.09	8.28	3.79	6.25	3.91	18-item
B. Students	423	2.23	2.01	10.27	3.62	8.59	3.90	scales
C. Industrial apprentices	185	1.85	2.04	11.58	3.25	7.26	3.67	
Prisoners	603	6.25	3.01	12.75	3.52	11.04	4.75	
A. Married men	534	3.54	2.40	9.71	4.22	8.25	4.57	24-item
B. Students	423	4.36	2.46	12.28	4.07	11.24	4.57	scales
C. Industrial apprentices	185	4.24	2.55	13.57	3.67	9.68	4.28	

These results strongly support our prediction as far as P is concerned, moderately strongly our prediction as far as N is concerned, and rather weakly, if at all, our prediction as far as E is concerned. We have already mentioned our reasons for believing that questionnaire measurement of E in prisoners presents certain problems which make verification of our hypothesis more difficult, and we have presented evidence (differential reliability of the E scales in prisoners and controls) which supports this belief. It seems possible that item comparisons between experimental and control groups may throw some light on these hypothetical difficulties, and such a comparison will be presented in a subsequent paper. For the moment, the results must be accepted as they stand.

One point might, however, be worthy of consideration. The results reported suggest that prisoners *as a whole* differ in their personality make-up from non-criminal controls, and that these differences are predictable from theory. Now it seems unlikely in the extreme that there are no personality differences between different types of criminals; some suggestions in this direction have been made in *Crime and Personality*. Gang crimes would appear likely to involve high E personalities; aggressive crimes and crimes involving unnecessary cruelty seem to carry implications of high P; the ineffectual crimes often committed by ageing recidivists might be due to the social incapacities of the introvert. It would seem to follow that by paying attention to differences *within* the criminal group in respect to P, E and N, i.e. by constructing a typology of crimes to take its place beside our typology of people, we should be able to get much greater differences between controls and homogeneous groups of criminals than we have obtained from our total group of criminals.

Some evidence for this hypothesis has been given in a recent paper (H.J. Eysenck and S.B.G. Eysenck, 1976), in which were compared the P, E and N scores of five different types of criminals, viz. conmen, inadequates, those guilty of crimes of violence, crimes against property and a residual group guilty of various different types of crimes. The results of this study are shown in Figure 34. Conmen are separated out from the beginning, as they have low P scores, as opposed to all the other groups. (They also have unusually low N scores and unusually high E scores.) We then separate out the high N scorers (inadequates and residuals) from low N scorers (violence and property offenders). Last, each of these two groups is subdivided into high and low E scorers. The mean scores of the different groups on these variables are indicated in the diagram. The results are suggestive rather than conclusive, but they do suggest that prison populations can be subdivided according to crime and personality structure. This is also suggested by a study in which H. Marriage (unpublished) found that when for a group of 228 long-term prisoners a factor analysis was carried out on twenty-two variables including personality factors, crimes committed, age, class, etc., there emerged a clear-cut factor (among others) with the following loadings: violence, .53; sex crimes, .79; conmanship, −.78; P, .51. This positive relation between P and crimes of violence, and the negative relation between P and conmanship, agree with our own data (see also Sinclair and Chapman, 1973).

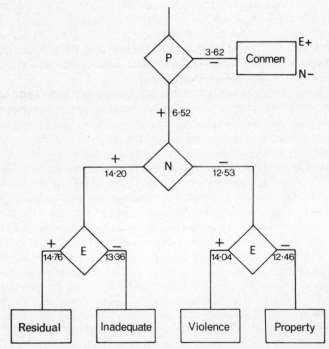

Figure 34   Discrimination on P, E and N between different types of felons

However that may be, the main fact of interest in connection with the theme of the present book is that criminals do indeed score significantly higher on P than do members of various control groups. The data were further analysed by taking each item in turn and determining its ability to discriminate between the criminal and control groups; this analysis made it clear that within the E scale it was items descriptive of impulsiveness, not of sociability, which discriminated between the groups. Within the P and N scales, some items did and others did not discriminate; it was difficult to formulate any strong hypotheses about the reasons for this difference. However, the existence of such differences did suggest the construction of a C (criminality) scale, made up of the forty items which best discriminated between criminals and controls. On this scale, which contains many P items, criminals scored 17 points, while the control groups averaged 10 (with a standard deviation of around 5). Details of these analyses are given in S.B.G. Eysenck and H.J. Eysenck (1971a). The reliability of the C scale was between .7 and .8 for the different groups. There seems to be no doubt that criminals and controls score quite differently on the P, E and N scales, and that P in particular shows marked differences between the groups.

Our next study was designed to provide information on female prisoners, to compare with the males reported above. Somewhat different scales were used for this study, so that results are not strictly comparable with those of our previous study. However, to make up for this difficulty, we have provided scores for various male samples, with many of the subjects identical with those in our previous study; the scales used in the present study were derived from the same questionnaire, but we scored a number of items previously left in as buffer items.

Our experimental population consisted of 264 female prisoners in Holloway Prison, London. Of these women, two-thirds were over 21 years of age, one-third under that age. Two-thirds had been sentenced, one-third were on remand. Differences on P, E and N were negligible and have been omitted in the computations to follow. Prisoners were tested without compulsion, in small groups, by a member of the Psychology Department.

There were three control groups in all; these have been kept separate in the Tables in order to overcome some of the difficulties which arise from the impossibility of obtaining a properly matched sample. These three samples were as follows: (1) Random sample. This was a group of 357 women approached by a market research agency in an attempt to obtain a quota population sample; these women were group tested in a special hall hired by the agency. Testing included appraisal of advertisements and other commercial tasks; the personality inventory was included among other types of tests. This group approaches a random sample quite closely, although the very top and the very bottom 5 per cent of the population are probably under-represented; we have in the past found that mean personality test scores so obtained agree very well with other random samples obtained by different methods. (2) The second sample was made up of mothers of a random sample of schoolchildren; the children had been approached first, in connection with an entirely different research, and the parents were later approached and filled in the questionnaires. There were 577 of these mothers, whose mean age would of course be higher than that of the prisoners. (3) The third sample was made up of 385 students, with a mean age below that of the prisoners. This sample included not only university students, but also students of nursing and various other non-academic types of course. It was hoped that, while none of these groups was identical with the prisoners with respect to age and social class, the differences in mean scores between the control groups would give a rough indication of the importance of these factors, compared with the differences between all control groups and the prisoner group.*

Means and standard deviations for the various scales and groups are given in Table 36; also given for the sake of comparison are scores for 1,301 male prisoners, for a random sample of 435 males, obtained in a manner similar to that used for our random sample of females, for a sample of 534 fathers, and for one of 423 students, these last two obtained in a manner similar to that used for our samples of females. Our first concern is with the P-scale scores. The following findings are very highly significant: (1) female prisoners have higher P scores than female controls; note the close similarity in size of mean score between the three control groups; (2) male prisoners have higher P scores than male controls; note the similarity in size of mean score between the three control groups; (3) male prisoners have lower mean P scores than female prisoners; (4) male controls have higher mean P scores than female controls. In other words, although generally males have higher P scores than females, yet female prisoners have higher P scores than male prisoners. This is an unexpected finding, but the figures leave no doubt about its accuracy. In as far as the high P scores of female prisoners go, the results are as predicted; it is the fact that the scores are in excess even of those returned by male prisoners that is surprising. However, it may be noted that prison psychiatrists have drawn our attention to the fact that female prisoners are psychiatrically much more unusual and disturbed than are male prisoners; the possibility should be considered that crime is so unusual an activity for women that only the most unusually high P scorers overcome the social barriers involved.†

As far as E is concerned, female prisoners have higher scores than any of the controls; even the students, who are younger than the prisoners, score below them, in spite of the fact that E scores decline with age. The significance levels of the three comparisons involved are respectively .05, .001, and .05. The female prisoners have lower E scores than the male prisoners; this sex difference is quite common, as can be seen from a comparison of the male and female control groups. In respect to E, Eysenck's original hypothesis is borne out. It should also be noted that the E score throws together sociability and impulsivity items; the difference would presumably have been greater had only impulsivity items been considered.

Concerning N, female prisoners score significantly higher than female controls; the only group which approaches the prisoners is the student group, and previous work has shown that students tend to be particularly high on N (see also data for

---

*As far as age is concerned, there was no difficulty in matching the samples precisely. As far as class is concerned, however, no great accuracy can be claimed. The reason for this is very simple: rating scales for social class are made for men, and do not apply at all well to women. Many of the prisoners had been prostitutes, often earning far more than a university professor. What social class would one put such girls into—compared, say, to a housewife whose father was a semi-skilled worker, and whose husband is a very highly paid salesman? We know of no way of overcoming these difficulties with any degree of exactitude; hence our purposely imprecise phrase. The difficulty here encountered was in part responsible for our decision to have three separate female control groups; these groups are differentiated with respect to social class and age, so that any marked effects of these variables could be noted.

†An alternative formulation might be that prison is so unusual a sentence for women that only the most unusually high P scorers pass through the screening processes involved.

TABLE 36 Scores on P, E and N scales of male and female prisoners and of various normal control groups

	n	P	E	N
Female prisoners	264	7.55±3.74	11.88±3.85	13.04±4.66
Controls:				
Random sample	357	2.89±2.11	11.20±4.28	12.01±4.43
Mothers	577	2.45±1.96	9.67±4.06	10.76±4.75
Students	385	2.42±2.11	11.25±4.14	12.79±4.75
Male prisoners	1,301	6.55±3.16	12.51±3.63	11.39±4.97
Controls:				
Random sample	435	4.52±2.64	13.41±3.88	10.09±4.49
Fathers	534	3.54±2.40	9.71±4.22	8.25±4.57
Students	423	4.36±2.46	12.28±4.07	11.24±4.57

male students). (Significance levels are .01, .001 and ns.) Male prisoners too have higher N scores than male controls. Females, whether prisoners or controls, have higher N scores than males; it is in good accord with previous experience. Results for N are in good agreement with prediction—with the proviso that N tested in isolation from E does not provide a proper test of Eysenck's hypothesis. We may conclude that, taken in isolation, scores on P, E and N discriminate between female prisoners and female controls of various kinds, with prisoners showing higher P, E and N scores.

Our next study was designed to provide a rather better control group than was possible before; we aimed to control for sex, age and social class in one single control group, rather than having different control groups making up in combination for the failure of each to control for all three factors.

Our criminal population was made up of 606 male criminals with a mean age of 26.53 (SD 10.00); these were a random population from several of the main British prisons. Our control population consisted of 518 white trainee railmen employed by London Transport, all male and with a mean age of 25.85 (SD 10.69). The two samples are thus reasonably well matched on sex, age and social class; they differ in that all coloured members had been removed from a somewhat larger total sample of controls. In all, 140 of these coloured trainee railmen were removed because they were found to have significantly different scores on some of the scales; details regarding these differences will be given presently. Coloured persons could not be removed from the prison sample because no record was available to identify them by colour; in any case, the proportion of coloured to white prisoners would most certainly be smaller. The age of the coloured controls was 30.83 (SD 9.42).*

Table 37 gives the means and standard deviations of these various samples for P, E, N and L. It will be seen that prisoners are significantly higher than controls on P and N, and significantly lower than controls on E; there are no differences on L, suggesting (if we are willing to assume that L is at least in part a measure of dissimulation) that deliberate falsification did not play an important part in the

*Unselected inventories were received from London Transport, and the allocation of the groups was undertaken by us.

production of these differences. Coloured people are much higher on the L scale than white controls; they are also higher on P ($p < .05$) and lower on N ($p < .01$). There are no differences on E.

TABLE 37 Means and standard deviations of 606 prisoners, and 518 white and 140 coloured London Transport employees on P, E, N and L scales

	Prisoners		London Transport employees			
			White		Coloured	
	Mean	SD	Mean	SD	Mean	SD
P	4.81	3.95	3.14	2.85	3.74	2.50
E	12.43	3.95	13.58	3.59	13.58	2.83
N	9.56	4.46	7.53	4.40	6.38	3.83
L	5.48	3.32	5.44	3.26	8.96	3.63

The need to match samples for social class is brought out clearly if we compare the data given in Table 37 with the norms of a more representative population sample of 1,012 male subjects. These score lower on P (2.50; SD 2.71) and on E (12.75; SD 4.12) than our working-class white controls; on N they score only fractionally lower (7.33; SD 4.37). These results are in reasonably good agreement with the social class comparisons made in our previous paper (S.B.G. Eysenck and H.J. Eysenck, 1969a). On L we have available results from two samples: a random sample of 152, and a somewhat more middle-class one of 329. L scores were 4.56 (SD 2.95) and 3.56 (SD 2.48) respectively, suggesting that L scores are higher in working-class groups. This does not necessarily mean that working-class subjects lie more; alternative and possibly more likely reasons for this difference are given in Michaelis and Eysenck (1971).

A further study which is relevant to our hypothesis has been reported by H.J. Eysenck (1974c). The data were collected by A. Maclean, in an unpublished study in which he used as his control group London Transport trainee bus crews of similar age and social class to the criminals; the results are very similar to those of our previous study. For the sake of comparison we have put together several of the groups previously discussed and collected by S.B.G. Eysenck, so that the numbers should be adequate for a reasonable estimate of the population parameters. Table 38 gives the results of the two sets of studies; it will be seen that on all three variables (P, E and N) the prisoners have higher scores, in both studies, with p values $< .001$ for each of the six comparisons. Taken together with our results for women prisoners, we believe that the results leave little doubt that the available data do not infirm our main hypotheses regarding the relation between personality and criminality. In adult criminals, P is clearly related to criminal activity.

Slightly different in kind is another study dealing with recidivism in Borstal boys (S.B.G. Eysenck and H.J. Eysenck, 1974).

The prediction made was that if a group of Borstal boys were tested with our personality inventory and followed up over a period of three years after discharge, then those reconvicted would have higher scores on P, E and N. It was not expected that the differences would be large. Environmental factors must play an important

TABLE 38   P, E and N scores of groups of adult male prisoners and controls; data from two independent investigations

		n	Psychoticism	Extraversion	Neuroticism
S.B.G. Eysenck					
(a)	Prisoners	1,301	6.55±3.16	12.51±3.63	11.39±4.97
(b)	Controls	1,392	4.10±2.53	11.65±4.37	9.73±4.71
			$p < .001$	$p < .001$	$p < .001$
A. Maclean					
(a)	Prisoners	569	6.65±3.12	12.47±3.67	11.77±4.98
(b)	Controls	595	4.38±2.32	11.54±3.62	8.82±4.50
			$p < .001$	$p < .001$	$p < .001$

part in causing recidivism; in addition, there is a large amount of simple unreliability attached to the determination of the dichotomy 'recidivist vs. non-recidivist'. Not all crimes are notified to the police; not all crimes notified are solved. (In fact, of the sort of crimes committed by Borstal boys, only a small proportion is ever solved.) Thus luck would play an important part in deciding whether a given boy who had actually reverted to criminal activity would be caught and punished. Such unreliability in the criterion would of course affect the differences in personality inventory scores, attenuating them below the level representing the 'true' differences between recidivists and non-recidivists. This argument should perhaps not be taken too seriously. We would probably think of the post-release behaviour of Borstal boys not in terms of a simple dichotomy: recidivist vs. non-recidivist, but rather in terms of a continuum from no further criminal activity through ever-increasing numbers of crimes to a maximum of criminal activity, with the probability of being caught increasing monotonically in accordance with the amount of criminal activity. Under these conditions, unreliability, while still an important factor, might not make it possible to discover significant differences in personality between extremes along this continuum.

One hundred and seventy-eight boys in a Borstal institution were administered the questionnaire, and their P, E and N scores determined. Three years and nine months after testing, an effort was made to ascertain whether or not these boys had been apprehended and sentenced a second time, or whether no further convictions had been recorded against them. One hundred and twenty-two boys came into the recidivist category, while fifty-six were non-recidivist on this criterion. The scores obtained by these two groups are given in Table 39. It will be seen that in each case, as predicted, recidivists obtain higher scores; however, only in the case of extraversion is the difference significant. This is interesting because in Eysenck's theory (1970e) this variable bears the heaviest load in accounting for 'criminality'. However, it would be too early to dismiss the other two variables from consideration; the number of boys in the non-recidivist category was unfortunately small, thus making the achievement of statistical significance rather difficult, particularly when the criterion itself is likely to be unreliable. It would seem desirable to carry out another study with rather more adequate numbers before dismissing the contribution of P and N to recidivism.

TABLE 39 Scores of 122 recidivists and 56 non-recidivists on three personality inventory scales

	P	E	N
Recidivists	9.52±3.82	15.18±3.25	10.94±4.94
Non-recidivists	8.73±4.09	14.07±3.51	10.07±5.18
't'	1.25	2.07	1.07
p	ns	.05	ns

In addition to studies of criminals as compared with non-criminals, work on the correlation between our scales and other well-authenticated scales may be of interest. One such inventory related to criminal conduct is the Jesness (1966, 1969) Inventory; this has ten scales, and is used to classify juvenile delinquents into eight personality types called I-level subtypes. Smith (1974) administered the two inventories to 153 males aged 16 to 20 years who had been sentenced to Borstal training (or Borstal recall). According to Jesness's typology, they were placed into I-level 2, I-level 3, or I-level 4 categories. Those at I-level 2 are depicted as asocial, egocentric and impulsive, with little or no understanding of interpersonal dynamics. Subjects at I-level 3 have become aware of certain rules of conduct and can conform to these if necessary. Those classified as I-level 4 have adopted and internalized rules as personal standards of behaviour, feeling guilty when violating these standards and showing empathy for others. Table 40, taken from Smith's study, shows the P, E, N scores of subjects diagnosed into these three 'I' groups on the basis of their questionnaire scores; also given are scores for the sociability and impulsiveness subscales of the extraversion scale. I-level 2 boys are significantly high on impulsiveness ($p < .05$) and psychoticism ($p < .001$), very much as one might have expected on the basis of the description of I-level 2 behaviour.

TABLE 40 Differentiation of Jesness I-levels on P, E and N. Also given is eta as a non-linear measure of correlation (from Smith, 1974)

		I_2	I_3	I_4	Eta
		(n=24)	(n=96)	(n=32)	
I	(Impulsiveness)	6.3	5.2	5.5	.22
S	(Sociability)	7.5	8.6	8.2	.17
E	(Extraversion)	13.5	13.6	13.6	—
N	(Neuroticism)	13.5	12.2	15.0	.24
P	(Psychoticism)	9.7	6.8	7.2	.35

Before turning to the topic of antisocial behaviour in children, we will briefly examine a particular type of criminal behaviour, namely the illicit use of drugs (Teasdale, 1973). Teasdale *et al.* (1971) used four different groups of drug takers: (1) twenty-one provincial heroin-users living in an English provincial town; (2) twenty-two in-patient injectors from a London clinic; (3) eleven oral in-patients, mainly taking Drinamyl and amphetamines; and (4) ten students admitting to taking drugs (LSD, marijuana, or amphetamines). A control group of 210 apprentices was used, although this group was younger than the drug-users, and would consequently be expected to have higher P scores as well as higher N and E scores. However, as this error in proper matching would bias the results against the hypothesis, it was decided to go ahead and make the comparisons anyway. The PEN scales were employed in this study.

The results of the comparisons revealed very clearly that drug-using in all these groups was significantly related to P, even when items whose content might have been relevant (e.g. 'Would you take drugs which may have strange or dangerous effects?') had been removed. An item analysis singled out eleven items, each of which discriminated at a $p < .01$ level or better between the users and non-users. Users in addition had high N scores in three out of the four groups, but for E the results are not clear, with two groups having significantly low scores, the other two not differing significantly from the controls. Teasdale's paper leaves little doubt about the relevance of P to crimes relating to drug usage, and also suggests the importance of N; the data on E are a little unexpected, but may be rationalized by suggesting that perhaps the drugs themselves may lead to more introverted behaviour. We would of course have to know the pre-morbid personality of all our drug-users in order to rule out this possibility of contamination for all our scales.

Validation of the findings reported above come from Czechoslovakia (Cepelák, 1973), where the PEN was administered to twenty-five prisoners dependent on drugs (called toxicomans by the author) and twenty-five non-addicted prisoners. Cepelák used two methods of scoring, namely that suggested by the authors of the PEN, and an extended one in which some of the buffer items were scored for those factors on which they had sizeable loadings. Figure 35 gives the main results of the study for P, E, N, and the C (criminality) score. These results are summarized by the author as follows: '(*a*) In factor P toxicomans scored significantly higher, especially when we extend the items of the P factor with other items in the questionnaire that have an affinity to P. The difference between the groups is significant even when we exclude the influence of the items relating to the use of drugs and of items that could be regarded as a consequence of drug dependence. (*b*) The higher values in extraversion of toxicomans may be attributed primarily to impulsiveness and not to sociability. (*c*) In the factor neuroticism there was only a slight difference between the groups, which contradicts the argument that higher values in P may be the result of high N. (*d*) In the individual factors as well as in the "scale of criminal propensity". . .toxicomans scored higher values thus showing the significance of toxicomania in the etiogenesis of criminal behaviour.'

Cepelák, as well as Teasdale, makes the point that drug users are a heterogeneous group (see also Hill *et al.*, 1962). These latter workers found several different types of MMPI profile in a population of drug addicts; however, they also found that all but one were characterized by higher Pd scores than the normal population. Thus the psychopathic aspect of the schizophreniform (psychotic?) syndrome clearly has a fundamental importance in the predisposition and maintenance of the drug-using habit. This emerges even when the control group is made up of criminals who themselves have elevated P scores.

The study by Cepelák is not the only one to indicate that the relationships between personality and criminality uncovered in the UK can also be found in a communist state. A study by Münnich has been described by H.J. Eysenck and S.B.G. Eysenck (1976); in this he compared 138 Hungarian criminals with 96 Hungarian controls on the EPQ (in translation). P scores for controls averaged 4.3, for criminals 7.1; the difference was fully significant statistically. For E and N, also, criminals showed higher scores than controls. For the C scale comparative scores were 9.8 as opposed to 15.0; all these differences are very similar to those found in the UK. These subjects were all male, aged 18 to 25 years. For two small female groups of criminals, Münnich also found very high P and C scores. The suggestion, frequently made by sociologists, that criminality is a function of the social system under which a person grows up, would predict that in two so very different systems as the capitalist and the communist, no such similarities should be found; the facts tend to disprove the hypothesis.

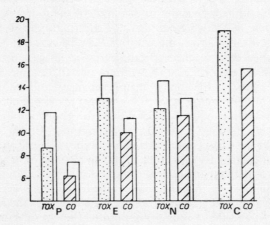

Figure 35   Mean scores on P, E, N and C (criminal predisposition) of two groups of prisoners: drug users (TOX) and controls (CO). The stippled and striped columns give PEN scores, the white columns give scores obtained by including appropriate 'buffer' items in the scales (from Cepelák, 1973)

We must now turn to the question of personality in children who behave in an antisocial manner. Of most importance and relevance here is the work of Allsopp (1975). In his studies he used two different indices of antisocial behaviour. The first of these is a self-report measure of antisocial behaviour (ASB), constructed by Feldman (Allsopp and Feldman, 1974, 1975). This subjective index is supplemented by objective records of classroom detention and other punishments inflicted by teachers for misbehaviour (NA = naughtiness score). For all the groups studied by Allsopp, these two indices were found to correlate together quite well, and to give similar personality differences between normal and antisocial children. This fact gives us confidence that the apparent subjectivity of the ASB questionnaire does not preclude considerable empirical validity.

In their first study, Allsopp and Feldman (1974) studied four groups of subjects, ranging from 11- and 12-year-old schoolgirls to 14- and 15-year-olds. One hundred and ninety-seven subjects took part, and the major outcome of the study is shown in Figure 36. This groups together children who show high scores on none, one, two, or all three of the personality scales (P, E and N); on the abscissa are given the mean ASB and NA scores for these four groups. It will be seen that there is a linear or at least monotonic increase in antisocial behaviour with increase in P, E or N; all three scales contribute about equally to the total result.

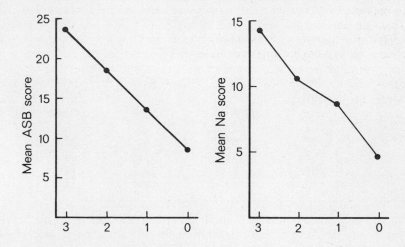

Figure 36 Mean ASB (self-rating) and NA (objective) antisocial behaviour scores of children scoring high on 0, 1, 2, or all 3 of the P, E and N scales (from Allsopp, 1975)

A second study (Allsopp and Feldman, 1975) used 385 boys ranging in age from 11 to 16 years; these were tested in a grammar school. The analysis in this case was carried out for individual items of the various personality scales, which makes summary of the results somewhat difficult. However, as far as P is concerned it was found that all seventeen P items differentiated between high and low ASB scorers in the predicted manner. On E, all but three of the items differentiated the groups in the predicted manner, the only one showing more than minimal discrimination in the wrong direction being concerned with participation in hobbies and interests, a finding easily explained. On N, the hypothesis is upheld for most items, but there are several which do not conform, for reasons which are explained by the authors. However, it would be safe to assume from this and other studies that the importance of N is greater for older subjects, and less for school children. The general outcome of this study cross-validates the results reported in the earlier work.

Allsopp (1975) reports two further studies, the first employing 347 boys and girls aged between 9 and 11 years from two primary schools. Some of the children were coloured, and as the coloured children showed significantly worse behaviour, their scores were treated separately. The results are presented in the form of correlation coefficients; these are given in Table 41. It will be seen that all correlations with ASB are positive with P and with N; for E there is no definite trend. This result goes counter to the usual finding that E is more closely related to antisocial behaviour in children than N, but of course this is a much younger group than the others studied, and possibly the meaning of extraversion has not yet properly consolidated before secondary school is reached. Nevertheless, as Burgess (1972) has shown, it is the combination of N and E which according to theory is the crucial factor in promoting antisocial conduct, and for white children at least this expectation is borne out by the data.

TABLE 41 Correlations of P, E and N with ASB (antisocial behaviour scale) in six groups of children (from Allsopp, 1975)

	A Boys	A Girls	B Boys (White)	B Girls (White)	B Boys (Coloured)	B Girls (Coloure
df	77	82	58	54	28	36
P	.37	.62	.51	.38	.67	.59
E	.02	.02	−.21	.22	−.11	.19
N	.21	.20	.45	.33	.43	.24

Allsopp's second study used 461 children between the ages of 13 and 16 years; of these, results will here be reported only on the 368 white boys. Teachers were asked to rate the behaviour of the boys; on this basis, they were divided into well and badly behaved. When these ratings were compared with the personality scale scores, the results indicated that 'badly behaved boys predominate at the high level of P, and at the low level of P where there is a combination of high E/high N scores; well behaved boys predominate at the low level of P except where E and N are

TABLE 42 Correlations of ASB sub-scales with P, E and N (from Allsopp, 1975)

Scale:	No. of items scored	P	E	N
Vandalism	7	.48	.20	.11
Stealing large objects	4	.33	.10	.09
Precocity	4	.33	.23	.00
Violence	4	.49	.14	.10
Serious school misbehaviour	5	.43	.13	.16
Breaking and entering	3	.24	.09	.07
Minor school misbehaviour	4	.35	.14	.10
Stealing	4	.39	.10	.17
School acts	16	.52	.18	.16
Other acts	36	.56	.22	.12
Total Score	52	.57	.22	.14

simultaneously high' (p.112). When we turn to the ASB, we may use a factor-analytic subdivision of the scale into ten factors, as shown in Table 42; this Table sets out the correlations of P, E and N with each of the subscales, as well as with the total scale. It will be seen that all the correlations are positive, being highest with P, and lowest with N. The results certainly bear out the general hypothesis in considerable detail.

The agreement found in the data for children and for adult criminals not only support the general theory of criminality which we have adumbrated; they also suggest that the children's P scale is valid as a measure of psychoticism. It is difficult to see how else we could obtain results supporting a prediction based on the validity of the scale. Provided that our general theoretical network is along the right lines, and given that for adult criminals a strong relation obtains between antisocial conduct and P, then it follows that a similar relation should obtain for children; the fact that such a relation is found supports both the general hypothesis and the validity of the Junior EPQ. This is an important point because there is much less external evidence for the validity of the children's scale than for that of the adult scale. Also, for children there is no obvious comparison group (psychotics) as there is for adults; childhood psychosis is an even more turbulent and unreliable field than adult psychosis.

9

Psychoticism, arousal and 'maleness'

As we have seen in Chapter 7, many theorists have tried to account for psychotic phenomena in terms of arousal, postulating either over- or under-arousal as a causative agent. We have also tentatively suggested in that chapter that possibly extraversion-introversion differences might be responsible for the direction of the arousal dysfunction, extraverts suffering from under-arousal, introverts from over-arousal of a chronic sort. There are in existence, however, data which suggest a much more complex relationship, and as these data and the theories which they give rise to are very relevant to the concept of 'psychoticism' they will be treated in some detail in this chapter. As Claridge (1972) has pointed out, we may look at the relation between arousal and psychotic behaviour in two ways. The first, already attempted in Chapter 7, involves the careful examination of arousal variations *within* groups of schizophrenic patients. We have already referred to the finding of Venables and his colleagues of relationships between arousal level and narrowly defined characteristics of schizophrenia, such as behavioural withdrawal and paranoid *vs.* non-paranoid symptomatology (Venables and Wing, 1962; Venables, 1967). Similarly, Herrington and Claridge (1965), finding a wide range of arousability in early psychosis, were able to demonstrate that differences in psychophysiological status were associated with such clinical features as thought disorder and mood disturbance. Whether work of this kind can be accommodated within the narrow confines of a P + E model remains to be seen. The second way of looking at the relation between P and arousal suggests that any such attempt will have to take into account a rather curious set of interaction phenomena.

Claridge (1972) puts it this way: 'The second and perhaps more interesting development has been the demonstration that schizophrenic patients differ from others, not so much in their absolute levels on given psychophysiological measures, but rather in the way in which different measures co-vary together; suggesting that it is the organization, not the deviation, of central nervous activity that is critically important in the schizophrenias. Empirically this difference in central organization is reflected in the correlations between measures that are considered to tap important aspects of psychophysiological function. Thus, some years ago Herrington and Claridge (1965) reported that the correlation between two such measures—the sedation threshold and the Archimedes spiral after-effect—was significantly negative in early psychotics but significantly positive in neurotic patients; yet the range of scores on each measure taken individually was identical in both groups. Around the same time Venables (1963) described a similar reversal of correlation using two quite different measures, skin potential and the fusion threshold for paired light flashes (two-flash threshold). Comparing normal subjects and chronic schizophrenics, he found correlations of opposite sign in the two groups, the direction of the relationships indicating that high autonomic activity was associated with poor perceptual discrimination in the former and heightened discrimination in the latter. Again both schizophrenics and normals spanned similar ranges on both measures' (p.8).

These results proved difficult to replicate, unfortunately. 'The result for the sedation threshold and spiral after-effect was later confirmed by Krishnamoorti and Shagass (1964), though Venables' finding has proved more difficult to replicate exactly. Lykken and Maley (1968) compared schizophrenic and non-psychotic patients on two perceptual measures, two-flash threshold and critical flicker fusion, and two autonomic indices, skin potential and skin conductance. They found that the perceptual and autonomic measures were certainly associated differently in the two groups, but that the pattern of correlations was diametrically opposite to that reported by Venables. The Lykken and Maley result with non-psychotics confirmed those obtained in an earlier series of studies by the same group of authors (Lykken *et al.*, 1966) and that reported by Hume and Claridge (1965) for normal subjects. To complicate matters further, Hume (1970) recently replicated Venables' original findings in schizophrenics but found zero correlations between two-flash threshold and skin potential in normal and neurotic subjects' (p.8).

Claridge believes that it is possible to reconcile some of these differences, and to throw further light on the nature of central nervous organization of schizophrenics, in terms of results found in a study of LSD responses in normal volunteers (Claridge, 1972). 'The aim of the experiment was to set up a drug model of Venables' comparison of schizophrenic and normal subjects. It was predicted that the overall effect of LSD would be not so much to produce a change in arousal per se but rather to alter the co-variation between autonomic and perceptual function, as reflected in the correlation between skin potential and two-flash threshold. A recent re-analysis of the data from this experiment has unearthed some interesting relationships, shown in the accompanying figures, which bear out this prediction. It can be seen that when the placebo and LSD conditions are compared there is indeed a systematic association between two-flash threshold and skin potential, the relationships being curvilinear but of opposite direction under the two conditions. That for placebo [Figure 37] is of the more usual inverted-U type, perceptual discrimination improving up to an optimum level of autonomic arousal and then deteriorating. Under LSD [Figure 38], on the other hand, heightened perceptual sensitivity appears to occur when the concurrent level of arousal is either very high or very low, being poorest at a moderate arousal level.'

'These results clearly help to account for the contradictory findings obtained in the group comparison studies described a moment ago. Thus, whether positive, negative, or zero correlations appear in particular groups may depend critically on the range of arousal over which subjects are tested. The point is well illustrated in Figure 39 where the placebo and LSD data from Figures 37 and 38, up to a skin potential level of 25 mv, have been superimposed. It can be seen that the correlation between two-flash threshold and skin potential is significantly negative under LSD ($-.82, p < .01$), but significantly positive under placebo ($+.74, p < .01$). In the upper range of skin potential, however, the correlations, while much lower are reversed in sign, now being positive for LSD ($+.11$) and negative for placebo ($-.32$)' (p.10).

This curious effect of LSD Claridge regards as a remarkable pharmacological parallel of the naturally occurring psychosis. Both can be regarded as evidencing a

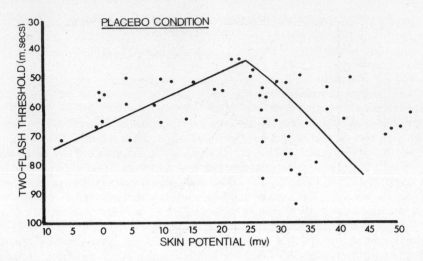

Figure 37 Measures of two-flash threshold and skin potential taken from ten subjects during the first hour under a placebo condition. Note that for convenience the signs of skin potential readings have been reversed. The scale for two-flash threshold is arranged so that changes in the upper direction indicate improved perceptual discrimination (from Claridge, 1972)

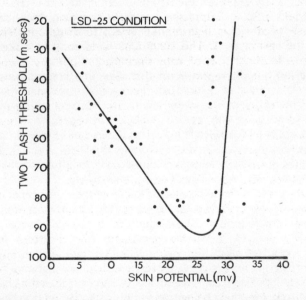

Figure 38 Measures of two-flash threshold and skin potential taken from ten subjects during the first hour under 100 μg LSD-25. Interpretation of the scales is as for Figure 37 (from Claridge, 1972)

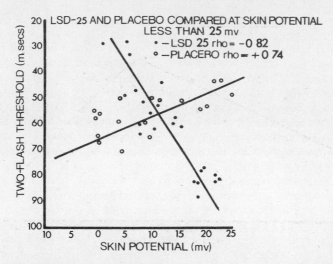

Figure 39   Data from Figures 37 and 38 up to a skin potential value of 25 mv, demonstrating how two-flash threshold and skin potential co-vary in opposite directions under LSD-25 and under placebo conditions (from Claridge, 1972)

weakening of central nervous homeostasis. The deterioration in perceptual sensitivity found in the LSD experiment at very high arousal levels in the placebo condition might be regarded in the Pavlovian fashion (Gray, 1964) as the intrusion of homeostatic or 'protective' mechanisms, activated once arousal reaches a critical level. Under LSD, or in psychosis, it might be argued that such mechanisms work in reverse, leading, at high arousal levels, to inappropriately heightened sensitivity to the environment. This condition would seem to represent a highly unstable 'positive feedback' sort of state, since marked changes in arousal in *either* direction could result in disproportionate alterations in perceptual sensitivity which would be very disruptive of mental functioning. Such a model, Claridge argues, might account for many of the symptoms of the schizophrenic patient, and the notion of altered feedback was, in fact, implicitly incorporated in his 'dissociation theory' of schizophrenia (Claridge, 1967). This theory, which attempted to account for the inverted relationship between sedation threshold and spiral after-effect observed in schizophrenic patients, was based on a long series of psychophysio-logical studies of neurotic, normal, and psychotic subjects.

'This research, which included two factor analyses of some of the more important measures, demonstrated two recognizable components of psychophysio-logical activity. One, clearly identifiable as a classic factor of arousal, as conventionally defined, accounted particularly for variations in autonomic responsiveness and sedation threshold. The second was mainly associated with EEG, particularly alpha rhythm, variables which, in turn, were related to the spiral after-effect. This latter component was therefore regarded as having a partly inhibitory feedback function, being concerned with the modulation of sensory input into the nervous system and with the selectivity aspect of attention. The model proposed that these two mechanisms are functionally related in the sense that variations in one are linked to variations in the other. The direction of this co-variation was considered to provide the nervous typological basis of the major neurotic and psychotic syndromes. One mode of co-variation was that postulated in neurotics and reflected empirically in the positive correlation between sedation threshold and spiral effect. There it was considered that the high levels of arousal (sedation threshold) found in dysthymic neurotics are associated with extreme selectivity or narrowing of attention, leading to prolonged spiral after-effects. The opposite would be true of hysterico-psychopathic individuals. The model further proposed that the reverse situation could occur, namely that high levels of arousal could co-exist with poor modulation of sensory input and vice versa; thus leading to negative correlations between sedation threshold and spiral after-effect. It was this dissociation of psychophysiological function—dissociation, at least, as judged against the neuroses—that was considered characteristic of schizophrenic patients.'

'A further feature of this model was the proposal that the dissociation of function found in the schizophrenias could occur in one of two directions, leading to different clinical syndromes. That conclusion was based on experimental evidence concerning the clinical and behavioural correlates of sedation threshold/ spiral after-effect variation. Thus, it was found that schizophrenics showing evidence of high arousal and poor selective attention—high sedation threshold/low spiral after-effect—were more often paranoid, behaviourally active, emotionally reactive and, consistent with their weak attentional control, more overinclusive in their thought disorder. Those in the opposite psychophysiological state—poorly aroused (low sedation threshold) and with highly narrowed attention (high spiral after-effect)—tended to be retarded, affectively flattened, socially withdrawn and, if thought-disordered, more often concrete and overexclusive' (p.11).

Claridge draws three main conclusions from the work here summarized. In the first place, he believes that the differences between schizophrenic disorders and other psychiatric disorders, as well as the reasons for variations within the schizophrenic syndromes themselves, seem to lie in the way the central nervous system is organized, rather than in any single disturbance of function. In the second place, the two main processes involved seem to be those of arousal and attention. And in the third place, the organization of central nervous function in patients and subjects can be most usefully examined by looking at the functional relationship between carefully chosen measures of psychophysiological activity. This emphasis on organization, rather than deviation, has actually been neglected by most psychophysiologists working in the field of individual differences. Claridge finds this lack of attention curious, because, as he points out, there are at least two well-established examples of such an approach to behavioural analysis. The first is the much-studied Yerkes-Dodson Law, alternatively known as the inverted-U function relating arousal to psychological performance (Hebb, 1955), and the second is the 'narrowed attention' hypothesis, suggesting that the range of cues to which the individual responds diminishes as arousal rises, and vice versa (Callaway and Dembo, 1958; Easterbrook, 1959). It is of more than passing interest that the two principles in question seem, if anything, to work in reverse in schizophrenia.

The interesting question which is posed by this theoretical discussion, and the experimental evidence reviewed, is clearly this: do high P scorers, as compared with low P scorers, behave in the same manner as do schizophrenics as compared with normals (or neurotics), and as LSD subjects behave as compared with placebo subjects? Claridge and Chappa (1973) attempted to answer this question in an experiment employing sixty-one normal subjects, who were administered the PEN inventory. Three groups were formed. One consisted of high P scorers; the other two groups were formed by subdividing the low P scorers into high N and low N scorers. There were eleven, fourteen, and twenty-one subjects respectively in the final groups so formed. Two experimental tests were administered, the two-flash threshold and the skin conductance level being determined. Results will be shown in graph form, and it should be noted that changes in an upward direction indicate improvement in perceptual discrimination; in other words, positive relationships indicate improvement being a positive function of increased arousal.

The results are shown in Figure 40; it will be seen that high P scorers show a negative correlation, as did psychotics and LSD takers. High N scorers (who also have low P scores) show a positive correlation. Low N scorers, curiously enough, align themselves with the high P group. These regression lines apply to all subjects except a very small number having very high skin conductance scores; when these are plotted they show the expected reversal from the direction taken by the regression line for low conductance scorers, i.e. inverted-U shape graphs for high N subjects, and U shape graphs for high P subjects. The numbers involved are too small to make much of this striking confirmation, and consequently they have been omitted in this summary of the Claridge and Chappa results.

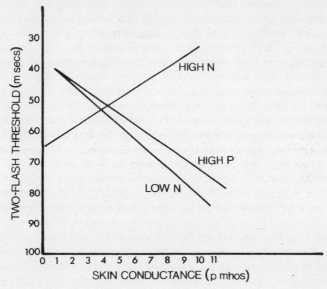

Figure 40 Regression lines relating skin conductance level and two-flash threshold in high P, low N and high N subjects in skin conductance range up to 10.25 micromhos (from Claridge, 1972)

Figure 40 may with advantage be compared with Figure 39 showing similar results for the comparison between LSD takers and placebo takers. For LSD takers the correlation was −.82, for placebo takers +.74. Comparable figures for the high P and high N groups are −.78 and +.64, with the low N group resembling the high P scorers ($r = -.58$).

Claridge and Chappa make two comments. First, they point out that they and Venables, in his 1963 study, employed identical techniques for measuring both skin potential and two-flash threshold. It is therefore possible to compare, across the two experiments, the direction of covariation between two-flash threshold and skin potential for equivalent ranges of electrodermal response. 'When this is done it emerges that most of Venables' subjects—both psychotic and normal—had a skin potential level of more than 25 mv, that is beyond the upper cut-off point used to define the high range in our LSD experiment. In other words, Venables seems mainly to have tested subjects in a state of *high* autonomic arousal. The direction of correlations he reports for normal and non-paranoid schizophrenics is therefore directly in line with those that would be predicted from our data for LSD and high P subjects' (p.184).

Second, Claridge and Chappa also comment on the curious resemblance of the reactions of high P subjects, and low N—low P subjects. They suggest that 'individuals reporting low neuroticism scores could be regarded as having the lack of anxiety and emotional responsiveness appropriate to certain forms of psychoticism which are not tapped by Eysenck's P scale. Inspection of the latter's item content, for example, reveals that many of its questions reflect paranoid tendencies. . . . In addition, several other items could be construed in a similar way, namely those referring to excessive concern with ill-luck and with contagion from disease. What seems most obvious is an almost complete absence of questions concerned with other prominent signs of psychosis, namely withdrawal, flatness of affect, lack of interest and drive, and the inability to express emotion. It is these characteristics which could be reflected in abnormally low levels of neuroticism and, while it seems unlikely that all low N scores can be interpreted in that way, the tendency in the present sample may have been sufficiently strong to bring out the psycho-physiological relationships observed' (p.185). Claridge also refers back to his suggestion that the dimension of psychoticism runs from an active (paranoid) pole to an inactive or retarded (non-paranoid) pole; he suggests that the P scale reflects only that group of personality traits clustering at the 'active' end of his dimension (Claridge, 1967).

Interesting as this suggestion is, it is not in line with the results of our factor-analytic studies. If Claridge's hypothesis were true, then clearly N items should correlate negatively with P; this they do not do. The P items make up a pool of questions which intercorrelate positively, and which do not intercorrelate at all (within the limits of chance errors) with the pool of N items. Furthermore, Claridge's low N scorers in this experiment also had low P scores; in other words, even his own data do not give us any reason to expect some sort of functional unity between high P and low N. Even if there were such a functional unity for a subgroup of low N scorers, this should be sufficient to produce negative correlations between P and N items, and between the scores and factors. The failure of such correlations to appear makes Claridge's hypothesis unacceptable.*

How can we evaluate the material summarized so far in this chapter? There are too many data indicating a reversal of relationship between arousal and sensitivity, or attention, when we go from normal people, low P scorers, or placebo takers to

---

*An alternative possibility to that suggested by Claridge is that low P—low N scorers might have had unusually high L scores; in other words, this group might be erroneously classified due to dissimulation. There is of course no way in which this possibility could be demonstrated to have obtained in this particular experiment. Replication with the inclusion of the L scale would seem the only way of deciding (a) whether there is in fact anything to be accounted for, and (b) whether abnormally high L scores might be responsible for this oddity.

schizophrenics, high P scorers or LSD takers, to make it possible to reject the theories here considered. However much in need of replication the experiments may be, and however much in need of verification the theory may be, the data already seem to indicate an important novel way of looking at the biological factors underlying psychotic disorder. It would take us too far to discuss in detail possible criticisms of the theory, and possible alternative ways of constructing hypotheses in this field; we are here much more concerned with the light the experiments throw on the nature of P. If P is properly conceived as a measure of psychoticism, then it must follow that high P scorers should in experimental situations behave like psychotics, compared with normals, or as LSD takers, compared with placebo takers. The fact that on the whole this seems to be true with respect to this very complex interaction of arousal and sensitivity (or attention) must be regarded as support for the interpretation of P put forward by us, although of course it must be added that replication of these studies, involving much larger numbers of subjects, and other types of experimental paradigms, is urgently needed before they can be adduced as strong proof. Nevertheless, as far as they go, they do lend some support to our hypothesis.

In one sense of the term, Claridge's theory might be regarded as a causal theory of psychoticism, although we have here used his experimental work rather to demonstrate the similarity of reaction pattern of psychotics, LSD takers, and high P scorers. Quite a different approach to the causal problem is afforded us by the observation (supported by numerous studies cited in previous chapters) that males tend to have much higher P scores than females. This immediately suggests a causal theory in terms of hormonal secretions associated with sex. Does such a theory, in its broadest aspect, find any support in data linking incidence of psychosis with sex? In the case of schizophrenia, there is initially a high incidence in males, who show a particularly marked rise in first admissions between the ages of 15 and 25 years; females begin to catch up with males at about the age of 35, and there is a marked preponderance of females after age 45 (Mayer-Gross, Slater and Roth, 1969, p.239). As Gray (1973) comments in an article discussing the 'maleness' hypothesis in this connection, 'a natural implication of this pattern is that the onset of full male sexuality, and of the social interactions which entry into adulthood requires of the male, somehow facilitate the occurrence of a schizophrenic illness, while active female sexuality actually affords protection against schizophrenia, this protection being removed at the time of the menopause' (p.450). In this connection, we may also note the decline in P with age; this closely parallels the decline in virility in the male. As far as depression is concerned, Kendell (1968) in his studies showed that the psychotic form of this illness is associated with male sex, while the neurotic form is predominantly found in females. We may conclude that there is some apparent support for linking psychoticism with 'maleness'; can we go beyond this descriptive association?

Gray (1973), rather speculatively, has linked psychoticism with the third of his major physiological mechanisms subserving emotion. The first two, which he calls the 'approach' and the 'stop' systems, are linked with E and N; the major physiological focus of the approach system appears to lie in the medial forebrain bundle and the lateral hypothalamus, and more rostral points in the septal area, to which the medial forebrain bundle projects, while the stop system, which is involved with behavioural inhibition, involves a series of interconnected structures including the hippocampus, the medial septal area, the orbital frontal cortex and the caudate nucleus. The third system is involved in fight/flight behaviour of an intra-species type, and has its physiological representation in the amygdala, the medial hypothalamus (to which the amygdala is connected by the stria terminalis), and the central gray of the midbrain (to which the medial hypothalamus is connected by way of the dorsal longitudinal bundle of Schütz) (Deutsch and Deutsch, 1966). This fight/flight system is concerned only with the kind of aggression usually elicited by a conspecific; predatory aggression appears to be mediated more by the approach system.

Gray (1973) continues: 'There is reason to believe, therefore, that psychoticism has something to do with an excessive degree of intra-specific aggressive behaviour and it is facilitated by some aspect of male sexuality. The case would be stronger, however, if there were evidence of amygdaloid involvement in psychosis. Such evidence does not appear to be available' (p.450). However, the amygdala lies buried in the temporal lobe, and there is evidence which implicates the temporal lobe in psychotic behaviour. Mayer-Gross, Slater and Roth (1969, p.470) review a number of studies which have shown associations between abnormal electrical activity in the temporal lobes and psychotic, especially schizophrenic, disorder. Flor-Henry (1969) has recently found that after temporal lobe epilepsy there was an increased risk of the development of psychotic disorder, and that this disorder was likely to be of a schizophrenic variety if the epilepsy had been in the left temporal lobe, but of a manic-depressive variety if the epilepsy had been in the right temporal lobe. It would not do to take these associations too seriously, but they do tend to strengthen Gray's hypothesis. Whether they, or the more direct hypothesized links with androgens and other humoral secretions, can be supported by direct studies aimed at the verification or falsification of these theories must be left to the future.

There are a few more studies, however, which must be mentioned before leaving this topic. The whole question of the relation of sex to mental disorder, in its methodological and substantive aspects, has been treated by Reich et al. (1975) and Cloninger et al. (1975a,b); they describe a model with multiple thresholds which would fit our case remarkably well. They show that 'sociopathy in men and women clusters in the same families, though it is much more frequent in men than women. Sociopathy is more prevalent among relatives of sociopathic women than among relatives of sociopathic men, and sociopathic women have more disturbed parental home experiences than male sociopaths. These observations suggest that the sex difference in the prevalence of sociopathy is due to sex-related cultural or biological factors causing the threshold for sociopathy to be more deviant in women than in men' (Cloninger et al., 1975a, p.19). Hysteria was found to be associated with sociopathy, very much in the manner suggested by Eysenck (1957). An extension of their method to psychotics would be of great interest, particularly if the theories here broached were borne in mind.

The direct evidence on these 'sex-related cultural or biological factors' is not very extensive, but a few studies have been reported on the effects of plasma testosterone on aggressive behaviour and social dominance in man (there is a more extensive literature on animal work, reviewed in Ehrenkranz and Sheard, 1974). Persky et al. (1971) reported a significant relationship between testosterone production rate and a group of self-administered hostility and aggression inventories in normal young males. Kreuz and Rose (1972) found that plasma testosterone levels failed to correlate with the incidence of fighting in a young criminal population in prison, but did correlate with a history of aggressive antisocial behaviour early in life. Kling (1973) found a positive correlation between testosterone and individual aggression in psychiatric patients. Finally, Ehrenkranz and Sheard (1974) found a significantly higher plasma testosterone level in a group of chronically aggressive subjects in prison, as compared with a group of non-aggressive prisoners; socially dominant but non-aggressive prisoners were intermediate. The plasma levels for the three groups may be of interest; in terms of mg/ml they were respectively 5.99 for the non-aggressive group, 8.36 for the socially dominant group, and 10.10 for the aggressive group. These differences are roughly equal to one standard deviation in each case, and are therefore not only statistically significant, but also psychologically important. It is of interest that the aggressive group differed from the other two on a variety of psychological items that further served to differentiate it: 'Thus the members of this group reported less responsibility, were less socialized, less tolerant and were less likely to create a good impression. They also strove less for achievement through conformity or via independence. They were less flexible and reported themselves less feminine. On the other hand, they were autonomous and more aggressive' (p.474). These findings agree well with an interpretation of this syndrome in terms of P.

Second only to testosterone in being linked with aggression and other P activities is serum uric acid (SUA). The literature has been well reviewed by Stevens (1973), and only a brief account will here be given of some of the more relevant papers. McGilvery (1970) saw the aggressiveness of Lesch-Nyhan retardates as a distinct personality trait causally linked with the metabolic dysfunction of excess serum uric acid. This association of SUA and aggression was confirmed in a more normal sample of young children by Vee (1969). Leadership, which has often been linked with aggression (although perhaps a more refined form!), has also been found correlated with SUA levels (Brooks and Mueller, 1966; Gordon and Gordon, 1967; Gordon et al., 1967). Sales (1969) found that in an adult sample SUA levels were associated with style in handling aggressive feelings, and also found that persistence was positively correlated with urate levels. The relevance of these studies to P is brought out by the work of Pfeiffer et al. (1969), who found that schizophrenic patients have lower SUA levels on leaving hospital than on entering it; Tobin and Halgrimson (quoted by Pfeiffer et al., 1969) have observed the same reaction. Pfeiffer interprets this change (which is analogous to that found in P scores in our own work) in terms of reduction of stress. This hypothesis does not stand up to many experimental results marshalled by Stevens (1973), who concludes that 'the evidence reviewed here suggests that Pfeiffer et al. have misunderstood the significance of their data. Rather than assuming that serum urate levels passively reflect the psychological stress of schizophrenic patients, it is probably more profitable to postulate that SUA may actually be one of the contributors to the excessive cortical stimulation which Pfeiffer et al. saw as precipitating schizophrenic disorders. This argument is particularly tenable in the light of their own submission that increasing SUA levels via administration of adenosine appears to exacerbate schizophrenic symptoms, whereas the reduction of SUA levels by way of psychotrolip drugs is associated with symptom remission' (p.25).

We may conclude that a suggestive relation is indicated between SUA and P, although nothing definite can be said at the moment. (There appears to exist some association also between depression and SUA level, but this relation is not clearly enough marked to be adduced as evidence; Stevens, 1973, reviews the literature.) It is noteworthy, however, that uric acid levels are higher in males than in females, as would be required if there were some connection between SUA and P. Mikkelsen *et al.* (1965), in a study of 2,987 males and 3,013 females, constituting a 90 per cent sample of a community population, found the overall mean for males to be 4.91 mg%, while the females had a mean of 4.18 mg%. These sex differences appear to be age-bound, with the differences appearing at puberty and subsiding at menopause, when the female SUA levels rise to approach the male levels. It appears likely, for various reasons, that SUA levels are under endocrine control, and are strongly influenced by androgens (positively) and by oestrogens (negatively). Genetic determination, with heritabilities around 30 per cent, has been established for chronic SUA levels.

Finally, there is evidence for a differential sympathetic-adrenal medullary reaction induced by different stressors; males showed a significant increase after stress, whereas females did not. Noradrenaline excretion was not systematically affected by either of the two stressors used in either sex group (Frankenhaeuser *et al.*, 1974). This suggests that some at least of the sex related factors posited by Cloninger *et al.* may be of a biological nature, and it will be of great interest to trace the nature of the factors in much greater detail than is possible at the moment. One of the reasons for our lack of knowledge may lie in the fact that psychologists tend to believe in 'equality of the sexes' in the sense of actual identity, rather than in the sense of 'equal value but different'—hence the lack of work on observable differences in this field. It is to be hoped that this state of affairs will change in the near future; sex-linked differences are of considerable interest and importance for psychology, particularly for the psychology of personality.

10

The inheritance of psychoticism

The theory of psychoticism is based on genetic considerations, and consequently it can be falsified most easily by a demonstration that P has no, or a low, heritability. Falsification is one of the most important qualities possessed by scientific theories, as Popper and others have emphasized, even though this property has been played up perhaps too much (Lakatos and Musgrave, 1971). In this chapter we shall review evidence bearing on this question, and we shall attempt to set up and test a model of gene action compatible with our general theory. The result is not likely to be definitive, given the complexities of the task, but the outcome may be suggestive. The data collected, and the methods of analysis used, are quite sufficient to disprove the hypothesis; they are less capable of establishing the conclusions to which we shall be persuaded to give temporary credence. Before discussing the evidence, it may be useful to introduce the concept of 'heritability', a task made necessary by the fact that there is much confusion attending this notion, particularly among psychologists.

We start out with the measurement of a particular character (trait, ability, attitude, or what not); our task is to break down the total variance of this *phenotype* into various components which have genetic meaning. The general formula for this runs as follows:

$$V_P = (V_G + V_{AM} + V_D + V_{Ep}) + (V_E + Cov_{GE} + V_{GE}) + V_e$$

In this formula V_P denotes phenotypic variance, V_G additive genetic variance. The non-additive genetic components are given by V_{AM} (assortative mating), V_D (dominance), and V_{Ep} (epistasis, or interaction among genes at two or more loci). V_E denotes environmental variances, and V_e error variance (unreliability). There are two terms denoting interaction between environment and heredity. Cov_{GE} denotes the covariance of heredity and environment; it arises when genotypic values and environmental values are correlated in the population, as for instance when genotypically bright children are reared in homes with superior environmental advantages. V_{GE}, on the other hand, denotes a statistical interaction to the effect that different genotypes may respond differently to the same environmental effect. Some geneticists include Cov_{GE} as part of the total genetic variance, rather than as part of the environmental variance, because the causal element is genetic. Most formulae for the estimation of heritability include V_e as part of the environmental variance, but this is strictly speaking incorrect, and appropriate correction for unreliability in the measuring instrument should always be made, or else the portion of the total phenotypic variance due to error should be specified.

The major variance components in the above formula can be further partitioned into a 'between-families' component and a 'within-families' component. The 'between-families' component (G_2) in the case of the genetic variance is that proportion of the variance which relatives have in common by virtue of common ancestry; the 'within-families' component (G_1) is that proportion of the variance which they do not share in common, since relatives receive a random selection of genes from their ancestral pool. The 'between-families' component (E_2) in the case of the environmental variance is shared in common by virtue of the individuals' being reared in the same family setting; the 'within-families' component (E_1) is the variance not shared in common by individuals reared in the same family, since some environmental variation occurs within the family setting.

Heritability is defined as the proportion of phenotypic variance attributable to genetic factors; we may attempt to assess the narrow heritability, which includes only the additive genetic variance, or the broad heritability, which also includes the non-additive genetic variance. The formulae, accordingly, are as follows:

$$h_N^2 = \frac{V_G}{V_P}$$

$$h_B^2 = \frac{V_G + V_{AM} + V_D + V_{Ep}}{V_P}$$

The variances due to the correlation between heredity and environment, and to the statistical interaction of genetic and environmental factors, are not included in these fundamental definitions of heritability. It would seem equally appropriate, or even more so, if the interaction of G and E were included with the genetic components than if it were included with the environmental components. The matter is purely academic in the case of psychoticism, as there is no evidence for such interaction in any case. There are formulae, widely used, which do not in fact constitute proper genetic estimates of heritability, although the results are often presented as such; the formulae due to Holzinger (1929), to Neel and Schull (1954), and to Nichols (1965) fall into this group. Proper formulations of the biometrical genetical analysis of human behaviour have been developed by Mather and Jinks (1971), and a simplified account of these methods, together with an application to the analysis of the genetics of human intelligence and personality, will be found in Jinks and Fulker (1970). In the analysis presented in this chapter we shall be using these formulations, and explain in some detail our use of the concepts and formulae there developed, without entering into a detailed technical description of the method. The essential point to grasp about the methods of genetic analysis now coming to the fore is that different kinds and degrees of kinship can be used to give us estimates of the various portions of the general formula; in addition, it is sometimes possible to carry out direct studies to establish the likely size of particular contributions. Thus, to illustrate the latter point, it is possible to study the degree of assortative mating (V_{AM}) which is taking place in a given population, with respect to a particular trait, by direct study of the mating couples; as we shall see, there is very little assortative mating with respect to psychoticism, the correlation between couples lying between .15 and .19. To illustrate the former point, estimates of the dominance variance (V_D) can be obtained from a comparison of half-siblings (of the same mother) and full siblings.

The first published accounts of genetic studies of P are based on data collected by Dr J. Price on 101 pairs of twins of whom forty-five pairs were living together, while the others had been separated for varying lengths of time. All the twins were monozygotic, but the small number available precluded analysis from taking sex differences into account. Intra-pair correlations for responses by the twins on the PEN gave the following results (Eysenck, 1972a):

	All Pairs:	Living together:	Living apart:
Psychoticism:	.54	.56	.52
Extraversion:	.38	.29	.45
Neuroticism:	.65	.57	.69

The data were analysed in some detail by Eaves (1973). No evidence was found of any relationship between degree of separation and intra-pair differences for factor scores, suggesting that E_2 effects could be discounted as components of within-pairs variation for these data. The environmental influences determining variation for E and N were found to act in a unitary manner, but the analysis did not suggest that the P scores reflected any unitary environmental influence. The P items played a greater part in the determination of genotype structure, although the item vectors required more than one dimension for adequate representation. The correlation between P and N (which, it will be remembered, was characteristic of this early form of the scale) could be shown to reflect the correlated influences of both genotype and environment on these factors. A very rough-and-ready estimate of heritability (begging many questions) derived from the data amounted to 53 per cent for P.

The failure of this study to produce clear-cut results is probably due to three main factors. In the first place, the PEN was psychometrically inferior to later scales; in particular, N and P were significantly correlated. In the second place, there are profound sex differences on P, and the small size of the sample made it impossible to take these into account properly. And in the third place, the P scale has a J-shaped distribution which requires re-scaling for proper use in genetic analysis; in the absence of such re-scaling certain complications appear which at the time could not be coped with properly. This point will be brought out in some detail presently. This study demonstrates that there is some genetic contribution to P, but does not enable us to form a correct estimate of the contribution along quantitative lines.

The second study is of greater interest, for two reasons. In the first place, the selection of twins was more appropriate for a genetic study, and in the second place, an effort was made to test the genetic and environmental interaction between personality (P, E and N) on the one hand, and social attitudes on the other (Eaves and Eysenck, 1974). The personality inventory used was the PEN, and in addition a social attitude scale was used which gave scores for radicalism-conservatism (R), toughmindedness-tendermindedness (T), and emphatic (extreme) responses (Em). The scale used was taken from Eysenck (1954). The population tested consisted of 331 pairs of female and 120 pairs of male MZ twins, and of 198 female and 59 male DZ twins, making a total of 708 pairs of twins. As in the previous study, duration of separation of the twins (for those pairs which did not live together) was not related to intra-pair differences in personality, so separated and unseparated twins were pooled. We put up two alternative hypotheses which were simple enough to be tested with the data at our disposal: (1) All the observed trait variation and covariation is attributable either to differences between the environmental differences shared by members of the same pair (E_2), or to differences in the environmental influences specific to individuals within the family (E_1). This will be referred to as the simple environmental hypothesis. The alternative hypothesis, which we shall call the simple genetic hypothesis, may be phrased as follows: (2) All the observed trait variation and covariation is attributable either to the cumulative and additive effects of many loci for which the population is polymorphic (D_R), or to specific (E_1) environmental influences. The analysis is described in some detail in the original paper; it showed conclusively that the simple environmental hypothesis fails by a wide margin, and must be rejected. The simple genetic hypothesis gives a residual chi square which is just significant, suggesting that some E_2 parameters might with advantage be added to our simple genetic model; however, it was felt that this minor deviation from expectation did not invalidate the model, and accordingly we have used it for the calculation of heritabilities.

The most general result of this study is that about half the variation between individuals for the six traits has a genetic basis; in particular, the following heritability values were obtained: R = .65; T = .54; Em = .37; P = .35; E = .48; N = .49. It will be noted that, contrary to common-sense expectation, the social attitude variances show evidence of greater genetic determination than do the personality variances; such comparisons, of course, do not take into account the respective error variances, and may therefore be quite misleading. Furthermore, the scores were not re-scaled, but were used as they stood; this may lead to underestimations of heritability, particularly for scales like P.

Of particular interest in the analysis was the presence of several predictable significant covariance terms. The nature of the analysis underlying these findings has been discussed at some length elsewhere (Eaves and Eysenck, 1975). It had been hypothesized that the social attitude variable T was mediated by personality factors, in particular E (Eysenck, 1954); our analysis confirms the correlation between E and T, showing that it has a genetic rather than an environmental basis, since only the D_R component of covariance is significant. There is also a significant genetic correlation between P and Em. This suggests that individuals who achieve high P scores share the strong conviction of being right, which is characteristic of some psychotic behaviour. Even more significant is the tendency for high P scores to be associated with toughmindedness (T); this covariation is primarily due to genetic causes, but also extends into the environmental field. There are weaknesses in this study which have been pointed out in the article quoted; nevertheless, in so far as the results go, they verify the assumption that P has a genetic basis, and that P and T share strong genetic links. In view of the limitations of the analysis, we cannot regard the heritability estimates as serious attempts to quantify the exact degree of heritability of P; all we can conclude is that no purely environmental model is tenable. A more complex design and analysis are required to make possible a proper evaluation of heritability. Such an attempt is available in Eaves and Eysenck (1976).

In this study a total of 544 pairs of twins were used; the sex and MZ–DZ composition is shown in Table 43. These were administered the EPQ; in this chapter we are of course mainly interested in the P scale, and will concentrate our discussion on results of this scale. We have already shown, in previous chapters, that the slightly bizarre quality of 'psychotic' behaviour is to some extent reflected in the distribution of responses to P items; generally, these are endorsed only rarely in the 'psychotic' direction. This leads to a scale which is heavily skewed, approaching a J-shaped distribution. This makes proper genetic analysis of P scores difficult; the errors of measurement associated with a given P score increase as P increases. This means that one source of environmental variation in P, namely the unreliability of measurement, becomes more important when we consider individuals who are more 'psychotic' than others, as measured by their P scores. (In the traditional type of analysis, V_e is lumped with V_E simply because there was no way in which V_e could be separated out from V_E.) As a consequence of this, we shall find that to the degree that individual predispositions towards high or low P scores are genetically determined, genetic and environmental factors will be found to appear to interact; in other words, the observed interaction is an artifact of the scale construction. This means that any analysis of the raw scale into component causes is likely to lead to a very complex picture because of the large genotype-environment interactions created by the choice of scale. In the case of P, we can overcome these difficulties by a single transformation of individuals' raw scores on P by means of the square root transformation. This transformed P we shall denote P'. The logic of the procedure here adopted is derived from the statistical properties of the Poisson distribution, which the observed distribution of P values resembles; details of the argument will be found in Eaves and Eysenck (1976).

TABLE 43   Analyses of variance of twin pairs for transformed P scores (from Eaves and Eysenck, 1976)

Twin type	Item	df	mean square	F	p
Female monozygotic	Between pairs	240	.033891	2.41	10^{-11}
	Within pairs	241	.014087		
Male monozygotic	Between pairs	78	.051267	3.71	10^{-8}
	Within pairs	79	.013817		
Female dizygotic	Between pairs	132	.042274	1.99	4×10^{-5}
	Within pairs	133	.021206		
Unlike-sex dizygotic*	Between pairs	72	.036167	1.66	.016
	Residual		.021789		
Male dizygotic	Between pairs	50	.030715	1.53	.067
	Within pairs	51	.020092		

The first and simplest theory to test would attribute all the variance in P' to environmental influences which were quite specific to individuals, and shared with no one else, not even with members of the same family. On this assumption we could attribute the variation observed for P' in a given population simply to a parameter E_1, and write:

$$\sigma_P^2 = E_1$$

*The residual term is corrected for the mean difference between sexes. Results are pooled from two sets of data distinguished by the order in which the sexes were born.

We can test this model quite simply because if all our variations were due to quite unique individual experience, we would expect individuals in the same family to be no more and no less alike than families of individuals produced artificially by grouping our test scores at random. If we call the variances of such family-pairs σ_b^2, we would expect them to average around zero. Table 44 shows the form such an analysis of variance would take, and Table 43 shows the actual analyses of variance for five groups of twins which composed our sample. A variance ratio test (F) shows that in many cases σ_b^2 is significantly greater than zero, so that we must reject the simplistic model which equates σ_P^2 to E_1 only. We can pool our data by calculating a weighted least square: this procedure gives us a P value $< 10^{-6}$, strongly disproving the adequacy of the model.

Slightly more likely to prove adequate would be a more complex model of the form:

$$\sigma_P^2 = E_1 + E_2$$

When this model is tested, using the data from Table 43, we find that it too fails conclusively; the fit of the data to the model is very poor. A purely environmental model is hardly tenable in the face of these data, and we must seek a more adequate one, embodying genetic parameters. In doing so we specify a component 'D_R', which contains all the variation due to additive gene action, but in addition also contains some of the variation due to non-additive effects when the allele frequencies are unequal.

TABLE 44   General form of analysis of variance of paired observations (from Eaves and Eysenck, 1976)

Item	df	Expected mean square		
Between pairs	$n-1$	σ_w^2	$+$	$2\sigma_b^2$
Within pairs	n	σ_w^2		

A simple model only involving D_R and E_1 involves certain assumptions which may be worthwhile stating. They are as follows: (1) there are no common environmental effects $(E_2 = 0)$; (2) there is no dominance; (3) there is no epistasis; (4) there is no genotype-environment interaction; (5) mating is random (panmixia); (6) there is no sex linkage or sex limitation; (7) E_1 is the same for males and females; and (8) there is no Cov_{GE}. Some of these assumptions are testable. There is evidence, summarized in Eaves and Eysenck (1976), that there is very little assortative mating for P. Genotype-environment interaction can be detected by plotting the sum of twin pair scores against the differences; it was in this way that we discovered the artifactual interaction effects due to faults in the original scale. Most important, however, is the consideration that departures from the model along some of the lines expressed in the form of assumptions above would lead to the failure of the model; we would not be able to say why the model failed, but we could detect failure by statistical testing of the fit of the data to the model.

When the actual D_R, E_1 model is fitted to the twin data for the P' scores, the observed and expected values agree quite well; the twin data give us little reason to doubt the validity of the simple model for individual differences in P'. We may conclude that we can adopt a working explanation for variation in psychoticism which assumes that there is both genetic and environmental variation in P. Our model suggests that to a first approximation we may discount shared family environmental effects (since a large E_2 might cause the model to fail), and we might consider mating to be random as far as any genetical analysis is concerned (and as far as observational data are available). In addition, we have found nothing to suggest that gene action is anything but additive. The resolution of our study is sufficient for us to reject the simplest environmental explanations, but insufficient to reject the simplest equivalent explanation in terms of the joint action of genetical and environmental influences. On this simple model, the proportion of variation due to genetical causes amounts to 46 per cent, a figure not very different to that obtained in the two previous studies (in so far as these can justifiably be used to produce estimates of heritability).

The value of heritability indicated by this figure of roughly 50 per cent is a gross underestimate, unless the reliability of measurement is such that V_e is small or non-existent. No psychologist familiar with the complexities of questionnaire measurement would entertain such an hypothesis, and we must seek to correct our observed estimate for attenuation. Having measured P on the scale we have chosen, we are able to obtain from theoretical considerations a value for the sampling error to be expected on the basis of the model we have assumed for the raw responses to the items (Eaves and Eysenck, 1976). In our case, having assumed that the model of independent rare events applies to responses to the items, we expect the variance of $\sqrt{P/N}$ to be approximately $0.25/N$. We have attempted to estimate as precisely as we are able the average error variance of the P scores in our sample. When this is done, we find that 11 per cent of the total variation of P' can be clearly assigned to environmental causes over and above errors of measurement. Sampling variation, on the other hand, accounts for nearly 40 per cent of the total variance. This leaves us with 49 per cent of the total variance to be assigned to the effects of several, perhaps many, genes of independent and additive effects. If we are prepared to consider only those causes of variation which cannot be ascribed to sampling effects, then the relative contribution of genetical variation appears much greater since we must remove the contribution of σ_e^2 from our estimate of the total variation. Potentially identifiable environmental factors now account for 19 per cent of the *reliable* variation of P', the remaining 81 per cent being due to genetical variation. This figure of 81 per cent is our best estimate of heritability of P', after correction for unreliability of measurement.

The finding that by far the greater part of the environmental variation within families (in our case 77 per cent) can be attributed to errors of measurement is by no means new in quantitative genetics, although it may lack intuitive appeal to clinicians. Eaves and Eysenck (1976) give examples from work on *Drosophila melanogaster* to illustrate this point. The main conclusion to be derived from these computations is of course that the contribution of potentially identifiable environmental factors is desperately small. In fact, the figures for P' are almost identical with those for intelligence, as far as heritability is concerned; there also the difficulty of using environmental influences to effect changes in the trait in question has been well documented. To say this does not, of course, invalidate the possibility of achieving marked changes in behaviour by means of drugs, such as the phenothiazines; such drugs played no part in the 'environment' of the population here studied, and consequently our conclusions cannot apply to environments which include such drug administration.

It may be of interest to look at the results of a variance-covariance analysis of the EPQ data, using scores for P, E, N and L, rather along the lines of the Eaves and Eysenck (1974) study. We used the square-root transformation of P into P'; for E, N and L an angular transformation was employed. When tested for fit, neither a simple E_1, E_2 model nor a D_R, E_1 model was found to fit, although the latter was much more in line with the facts. A good fit was found for a model which allowed D_R, E_1 and E_2 as the sole parameters, with a chi square $p > .07$. The estimated parameters of this model are given in Table 45. As far as trait variation is concerned, we find highly significant E_1 effects for all traits, although it must be stressed that E_1 contains any variation due purely to chance. We also find significant additive genetical effects for every trait. Only L shows any indication of a common environmental component (E_2) above the contribution of genetical variation. There are significant covariations between the 'within family' environmental differences for P and E, and P and L, though not for E and L. The fact that we can detect significant environmental covariation between P and other traits confirms that not all the E_1 for P can be due to measurement error. However, the environmental correlations (r_{E_1}) are still comparatively small $(r_{E_1} = .14$ for P and E; $r_{E_1} = -.17$ for P and L), so that we may conclude that only 5 per cent of the environmental variation in P could be predicted from knowledge of the environmental deviations affecting E and L. This is quite consistent with the small excess of our estimates of E_1 over the value expected if the environmental differences within families were simply due to sampling variation.

All the traits show significant additive genetical components of variation, *but no pair of traits shows clear indication of genetical covariation.* Only L shows any sign of E_2 variation, which subsequent detailed analyses have shown to relate mainly to females. We shall discuss this effect in the next chapter.

The results obtained in this study, even though subject to future changes in the precise quantitative estimates, do demonstrate convincingly the major importance of additive genetic influences on variation in P', the relatively small direct and covariance effects of E_1, and the absence of E_2 effects. However, heritability, even though it be as high as that observed here, does not itself help very much in our understanding of the trait in question. It might indeed help us to predict a response to selection, at least in the short term, but this is more appropriate to the manipulation of cattle than to the understanding of people. Our purpose is to understand the biology of psychoticism, and we must ask ourselves whether the genetical model we have arrived at in our search for an explanation of the variation in P has any implications for understanding the polymorphism we observe for psychotic (and 'psychotic') behaviour. Experience of genetical analysis in other organisms has shown that the absence of strong non-additive components of genetic variation is typically associated with traits which are not subject to strong uniform directional selection; this absence of strong uniform directional selection, of course, is required to explain the relatively high incidence of a disease (schizophrenia, or psychosis as such) which is apparently debilitating in terms of reproductive fitness, and difficulties have always arisen in attempts to account for this high incidence.

TABLE 45 Estimates of genetical and environmental variation and covariation for transformed P, E, N and L scores from the EPQ (from Eaves and Eysenck, 1976). Asterisks denote level of significance

	D_R				E_1				E_2			
	P	E	N	L	P	E	N	L	P	E	N	L
P	.0228**	−.0155	.0038	−.0082	.0144***	.0033*	−.0021	−.0033**	.0020	.0071	.0038	−.0053
E		.1169***	−.0148	.0217		.0376***	−.0104***	−.0028		−.0163	.0012	−.0116*
N			.0999***	−.0221			.0416***	−.0023			−.0015	.0014
L				.0389**				.0260***				.0126*

Asterisks denote significance at the .05, .01 and .001 levels (one, two and three asterisks respectively)

The kind of genetical variation we observe for P' may be what we have come to associate with stabilizing selection, i.e. natural selection which favours individuals of intermediate predisposition rather than extremes in either direction (high or low P'). It is usually assumed that polymorphism can be maintained under stabilizing selection only when genetical variation is due to relatively few loci of fairly large individual effect. It is certainly possible to envisage a situation in which very low P' scores would be equally debilitating as very high scores; low scorers might be lacking in assertiveness, show little originality, and too much 'super ego' activity to compete successfully for food, shelter, and mates.

Of the consequences which follow from an adoption of our model for psychological theorizing, one of the most important is the simple deduction that any influences of the family environment, such as are shared by individuals reared by the same parents, are likely to be small relative to other causes of variation. This spells the death knell of such theories as those adopted by many psychoanalysts, who see family interactions, and particularly the influence of the mother, as causal in the production of schizophrenic and other psychotic disorders. Unless there is some fatal flaw in our data, such a theory is not tenable. If we are right in assigning the causes of P to the various parameters investigated, and extending this analysis to the variability underlying certain forms of psychopathology, then it is clear that these are not going to be amenable to analysis in terms of 'family history' regarded in purely environmental terms. The term 'family history' in this context extends to any features of the family environment which may be correlated with the genotype of the individuals studied; if we are justified in disregarding E_2 we must also discount any environmental influences of, for example, the parental genotype, since they are confounded with E_2 in twins reared together. Thus the contribution of psychotic parents to psychoticism in their offspring may not be in the quality of the environment they provide by virtue of their psychosis, but in the genes they transmit.

It may be thought that this is a large deduction to make from sparse data, but it is well in line with the results of a large body of empirical research which has been done on the environmental effects of 'between family' forces on psychotic behaviour. This field cannot of course be reviewed here; Hirsch and Leff (1975) have provided an excellent summary and discussion of all this large body of evidence, and their conclusion is in essence similar to ours. It is this agreement between two entirely different procedures, making entirely different assumptions, and using entirely different material, which lends some degree of support to our conclusion.

Our model also has consequences for within-families environmental variation. The small contribution of E_1 reflects environmental differences between individuals within the same family. The specific experiences to which individuals are exposed in this context must of course be the object of quite a different sort of study. However, the fact that they relate to differences between individuals even in the same family suggests that they are likely to be of an accidental rather than of a social or cultural character.* Again, the precise nature of the 'accidents' remains to be established; they may be physical or behavioural. Clearly, there is scope within

*It is interesting that almost the only really well-documented factors which distinguish between schizophrenic and not schizophrenic MZ twins are birth weight and birth size (Fischer, 1972), i.e. presumably accidental consequences of E_1 events happening within the womb.

E_1 for the discovery of 'traumatic' experiences, but any variation due to such experiences is expressed in addition to that already created by genetical polymorphism. This may furnish the explanation for the view that certain traumata only induce psychotic behaviour in certain individuals. If we regard overt psychotic behaviour as a threshold character, with an underlying continuously variable trait, it is easy to see how environmental accidents occurring to those predisposed genetically to be near the threshold of psychosis may be much more damaging than similar accidents occurring to those much further away from the threshold. Thus, although $G \times E$ interaction was eliminated by our present scale of measurement, we should not be surprised if our trait translated into terms of clinical diagnosis and aetiology showed substantial genotype-environmental interaction, with psychotics being relatively more sensitive to environmental experiences than normals. In this respect, our original (untransformed) P scale, for all its faults, simulates what we might expect on the basis of some kind of threshold model of variation in psychoticism, since genotypes who on average produce high P scores seem to show greater sensitivity to environmental influences.

Our theory postulates that actual psychotic disorders, in particular schizophrenia, are continuous with normal behaviour patterns; one deduction from this hypothesis would seem to be that the actual genetic and environmental causation of schizophrenia would be reducible to a model similar to the one we have built up for psychoticism. This is perhaps too strong a test for the theory; we have not ruled out the possibility that in addition to the additive genetic variance implied in P there might also be major genes determining the specific symptomatology of the psychotic patient's disorder. However, it may be of interest to take our general discussion of the genetic background of psychotic disorder, given in a previous chapter, a little further along the lines of quantitative analysis, and see to what extent the similarity of P and psychosis finds support in the details of genetic analysis. In our discussion we will make use particularly of the re-analyses of previous studies reported by Fulker (1973, 1974); as will be seen, his estimates agree remarkably well with our own. Table 46 shows the data on which Fulker has based his analysis. It is restricted to recent studies in which sampling biases, generally acknowledged to play a part in the older studies, would have been much reduced or eliminated. Diagnosis was reasonably objective and uniform. The concordances in the Table are simple pair concordances based on fairly clear-cut cases of schizophrenia. Heterogeneity chi-square tests suggest that samples within each of the three groups are sufficiently homogeneous to be pooled for the purposes of analysis, and a tetrachoric correlation was calculated for each. This correlation was based on a population incidence (p) for schizophrenia of 1.14 per cent. For MZ twins, the correlation turns out to be .76; for DZ twins, .35. Two studies involving parents and offspring reared apart (PO_A) are also given in the Table; they provide unique information about the effects of the common family environment.

Table 47, taken from Fulker (1973), presents a simple genetical model fitted to the observed correlations. The model omits any effects of assortative mating. This omission is justified because (1) on a strict threshold model no substantial effects can occur, and (2) data on assortative mating (Erlenmeyer-Kimling and Paradowski, 1966) suggest a 2 per cent rate for spouses, which implies a marital correlation of only about .1 (very similar to that we have found for P). This figure is so low that its effects may safely be neglected, as a first approximation. When we postulate

157

TABLE 46 Concordance rates from recent schizophrenia studies (from Fulker, 1973)

Source	Concordance		
	MZ_T	DZ_T	PO_A
Gottesman and Shields (1966)	10/24	3/33	
Harvald and Hauge (1965)	2/7	3/59	
Tienari (1963)	1/16		
Kringlen (1966)	17/55	14/178	
Heston (1966)			5/47
Rosenthal *et al.* (1968)			3/54
Heterogeneity			
χ^2	3.64 (ns)	0.57 (ns)	0.77 (ns)
df	3	2	1
% Concordance	29.41	7.41	7.92
Tetrachoric correl. based on p=1.14%	0.76±0.04	0.35±0.01	0.37±0.02

panmixia (or a close approximation to it), the biometrical model and its expectations holds for any number of loci, including the simple case of a single locus; the biometrical analysis presented therefore subsumes single-gene models as a special case: 'If we accept this model, the results of the analysis are very simple and suggest only additive variation with no effects due either to dominance or to a common or shared environment. Maximum likelihood estimation confirms this simple model, the chi square for failure of the model being nonsignificant' (p.274).

As Fulker points out, 'the absence of common family environmental influences, combined with a high heritability (73 per cent) seems to favour a biological rather than a cultural explanation for schizophrenia, and the absence of dominance

TABLE 47 A simple model for schizophrenia* (from Fulker, 1973)

Type of Family	Correlation	S.E.	Model		
			Additive Variance	Dominance Variance	Common Environment Variance
MZ_T	.76	.04	1	1	1
DZ_T	.35	.01	½	¼	1
PO_A	.37	.02	½	0	0

*Additive variance = .74 ± .07; dominance variance = .05 ± .12; common environment = −.03 ± .03; residual environment = .24 ± .06.
Maximum likelihood estimates: Additive variance = .73 ± .06; residual environment = .27 ± .06; model fit χ^2_2 = 1.64 (ns).

suggests an evolutionary history of stabilizing selection for an intermediate optimum, characteristic of other personality traits and in contrast to the picture for IQ'(p.274). The heritability of 73 per cent allows us to make an accurate prediction for the frequency of schizophrenia in the offspring of two schizophrenics. Slater and Cowie (1971) give an estimate of 37 per cent, a figure based on all available data; Fulker's model gives a predicted frequency of 39 per cent, a remarkably close prediction.

Existing data on schizophrenic patients thus result in a remarkably simple model, for which the following are the best obtainable estimates: $D_R = 1.46 \pm 0.12$, and $E_1 = 0.27 \pm 0.06$, with no other factors demanding inclusion. An approximate estimate of the number of loci controlling variability may be obtained from the expression: Number of loci = $(\frac{1}{2} \text{Range})^2/D_R$, which gives a minimum estimate of number of loci involved in excess of four; this calculation, like so much other evidence, clearly suggests polygenic rather than single-gene control. Obviously all these estimates are only approximations, and Fulker himself notes a number of possible criticisms that could be directed at the data used, and the analysis performed. Nevertheless, in broad outline these criticisms are not likely to affect the general conclusions. The analysis of schizophrenic heritability, and that of psychoticism, give remarkably similar results, emphasizing the paramount influence of D_R, the small contribution of E_1, and the failure of E_2 and shared environment effects. Both models show absence of dominance and epistasis, and very small assortative mating; the latter effect emerges both from direct study and from genetical analysis. Heritability for both is very similar, the difference not being significant on any reasonable assumption. We may conclude that the data do not contradict the strong hypothesis which is being tested, and that we would be justified in regarding schizophrenia in terms of a threshold model, with P measuring the underlying continuum.

This conclusion should not be overinterpreted. The number of models which might be considered at a first approximation is limited. We should therefore not be too surprised to find that the different approaches to aspects of psychotic behaviour gave fairly similar answers. Nevertheless, any marked inconsistency would have suggested that the different traits and analyses were not comparable, and that psychotic and 'psychotic' behaviour did not share common causal factors. The comparison puts our hypothesis at risk, because it could be disconfirmed by any failure to agree on important aspects; in this sense it does constitute a proper scientific test of the theory.

11

The nature of the Lie scale

There is no doubt that personality questionnaires are subject to faking, and that in fact such 'faking good' or 'faking bad' (malingering) is relatively easy, whatever the questionnaire concerned (Alex, 1965; Borislow, 1958; Braun and La Faro, 1968; Braun and Gomez, 1966; Dicken, 1959; Doll, 1971; Gomez and Braun, 1967; Kuder, 1950; Longstaff and Jurgensen, 1953; Norman, 1963; Power, 1968; Power and O'Donovan, 1969; Radcliffe, 1966). These studies are concerned with instructed faking, i.e. conditions in which subjects are explicitly asked to fake good or bad. Similar results are found under selection conditions (Gordon and Stapleton, 1956; Green, 1951; Heron, 1956; Werman, 1952). These data are sometimes misunderstood, and the suggestion made that because of faking personality inventories are of little use in research. Precisely the opposite conclusion is indicated. The fact that instructions to 'fake good' produce much lower N scores, say, than do the ordinary test instructions, indicates not only that faking can be induced by suitable instructions, but also that before these instructions were given there can have been only little if any faking! (S.B.G. Eysenck and H.J. Eysenck, 1963a,b). The fact that conditions of anonymity do not produce changes in personality test scores, as compared with name-signing conditions, also seems to indicate that under ordinary conditions subjects give relatively truthful answers (Nias, 1972a).

This conclusion was borne out by the fact that there is a great deal of direct evidence of validity for personality questionnaires. Ratings made by friends and close acquaintances agree very well with self-ratings (S.B.G. Eysenck, 1962; S.B.G. Eysenck and H.J. Eysenck, 1963c, 1966; H.J. Eysenck and S.B.G. Eysenck, 1969), and response sets do not seem to play much part in the determination of answer patterns (S.B.G. Eysenck and H.J. Eysenck, 1963a, 1963b, 1964a; Farley, 1966). Above all, it is possible to make predictions on the basis of theoretical formulations concerning the nature of the personality dimensions measured, and confirm these in experimental laboratory tests, using questionnaires to select subjects characteristically high or low in a given dimension (Eysenck, 1967b). Thus there can be no question of the at least partial validity of personality questionnaires, such as the EPQ.

Nevertheless, it also seems clear that under certain circumstances (e.g. when subjected to a selection procedure) many people will dissimulate, and even under ordinary experimental test conditions it seems likely that some people will dissimulate. Given that it is possible and indeed easy to dissimulate, it clearly becomes important to attempt the construction of scales for the measurement of dissimulation, in order to establish who has dissimulated when, and if possible to correct the measurement scales for this dissimulation. Several different methods have been tried in this connection, but the most important has undoubtedly been the construction of the so-called 'Lie' scales. O'Donovan (1969) has traced the history of these scales, which go back to the early twenties, but for practical purposes the first useful scales were constructed by Hartshorne and May (1928). Their original purpose was not so much to correct personality scale scores for 'faking' or other test-taking attitudes, but rather to measure the children's tendency to deceive. The method 'consists of a series of rather personal questions. There are many specific acts of conduct which on the whole have rather widespread social approval, but which at the same time are rarely done. The questions revolve around situations of this sort.' Lying is diagnosed when such rarely performed acts are endorsed by the child as being habitually done, or when frequently performed non-desirable acts are denied by the child. Validity was claimed for the test by its authors because it correlated with various other tests of deceitful conduct, such as classroom cheating, out-of-classroom cheating, and stealing; the correlations were not high, ranging from .11 to .40, but correction for attenuation might raise these observed correlations to some extent.

Scales of this kind have been used to correct other scales for test-taking attitudes; this use of the Lie scale has been pioneered by the authors of the MMPI (Dahlstrom and Welsh, 1960). The EPI and the Junior EPI contained rather short Lie scales, and in order to prepare a better Lie scale for the EPQ, several factorial studies were carried out with rather large numbers of items (e.g. S.B.G. Eysenck and H.J. Eysenck, 1970a; S.B.G. Eysenck, Nias and H.J. Eysenck, 1971). These studies attempted to establish the existence of the unitary factor of 'dissimulation', and its independence of P, E and N. This seemed particularly necessary in view of some results published by Rie (1963), who reported remarkable inconsistencies between different portions of a widely-used Lie scale, including negative correlations between one part of the scale and another, and even between two items which differed in form but not in content! It seems reasonable to say that any scale purporting to measure a single psychological tendency, such as 'faking good' under test conditions, should include in its validating procedures a set of factor analyses giving the actual observed correlations between the items and the factors emerging from such matrices; only in this way can mistakes like those pointed out by Rie be avoided.

Illustrative of our results is a study in which a sixteen-item Lie scale was constructed for use with children, and administered as part of the larger inventory to 2,500 children between the ages of 7 to 16 years. The actual items used are given below. Factor analyses were carried out separately on the different age groups, on the grounds that different ages might attach different meanings to the same question, so that what might be true of one age might not be true of another (S.B.G. Eysenck and H.J. Eysenck, 1970a).

Details of the analysis are given in the paper quoted, but the outcome is very clear, as shown in Table 48. There is at each age a single, strongly marked super-factor which loads appropriately on all the items, and which can be identified confidently with lying or dissimulation. Loadings are very similar from one age to another, and it is indeed surprising that even with seven-year-old children such clear-cut results can be obtained. Four items seemed less reliable as far as measurement of this factor is concerned; these have been indicated by putting brackets around the item number. For future use these items have been eliminated. This study shows quite clearly that L items can and do generate a single, strongly marked factor which behaves very much as predicted.

Sixteen Items of the Children's Lie Scale
1. Do you sometimes get cross?
2. Do you always do as you are told at once?
3. Have you ever broken any rules at school?
4. Do you like everyone you know?
5. Have you ever told a lie?
6. Do you always finish your homework before you play?
7. Have you ever been late for school?
8. Do you sometimes boast a little?
9. Are you always quiet in class, even when the teacher is out of the room?
10. Have you ever said anything bad or nasty about anyone?
11. Do you always eat everything you are given at meals?
12. Have you ever been cheeky to your parents?
13. Do you say your prayers every night?
14. Would you much rather win than lose a game?
15. Can you always keep every secret?
16. Do you always say you are sorry when you have been rude?

In another study with children, S.B.G. Eysenck, Nias and H.J. Eysenck (1971) tried out a somewhat longer L scale, together with E and N items; these three sets of items fell clearly into three independent sets, and it was apparent that there was

TABLE 48 Factor loadings of ten groups of children on sixteen items of Lie scale*

1	N	45	33	39	17	13	26	35	33	66	3!
2	Y	−44	−58	−56	−63	−52	−74	−56	−47	−52	−2!
3	N	20	43	50	44	51	50	41	37	53	46
(4)	Y	−14	−47	−34	−32	−37	−52	−26	−45	−40	−4!
5	N	59	49	62	54	37	43	50	46	57	4!
6	Y	−26	−38	−33	−45	−51	−56	−34	−53	−51	−5!
(7)	N	54	36	40	20	31	18	−02	27	22	3!
8	N	33	49	39	42	42	33	49	32	42	3!
9	Y	−34	−46	−58	−48	−64	−45	−50	−54	−55	−5!
10	N	60	57	57	68	57	58	50	57	67	4!
11	Y	−24	−34	−33	−39	−39	−46	−03	−41	−36	−3!
12	N	59	51	44	49	47	62	41	45	60	5!
13	Y	−45	−31	−41	−45	−46	−37	−27	−44	−52	−3!
(14)	N	19	−01	25	−15	18	24	−28	17	37	−2!
15	Y	−47	−42	−48	−50	−39	−41	−47	−48	−43	−4!
(16)	Y	−09	−44	−34	−46	−39	−52	−31	−36	−48	−3!
		16%	19%	20%	20%	19%	22%	15%	18%	25%	1!

*Decimal points properly preceding each entry have been omitted.

no less internal cohesion as far as the L-scale items were concerned, than was true of the other scales. Alpha reliabilities were .83 for N, .73 for E, and .83 for L. (The number of children involved was 390.) The scales were independent of each other, all correlations being below .20. Intelligence was measured with the Progressive Matrices; this variable did not correlate with E or N, but did correlate significantly with L ($r = -.29$). This correlation is typical of many others we have obtained in our work; quite generally there is a low but usually significant negative correlation between L and intelligence, however measured. The meaning of this correlation will be discussed later on.

Details of the Lie scales (adult and child) used in the EPQ have already been given in previous chapters; we shall here rather concentrate on evidence relating to the interpretation of these scales. Mention has already been made of the complexity of this problem. Dicken (1959) has suggested three possible and plausible reasons for high scoring on the L scale: (1) deliberate 'faking' with intent to deceive the user; (2) response in terms of an ideal self-concept rather than a candid self-appraisal; (3) response in terms of an 'honest' but inaccurate and uninsightful self-assessment. To these we might perhaps add a fourth possibility: (4) genuine conformity to social rules and mores. This was already suggested by Hartshorne and May (1928) when they found that girls had higher L scores than boys; they gallantly suggested that this might be due, not to more dissimulation in girls, but rather to their greater conformity which allowed them to answer more questions truthfully in the socially desirable direction.

In order to select between these various possibilities in any particular case, it becomes crucial to be able to ascertain the degree of motivation for dissimulation which is present in any particular situation; this should influence (1), but leave the other causes listed above uninfluenced. Michaelis and Eysenck (1971) have reported a series of experiments with this aim in mind. They tested 339 high-motivation and 225 low-motivation apprentices at a large motor-car works near London, using an early form of the EPQ. The HM group were under the impression that their scores would be used as part of a selection test to decide about their acceptance by the firm for apprenticeship training; they were therefore highly motivated to put themselves in a good light. The LM group were already employed by the firm, and were explicitly told that the scores would not be divulged to the management; they knew from long-continued earlier work by the authors in that plant that results were always used exclusively for scientific purposes. This group therefore had minimal motivation for dissimulation.

The major difference in scores between the two groups was in respect to the L and N scales—the HM group had higher L scores (7.0 as opposed to 3.1) and lower N scores (5.4 as opposed to 8.9). Thus, when motivated by the situation to dissimulate, most people increase their L scores and decrease their N scores; so far this experiment does not add appreciably to what had been found before. However, the authors went on to calculate the intercorrelations between the scales for the two groups, and found a significantly higher (negative) correlation between L and N for the HM group. (The correlation between L and P (negative) was also higher for this group.) Another difference became obvious when the items were intercorrelated and factor-analysed, separately for the two groups; the personality factors accounted for less of the variance, and the L scale more, in the HM group, as compared with the LM group. We may therefore have here a method of assessing the degree of 'dissimulation-motivation' inherent in a given situation; this would be assessed by means of the LN correlation—the higher the correlation, the more dissimulation can be expected. Clearly our data are in line with this hypothesis, but equally clearly more evidence is needed to support it.

Fortunately, there is a set of relevant studies available, carried out in our laboratories by Furneaux and Lindahl (unpublished), in which they demonstrated clearly that this hypothesis was in fact tenable.

Furneaux and Lindahl made use of the motivational situation also used in our study, but added three further groups, at two other factories, whose motivation they considered to be intermediate between the HM and LM groups similar to our own. Group 1 in their sample was similar (not identical) to our LM group, and Group 5 was similar to our HM group. Their Group 1, unlike our subjects, 'took part in the tests mainly because they were paid to do so, and because this gave them an excuse for missing a day's work, by visiting the Institute'. The apprentices making up Group 2, in addition to coming from another factory, 'were not paid, and lost comparatively little work-time by taking part in our experiment, which was conducted in their own factory. One would therefore assume that involvement in the tests was greater in Group 2 than in Group 1'. One might add to this argument that apprentices in the factory from which Group 2 was taken had had no experience of psychological testing by outsiders, and consequently might be expected to have some residual qualification in mind regarding the communication of results to management. Group 3 was assured of non-communication to the management of results, but also came from a factory where no previous testing had taken place; in addition they were not volunteers, as had been members of Groups 1 and 2, so that their motivation might well have been raised by more definite suspicions about what the psychologists were up to. Group 4 was made up of selectees, as was Group 5, but whereas in Group 5 only a very small proportion of applicants was taken, nearly all those in Group 4 were taken (this fact was, of course, known to the candidates, and depended on the particular factory at which they were applying). Accordingly, Furneaux and Lindahl argued that the groups were ranged in order from lowest to highest motivation, with Group 1 having the lowest and Group 5 the highest motivation. The instrument used for testing was the MPI, to which was added a 38-item Lie scale; a score of ten was used to split the population into 'Liars' and Nonliars'.

Table 49 shows the increase in the proportion of liars with increase in (hypothetical) motivation, and the correlation between L and N for each group; correlations with E were not affected, as in our own study. It will be seen that these correlations become increasingly negative, as motivation increases. Furneaux and Lindahl put forward the hypothesis that in Group 1 'only those lacking insight gained high lie scores, and the similarity of the two distributions of neuroticism scores in this group (i.e. that of "liars" and that of "nonliars") suggests that such subjects have little systematic tendency to deny neurotic attitudes and behaviours. Within the group of applicants there must also have been a proportion of subjects gaining high lie scores for the same reason. In addition, however, because of the strong press of the selection situation, a substantial number probably resorted to deliberate lying, or were influenced by an increased tendency to respond in terms of an ideal self-concept. In contrast to lack of insight, these two attitudes do seem to result also in a strong tendency to deny neurotic characteristics. We can in fact postulate a general rule, to the effect that a large proportion of high lie scores, together with a strong negative correlation between scores for lying and neuroticism, will usually be found in groups completing tests under certain conditions of high motivation. Their presence, in fact, might even be used as a measure of motivation.' The regular progression of values for the intermediate groups in Table 49 lends some support to this notion.

TABLE 49   Percent of 'Liars' and tetrachoric correlations between L and N for five different groups of apprentices in increasing order of motivation to dissimulate (from Michaelis and Eysenck, 1971)

Group	Percent liars	r_{LN}
1	38%	.07
2	53%	−.36
3	56%	−.45
4	67%	−.52
5	77%	−.58

These data are in good accord with the Michaelis and Eysenck data; the LM group used by them is more similar to their Group 2 than to their Group 1, which was tested individually, and the two groups give very similar correlations. We may conclude that there is good evidence for using the LN correlation as a measure of the situation-inherent motivational tendency to dissimulate.

Unfortunately, this general conclusion is in fact untenable. In an unpublished study Dr L. Montag, Chief Psychologist to the Israeli Ministry of Health Medical Institute of Road Safety, gave EPQ questionnaires to 400 male subjects, mean age 25 years, all of whom had been referred to the Institute for a physical and psychological assessment in relation to their driving fitness. These subjects had either been discharged from the Army with a psychiatric diagnosis, had had their licence suspended after being involved in an accident and being found guilty by the Court, or were applying for a public vehicle driving licence according to a new Government regulation, in spite of a clean driving record. These subjects were all very highly motivated to do well as they were under great pressure (social, professional, etc.) to obtain a driving licence, and considered that the personality test would be an important element in coming to a decision about their application. This group might therefore be considered very highly motivated (VHM), and in accordance with our hypothesis, the correlation between N and L should be very high; in actual fact it was only −.17! The actual values of the scores obtained bore out the hypothesis that the group was highly motivated to suppress admission of N items; the score was 3.93 only, as compared with scores in excess of eleven for non-motivated subjects.

The explanation for this state of affairs probably lies in the presence of threshold and ceiling effects. Consider Figure 41, which contains hypothetical plots (scatter diagrams) of subjects' scores in a low motivation, a high motivation, and a very high motivation group. The scatter diagrams for both the LM and VHM groups are circular, illustrating the fact that at very low and very high values of L, and correspondingly very high and very low values of N, there is no effective correlation between the two variables. It is the middle group, i.e. the HM subjects, who have a larger variance, and consequently demonstrate a high correlation between the two variables. With LM or with VHM, nearly all the subjects are similar in motivation to dissimulate; in the middle HM group, some individuals are highly motivated, others very little, with others still having intermediate levels of motivation. It is this hypothetical spread of motivation in the HM group that is responsible for the observed high negative correlation in this group, as compared with the hypothetically more homogeneous LM and VHM groups.

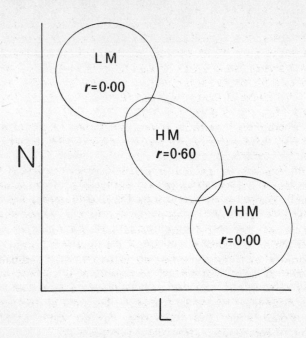

Figure 41 Hypothetical correlations between N and L in groups respectively low, medium high and very high on motivation to dissimulate

The Lie scale can measure conditions productive of dissimulation, by a suitable combination of the mean score on the scale, and the observed correlation between N and L; it can also be used to correct for the presence of such conditions. Power (1968) and Power and O'Donovan (1969) have shown that by warning subjects of the existence of an L scale, or by giving them information about its rationale, subjects can escape detection of instructed 'faking' better than when ignorant. Montag, in some unpublished research, has used the warning of the presence of the scale as a means of dissuading subjects from attempting to dissimulate, and has found that with this warning (in the sort of situation described above) there is a definite drop in the amount of faking; L scores go down, and N scores rise.

Nias (1972b) has reported an experiment with children in which 262 school pupils aged 12 and 13 years completed an early version of the Junior EPQ. Half the group were given normal instructions, while the other half were warned of the existence of the Lie scale. In the experimental condition, L-scale scores were significantly lower for both boys and girls, indicating some success for the method. There were also significantly higher scores for P under the experimental condition.

In the case of the boys N scores were significantly higher in the experimental condition, and there was also a drop in the (negative) correlation between N and L.

Another use of this method of reducing the effects of dissimulation, with adults this time, has been reported by S.B.G. Eysenck, H.J. Eysenck and L. Shaw (1974). Three experiments are reported in this study, comparing the effects of ordinary instructions with those obtained under special 'honesty' instructions (i.e. warning of the presence of the Lie scale). In the first experiment, random samples of subjects were tested under conditions of low motivation for dissimulation. As expected, little in the way of difference in N or P was found, although the L-scale scores did change, scores going down significantly for both men and women. (For women only, there was also a significant increase in the size of the N scores.) In the second experiment, samples of black South African subjects were tested under conditions of high motivation for dissimulation; quite considerable changes in scores on N, P and L scales were found. P scores increased from 4.64 to 5.65; N scores increased from 7.95 to 9.44; L scores decreased from 6.13 to 4.52. As usual, there were no changes in E. Where there is motivation for dissimulation (in this case provided by a selection process), there is clearly an effect upon scores on N, P and L which can be partly reversed by 'honesty' instructions.

In the third experiment, groups of prisoners were employed; here 'honesty' instructions produced a sizeable change in N and L scores. There were no changes in P scores, or in E. The prisoners have average LM group L scores, but the correlation between N and L is significantly higher than for the LM control group used in the first experiment of the series; thus simple recourse to mean L would have misinterpreted the motivational properties of the situation. Possibly this is due to the 'nonconformity' of criminals, which would give them an unusually low L score (granted, as we shall argue, that part of the variance of L is generated by individual differences in conformity). Starting out with such a very low 'true' L score, motivation to dissimulate would push this up, but only to the level reached by non-criminal groups under LM conditions, due to their 'conformism'. This interpretation is of course speculative, and requires support.

We have so far reviewed the evidence suggesting that, under certain conditions, L-scale scores may serve as indicators of dissimulation; this evidence is fairly conclusive, even though there are still some odd findings which are difficult to integrate with our model. What is the evidence to suggest that L measures something over and above dissimulation? Our first argument would be that even under extremely LM conditions, L-scale scores do not drop to zero, but remain well above it; clearly the scale is still measuring something that exists even though motivation for dissimulation has been removed. Furthermore, variances are still quite large; in other words, individual differences have not been abolished by maximum reduction of motivation for dissimulation. It could of course be argued that even under these conditions, many people still feel under pressure, and dissimulate to some extent. Our second argument would seem to militate against this suggestion. The internal consistency of the scale (K.R. 20; alpha coefficient) seems quite independent of the degree of motivation for dissimulation; the scale is highly reliable whether administered under LM, HM or VHM conditions. If variance were produced entirely by individual differences in degree of dissimulation, then manipulating this variable should produce changes in the covariances observed between items, and thus in the reliability of the scale; this is typically not found. It could be that people differ in respect to some sort of 'defensiveness'; they respond with dissimulation to any request for disclosure, and the degree of dissimulation depends partly on stable individual personality structures, partly on external motivating conditions. Conditions determine the mean score, but shift everyone's score up or down by an equal amount, thus preserving reliability from one condition to another. This is not impossible, but it seems rather unlikely, particularly as defensiveness seems itself correlated with N (Coan, 1974). L, as we have seen, is not so correlated.

There is some evidence also that 'defensiveness' is dependent on a person's particular position or situation; high defensiveness is found when a person is in a vulnerable position. Thus Morgenstern (unpublished) found that amputees suffering from referred ('phantom limb') pain scored abnormally high on the L scale, and other (unpublished) studies have shown other patients suffering from physical illnesses to react in a similar manner—almost as if to say: 'I am ill now, or disabled, but look at my wonderful personality!' It may be for the same reason that older people have elevated L scores; what they are saying in effect may be something like: 'I may be old now, and unable to do some of the things I used to do, but my personality is still as good as ever.' We would thus consider 'defensiveness' as simply another word to denote motivation for dissimulation; HM situations produce more defensiveness than LM situations. This would not produce the effects under discussion, such as equal reliabilities under different conditions of motivation.*

An alternative hypothesis could be phrased in terms of another personality dimension, or set of characteristics, independent of P, E and N, and stressing such traits as conformity, orthodoxy, conservatism; in other words, perhaps the high L scorer actually does behave in a manner more conforming to the present social mores! The reliability coefficients certainly strongly suggest that underlying the scale there is some consistent personality attribute; the notion of 'readiness to dissimulate' would not seem to fill the bill, in spite of the slight correlations which Hartshorne and May (1928) found between high L scores and actual dishonesty. These findings would also find an explanation in terms of our hypothesis; high L scorers are not conforming to socially acceptable mores, and consequently they indulge in other, equally unacceptable types of conduct, such as stealing, etc. The fact that women and girls tend to have higher L scores also fits in with this view; females are known to be more law abiding and conformist than men. If the L scale measured a personality trend to lie and behave dishonestly in general, then one would expect males, who are far more prone to commit criminal acts of one kind or another, to have higher L scores. An explanation in terms of conformity seems much more likely to cover these facts.

This general suggestion that the L scale measures, in addition to a tendency to dissimulate in a particular set of circumstances, a consistent personality variable, would of course be strengthened considerably if it could be shown that the L-scale scores are to a marked extent determined by genetic causes. We shall next turn to an investigation of this possibility; before doing so we may perhaps reflect that the

---

*A somewhat different formulation was used by Taylor and Marsh (personal communication), who investigated patients who had undergone anterior temporal lobectomy for the relief of intractable psychomotor epilepsy. Finding exceptionally high L scores, particularly in females operated on the left side, they concluded: 'It seems to us unlikely that these very high lie scores are the result of dissimulation, but rather that this scale relates most meaningfully to the clinical impression we gain that many of our patients live in a world of tolerable fantasy rather than unbearable reality.'

dual nature of the L scale produces considerable difficulties in its use. The scale, if our hypothesis be accepted, measures first of all an underlying personality trait of conformity; highly conformist persons obtain high scores, less conforming persons lower scores. But in addition, under conditions which motivate people to put their best foot forward (selection pressures, need to obtain a driving licence, etc.), there is external stress to appear more conformist than the person really is. (The terms 'conformist' and 'putting oneself in the best light possible' are almost synonymous, by definition—conformity is defined in terms of the existing set of rules and regulations which a person is supposed to observe, and by means of which he gains public approval.) Thus a score can only be evaluated under conditions where external motivating conditions are roughly equalized; when this is done, then the L score can be used as a measure of the personality trait of 'conformity'. When conditions are motivating to dissimulation, the score becomes a proper Lie score, and can be used to detect dissimulation. There may be other conditions which determine L scores, and there may be other traits measured by this scale, but it is doubtful if they exert enough influence to determine much of the variance. The determination of correlates of L and LM conditions, in order to throw further light on the nature of this personality trait, is largely in the future; here we have merely discussed the possibility that this scale may in due course become a useful personality scale in its own right, and under conditions which rule out dissimulation for the majority of subjects.

In essence, the genetic determination of L has already been indicated in Table 45, and the discussion regarding it. There is a strong genetic determinant (D_R) governing individual differences between persons; this is *independent* of the genetic factors determining individual differences in P, E, or N. There is a highly significant E_1 environmental effect (within families), and a marginally significant E_2 environmental effect (between families). Thus L is the only scale which shows any evidence of E_2; it is also the only scale to show significant covariation (with Extraversion), although we were unable to detect any significant E_2 variation for Extraversion. As both effects for E_2 are only just significant, and are taken from ten possible sources of significance, we may be permitted to disregard them until replication has confirmed their existence. If there is any reliance to be placed on the E_2 effect, it is notable that this is mainly due to the *female* sample. This may reflect in part the assumed greater social pressure for conformity in females. We hope to publish a more detailed account of the genetic analysis of the L data in due course; for the present purpose the data already discussed are sufficient to establish the major points of interest.

It is interesting that L has a significant covariation with P for E_1. Discounting shared family environmental effects (since E_2 covariation is insignificant), we would interpret this as suggesting that environmental influences making for conformity (high L) operate in the opposite direction for P (low psychoticism). This is intuitively obvious: P behaviour is certainly nonconformist, odd, and unorthodox, and would be disfavoured by environmental factors encouraging L behaviour (conformity). It is interesting that this effect is environmental not genetic; there is no covariation of any kind in the analysis of D_R effects. The effect is sufficiently large (being at the $P < .01$ level) to make it seem fairly secure; it presumably accounts for the usually slight but ever-present negative correlation between P and L.

We would like to take the discovery of this covariation between P and L as an occasion for stressing a point which has been made before, namely that interpretations of single-scale results are dangerous unless reference is also made to other scales. In particular, psychotic individuals frequently have only moderately high scores on P, marginally above normal or neurotic groups, but they also usually have very high L scores. It is this combination of high L, and elevated but not exceptionally high P, that characterizes psychotics (particularly schizophrenics); prisoners would tend to have higher P scores, but low L scores, as would psychopaths. The clear separations achieved in Figures 32 and 33 between different clinical and normal groups is due, not to single scales, but to *combinations* of scales, particularly P and L. High L scores should always act as a warning light; they do not necessarily invalidate the study, but they must on no account be disregarded. The interpretation must of course depend on the precise circumstances, the samples used, and the hypotheses tested; what is certain is that a proper consideration of high L scores is vital. The L scale is the least well understood of all our scales, and future research may with advantage be directed towards a better understanding of its properties; nevertheless, enough is known to suggest that no personality inventory is likely to prove satisfactory unless it contains a properly constucted L scale. Furthermore, no interpretations of individual scales is likely to prove satisfactory unless L-scale scores are taken into account.

12

Clinical, experimental and correlational studies of psychoticism

The previous chapters have given some support to the general hypothesis which forms the basis of this book, and we have quoted a number of published studies on such topics as the relation between P and psychosis, criminality, sex, originality, etc. In this chapter we shall attempt to survey a series of mainly unpublished studies which have looked at a variety of different aspects of P, from its role in mediating failure in therapy to its role in drug usage, from its relation to body build to its connection with the XYY caryotype, and from its role in V.D. to its role in meditation. Inevitably this chapter will be less well organized than the previous ones; the author of a book has no control over the diversity of material produced by experimentalists interested in different aspects of a given subject he is trying to review! Nevertheless, there is one strong point of unity: all the studies are relevant to a better understanding of the nature of P, and many of them make an experimental attempt to test certain theories about the nature of P.

Could it be said that we have here a paradigm of scientific research, i.e. the statement of a clear hypothesis, followed by an attempt to test deductions from this theory, and falsify the theory itself? The answer must of course be that such an idealistic picture of Popperian procedures is only very partly what happens in actual research, particularly when new concepts are in question. Without wishing to enter into philosophical disputations about the nature of science, we believe that it is more realistic to think of a gradual development of scientific theories, from 'hunches' through partial hypotheses, to genuine theories, and finally to scientific 'laws'. Parallel with this development is a set of appropriate experimental paradigms, ranging from simple observation in the service of induction, through attempts at verification at a low level, to falsification (along the lines made familiar by Popper), to systematic hypothetico-deductive testing of alternative theories. Figure 42 shows in outline the sort of growth we have in mind. Observation suggests, through a process of induction, certain hunches; these lead to further, more controlled observations which in turn suggest partial hypotheses. Attempts are then made to verify at least some of the consequences and deductions which this hypothesis gives rise to, and gradually a more general theory suggests itself. When this is set down in more or less rigorous fashion, we can begin the process of falsification; critics will begin to make deductions from the theory and attempt to demonstrate its insufficiencies. When finally such attempts are found to fail (on the whole, and probably still leaving many inconsistencies and anomalies to be explained away), the theory may finally aspire to become a 'law', particularly when it is properly quanticized, as for instance in the case of Newton's law of gravitation. Even then the theory is not immune, although falsification does not usually harm it very much; the aberrant precession of Mercury's perihelion, although contrary to prediction from Newton's theory, did not cause anyone to abandon the theory! What may happen, however, is that an alternative theory will be proposed which, if it is more inclusive and/or more accurate, dethrones the previous one and its 'laws'; thus Einstein replaced Newton. It is unrealistic to think of the development of scientific theories in terms only of one or the other of these stages (as most philosophers are wont to do); usually, dealing for the most part in highly developed sciences, philosophers base their theories on the upper end of our continuum. This is not appropriate for newly developing sciences, and it will not do for psychology; by making conditions of recognition too difficult, we may easily prevent the growth of worthwhile theories altogether.

The general level of the views proposed in this book lies somewhere between *ad hoc* hypotheses and theory; that means that the appropriate experimental paradigms are verification and falsification. We can make certain deductions from our theories, although without much certainty; that means that verification counts in favour of the theory, but falsification does not hurt it as much as it would a more developed theory. Of course, certain kinds of falsification would destroy the very basis of the theory; thus if psychotics and criminals did not have high P scores we would obviously have to reconsider the very meaning of high P score. But for the most part we are concerned with widening the empirical basis of the concept, and with attempts to verify cautious predictions which partake of the nature of hunches, but which occasionally may be aspiring to the rank of hypotheses or even theories. It is important to be clear about the rather lowly status of the concepts and views put forward in this book. Psychologists are often tempted, by looking at the pinnacles of scientific achievement in the hard sciences, to put their level of aspiration too high. Psychological theories cannot rival those of physics or chemistry at the moment (possibly ever) for consistency, accuracy, and predictive power; to attempt the impossible would not be in the best interests of the subject. Science, as Medawar pointed out, is the art of the possible. We must try to advance as far along the continuum of Figure 42 as possible, but we cannot hope to leap, with one tremendous insight, from one end to the other.

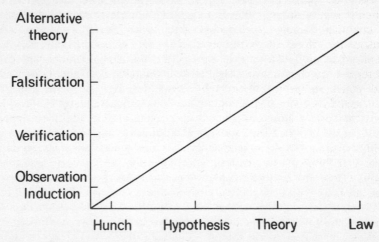

Figure 42   Relationship between stages of development of a scientific theory (abscissa) and appropriate testing paradigm

The most general argument, in constructing our experimental paradigm, is in fact an analogy which forms the basis of the method of criterion analysis, already discussed in an earlier chapter. What the theory suggests, in brief, is that any given behaviour which distinguishes psychotics from non-psychotics, should also distinguish high P scorers from low P scorers, in such a manner that high P scorers behave like psychotics (but less so), and low P scorers behave like non-psychotics. Thus we would expect, on any particular test which clearly discriminated psychotics from other groups, that scores on this test would follow a sequence:

Psychotics . . . High P Scorers . . . Low P Scorers.

There are, of course, precautions which require to be taken in order not to allow irrelevant artifacts to obscure this equation and its proper testing. Thus it may be that the distinction between psychotics and controls is mediated by the fact that the psychotics are institutionalized, the controls not; if this, rather than their psychotic behaviour, is at the basis of the experimental discrimination, then the formula might easily break down—in fact, it should break down. It may not always be easy to be certain on this point, and the possibility must always be borne in mind that artifacts may affect the measurement in question. But if the paradigm failed in most cases, or even in a large minority, we would certainly feel less happy with the adequacy of our hypothesis.

Another mode of arguing stems from the high correlation between P and maleness. We can advance another paradigm, using the following equation:

High P Scorers: Low P Scorers = Males: Females.

We have already seen one example of this argument, in our consideration of sexual attitudes; it will be remembered that indeed high P scorers (in both the male and the female population) reacted in the typically male fashion, and that low P scorers (again in both the male and the female population) reacted in the typically female fashion.

These two paradigms may point in different directions upon occasion, and then it is very difficult to make any reasonable prediction. Thus, for instance, from our first paradigm, we would argue that high P scorers should be less muscular; the work of Kretschmer and his successors has suggested that schizophrenics are leptosomatic, and even the pyknic manic-depressives are characterized by fat, not muscle development (Rees, 1973). However, on our second paradigm we would probably argue that men are more muscular than women, and that hence high P scorers should be more muscular than low P scorers. Perhaps the former argument has greater potency, being more directly concerned with psychosis, but the conflict remains. Segraves (1970) has in fact carried out the experiment, using 100 male students, and found significant negative correlations between P and muscularity; in other words high P scorers are less muscular than low P scorers. They did not differ on various other indices of body build, or fat, or surface area, and of course these results from a student population cannot be generalized to other groups, or nationalities. The finding is mentioned primarily because of the different predictions generated by our two paradigms, rather than for any particular substantive interest they might have.

Even more in the nature of a hunch would be the notion that perhaps prisoners of XYY caryotype would be more likely to be high on P than low. The only reason for this belief stems from the general impression (possibly false and due to faulty sampling) that XYY caryotypes are characterized by behaviour that would resemble that of high P scorers. In actual fact, a small sample of prisoners showing this caryotype was found to be significantly higher on P than a control group (Griffiths, 1971; H.J Eysenck and S.B.G. Eysenck, 1972), as already mentioned. Such a finding would require replication before it could be accepted, and in any case it would not be of broad theoretical interest; it would add slightly to the general inductive basis on which in due course a more causal theory of P may be built.

If the caryotype research is situated somewhat to the extreme left of our diagram (Figure 42), with the work of sex attitudes a little further to the right, then such studies as those of Stroh (1969, 1971) to be discussed below, on vigilance, are as far to the right as the present status of the subject allows.

These various experiments demonstrate the boundaries within which our various efforts to validate the P scale have lain. They vary from well-controlled laboratory studies, such as that of Stroh, to the simple observational or questionnaire type of study. Some, again like the Stroh study, can be seen to be based on predictions from widely accepted theoretical frameworks; others depend on hunches or *ad hoc* hypotheses. It would be idle to claim that all studies should be of the experimental type, and deal with proper deductions from theory. Not all investigations of human conduct lend themselves to the experimental, laboratory paradigm, and the attempt to *create* a theory must precede the *application* of such a theory. Consequently many of the studies to be mentioned fall short of full experimental rigour, and cannot be taken as good examples of the hypothetico-deductive method. They may nevertheless serve to extend and confirm certain aspects of the concept of psychoticism, delineate it more clearly, and suggest new approaches of a hopefully more experimental kind.

(a) Clinical studies

Following what seems a more or less natural order, we shall begin with a few additional studies looking at the P scores of psychotic patients. In the first of these, John Clements (1970) studied twenty-eight acute schizophrenics (less than two years of continuous hospitalization), twenty-eight chronic schizophrenics (more than two years of continuous hospitalization), and fourteen non-schizophrenic psychiatric patients. A variety of test scores and psychiatrist's ratings was available, and the following correlations are of some interest (there were no significant differences between the three groups on P or E, with the chronics significantly lower on N than the other two groups). Among the acute, P correlated .45 with doctor's rating of poverty of speech, .36 with rating of incoherence of speech, and .36 with rating of retardation. A principal components analysis gave rise to a component showing high loadings on P and on doctor's ratings of symptomatology, i.e. high P was associated with florid clinical state.

Among the chronic schizophrenics, P correlated .58 with evidence of coherent delusions; a principal components factor again associated P with poor premorbid adjustment, ward ratings of paranoid symptoms, and doctor's ratings of coherent delusions, incoherence of speech, and flatness or incongruity of affect. Again, therefore, P loads highly on a symptomatology factor. When the schizophrenic groups were combined, P was also found to correlate with slowness on a reaction time task. In this study the PI was used, and there were some moderately high correlations between P and N. The data support the generalization that higher P signifies greater severity of psychotic symptomatology.

In another study, John Griffiths (personal communication) tested eighty-eight normal, thirty-seven neurotic, and fifty-one psychotic men and women, using the EPQ scale; he also used the Foulds Hostility and Direction of Hostility Scales. P was found to be independent of E and N, and the P scale distinguished significantly between psychotics and normals and psychotics and neurotics, but not between normals and neurotics. This finding reinforces the specificity of the P scale in relating discrimination to psychotic groups only, not to neurotic groups. Both the psychotic and the neurotic groups were retested after between one and three months, during which time psychiatric treatment had been carried out, consisting in the case of successfully treated psychotics mainly of phenothiazine administration, in the case of unsuccessfully treated psychotics of monoamine oxidase inhibitors, and in the case of neurotics of ECT and anti-depressants. Table 50 shows the results. These may be summarized as follows: (1) improved psychotics showed a significant drop in P scores on retest; (2) improved psychotics showed significantly higher E scores on first test; (3) improved psychotics scored significantly lower on P on retest than non-improved psychotics. Thus low P was not prognostic of improvement in psychotics (if anything, the improved psychotics had slightly but not significantly higher P scores), but improvement is reflected in change in P score. This supports the Verma and Eysenck findings discussed in a previous chapter. It is interesting to note that improved psychotics are lower on N than are unimproved psychotics; although this difference falls short of statistical significance, it suggests that admixture of N may retard recovery in psychotics.

TABLE 50 Test and retest data on P, E and N for improved and non-improved psychotics and neurotics

		Test			*Retest*	
	n	P	E	N	P	E	N
Improved Psychotics	22	7.32	13.41	14.59	4.45	13.95	15.41
Non-improved Psychotics	18	6.62	9.50	17.06	7.78	10.83	17.06
Improved Neurotics	16	4.94	9.06	18.19	3.44	11.62	16.50
Non-improved Neurotics	8	5.00	13.62	15.50	6.25	12.50	17.37

The improved neurotic group shows a significantly greater drop in P than does the unimproved group. The improved neurotic group is also somewhat higher on N, and lower on E, than the unimproved group; these differences fall short of statistical significance. In any case, our main interest here is in the psychotic groups, rather than the rather small neurotic ones, so these differences will not be discussed in detail.

However this may be, the question may arise of what precise influence the presence of P may have on recovery after therapy in neurotic patients. Given the nature of the psychotherapeutic (and to some extent even the behaviour therapeutic) process, involving as both do personal interaction, cooperation, trust, and the following of instructions and suggestions, it would seem that the high P personality would be much less well equipped to benefit from such interpersonal therapy than would the low P personality. Given also that P and N are orthogonal, and represent quite different causal processes, it would seem to follow that quite a number of neurotics, besides having high N scores, would also have high P scores, just as another number of neurotics, apart from having high N scores, would also have low P scores. This should enable us to study the performance of high *vs.* low P scorers in a neurotic population, with the provisional hypothesis in mind that response to psychotherapy or behaviour therapy would be less positive in high than in low P scorers. The complexity of clinical intervention, which makes it impossible to allocate patients to given treatment groups, which mixes personal therapy with drug therapy, and which allocates patients to diagnostic groups only with very low reliability, makes it difficult to design a convincing experiment to test hypotheses of this kind. In spite of this, an attempt to do so has been made in a study by A. Rahman (personal communication).

In this study, 116 male and 188 females diagnosed as neurotics were studied; psychotics and organics were excluded. The EPQ was administered at the beginning and at discharge (or after six months' treatment, if discharge occurred later). In addition, psychiatrists were asked to give a prognosis at the beginning, and an assessment at the end of each patient's period in the experiment; these assessments were on a numerical scale from 1 (good) to 6 (poor). Before turning to the effects of psychotherapy (which for the purpose of this discussion will include behaviour therapy), it is necessary to point out that 111 female and 73 male patients were on anti-depressant drugs, and that these patients had significantly lower P scores; the possibility cannot be ruled out that these drugs had the effect of lowering the P scores. This seems a more likely hypothesis than the alternative one, namely that low P scorers would be selected to be given anti-depressant drugs.

When the data were analysed, it was found that P correlated with length of treatment (number of days) for both males ($r = .21$) and females ($r = .36$). Both correlations are statistically significant beyond the .01 level. The number of appointments also correlates with P for both sexes, but the correlation is significant only for the women ($r = .15$). Prognosis (psychiatrist's rating) correlated with P for females ($r = .20$, which is significant), but only insignificantly for males ($r = .08$). The assessment at the end of the study gave significant correlations with P for both sexes ($r = .28$ and .43, respectively). The assessment figures are of particular interest here; when we consider the unreliability of the assessment, and also the unreliability of the scale, then it becomes clear that correction for attenuation would produce quite impressive relationships between P and failure to benefit from treatment. (N was also correlated with assessment for both sexes—$r = .25$ and .14, respectively; only the former figure is significant.) Just how accurate are prognosis and assessment, in terms of the observed changes taking place on the scales of the EPQ? Rahman correlated prognosis and assessment with the difference between the scores obtained on the first and second administrations of the questionnaire. For prognosis, results were significant only for the men, correlations amounting to .36 for P, .31 for N, and −.28 for L. In other words, subjects given a hopeful prognosis scored lower on P and N after treatment, as compared with patients given a bad prognosis; their L scores increased.

Correlations for assessment ratings were higher, but here also the females were conspicuously less well judged than the males. For males, the correlations were .51 for P, .44 for E, and −.22 for N; for females, the correlations were .26 for P, and

.26 for N. All the values for both prognosis and assessment were significant at or beyond the .01 level, except for the L score on assessment, which was significant only at the $p < .05$ level. It seems that psychiatrists can prognosticate with some success for men, but not for women, and that psychiatrists can assess improvement also better for men than women (against the criterion of the change in EPQ scores). It is not clear why there should be such a sex difference, and of course replication of the findings is essential before they can be taken too seriously.

It is interesting to look at the different groups included in the analysis by diagnostic label. All the groups (anxiety states, depressives, phobics, sex disorders, obsessionals) averaged mean scores between 2.3 and 2.6 (females) and between 3.1 and 4.2 (males) on P; the only group which consistently had higher P scores was that composed of the personality disorders (mean scores on P was 6.0 for females and 5.5 for males). This finding is in good agreement with our theory. Personality disorders had the worst prognosis and the worst assessment on the psychiatrists' ratings; the other groups did not differ much from each other. Personality disorders also differed from the other groups by having by far the greatest amount of intensive psychotherapy (60 per cent of females, 72 per cent of males, as compared with values half that size for anxiety states, depressives, etc.). Correspondingly, personality disorders had the least amount of drug therapy (40 and 33 per cent, respectively); only the small group of sex disorders showed a similar disproportion. If our general theory is correct, we would anticipate very little success for personality disorders with psychotherapy of any kind, and would expect instead that phenothiazine and other anti-psychotic drugs might be far more effective. The routine psychiatric intervention through psychotherapy in these cases would appear to be the worst possible choice, and the fact that psychiatrists rate prognosis and final assessment so poor suggests that they are themselves aware of the position. It is not at all clear why they do not take the alternative path open to them, and rely much more on intervention through drugs. A proper comparative study along these lines might furnish us with interesting evidence about the value of the general theory developed in this book.

The failure of high P scorers to respond well to therapeutic intervention is also apparent in a study by Russell, Armstrong and Patel (1975) on electric aversion therapy for cigarette smoking. Seventy heavy smokers (32 cigarettes per day) constituted the sample; electric aversion therapy was the technique used for cure. Several different contingencies were tried, but did not differ much in effectiveness. Failures had higher P scores than did successes, among the males and the females alike; for the groups combined, the scores on P were 1.29 (SD 1.22) for the successes, and 3.00 (SD 2.16) for the failures; $p < .001$. Neither E nor N showed any consistent effect in this connection. This study, then, confirms the finding that P has a negative effect on response to psychiatric treatment.

A final clinical study concerned with the relation between diagnosis and personality has been reported by J. Griffiths (1975). He studied groups of male and female patients diagnosed as personality disorders, paranoid schizophrenics, non-paranoid schizophrenics, psychotic depressives, and neurotic depressives. Each of the ten groups contained on the average twenty patients. These patients filled in the EPQ during the first four days after admission to a mental hospital; they were taken on a random basis, and only cases suffering from a known organic aetiology, or too disturbed to cooperate sufficiently to fill in the inventory, were excluded. The various groups differed in age, with the depressives being the oldest, and the personality disorders the youngest. In order to compare the different groups, each group was compared with the standardization group of the same sex and age, and the difference between the group mean and the standardization mean taken as the score of that group. For the sake of interest, we have plotted these different scores (which eliminate the influence of age) on P and L. There is not much variation in E between the groups; on N the neurotic depressives and the personality disorders have higher scores than the other groups. Figure 43 shows the position of the five male and five female groups; normal subjects would lie at the intersection of the ordinate and abscissa.

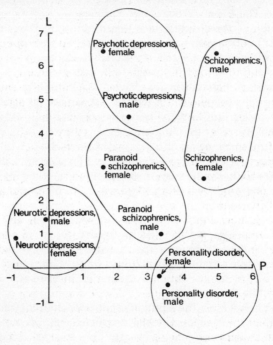

Figure 43 Position of five male and five female groups of psychiatric patients on P and L scales. Scores are expressed in terms of deviations from respective normal age means. Normals would be positioned at intersection of the two axes (drawn after figures supplied by J. Griffiths)

It will be obvious that the neurotic depressives have low (in fact, slightly negative) P scores; in other words, they score below the standardization groups on P. On L, they are very slightly above the normals, but essentially neurotic depressives do not differ from normals on L and P, for all practical purposes. Psychotic depressives, on the other hand, have clearly elevated P scores and very high L scores; they are very significantly differentiated from neurotic depressives on both these scales. Personality disorders have very high P scores, but normal L scores; schizophrenics have the highest P scores, and also high L scores, particularly the males. Paranoid schizophrenics have middling P and middling L scores. This is interesting as it has sometimes been suggested that the P scale is most representative of the paranoid type of psychosis; clearly this is not so. The data on the whole support the

178

interpretation of P as psychoticism, and suggest that psychotic depressives react similarly to schizophrenics.

Having dealt with psychiatric groups (psychotics, neurotics), we turn next to groups suffering from what are often considered psychiatric abnormalities which lie nevertheless outside the traditional categories of psychiatric nomenclature, e.g. drug users, alcoholics, patients in V.D. clinics, etc. Teasdale (1973) has given a review of the literature on the subject of drug dependence, included in which is a section on the personality of drug users. This suggests that drug users might be characterized by high P scores, but the evidence is equivocal because of the failure of investigators to use a proper P scale. This omission was rectified by Teasdale, Segraves and Zacune (1971), in a study using four separate groups of drug users. All four groups scored significantly higher than the comparison groups on P, and this was shown to be not simply the result of endorsement of items directly related to drug-taking, nor to the correlation between P and N scores. Item analysis showed that eleven of the twenty items significantly differentiated drug-using and control groups, and these items tended to be less homogeneous than those which failed to differentiate, and which tended to conform to a 'paranoid' stereotype. These findings agree with those of previous researchers using the MMPI, where drug users usually scored high on the Pd (psychopathy) scale. Three of the drug-using groups were significantly high also on N, the fourth approaching significance in that direction. Two of the drug-using groups were significantly low on extraversion, the other two not differing from the control population. These results suggest that drug users are similar in personality to psychiatric groups, and that P (predominantly) and N are involved in the causation of their behaviour.

This conclusion is borne out by a study in which Wells and Stacey (1976) approached 2,809 young people in Glasgow, aged between 16 and 24 years, and asked them to fill in questionnaires dealing with subjects' knowledge of drugs, personal experience, and other similar matters. Subjects were also asked to fill in the PEN, and it is the results obtained from this instrument, and the Cattell Anxiety scale, which will here be discussed. About one in three of the youngsters had taken drugs at some time, however infrequently, the incidence being higher among the males than the females. The highest incidence was in the offender group (56 per cent), with students only being average (32 per cent). Six per cent of the group took drugs regularly, according to self-report.

Table 51 gives the main results of the study, in so far as they are of concern to our argument. On P, N and Anxiety (which for all practical purposes is just another measure of N), drug users have higher scores than non-users, and regular users have higher scores than occasional users. These differences have good statistical significance, and leave little doubt that drug taking is related to psychiatric abnormality, with both P and N implicated, the former rather more than the latter.

In this study, greater psychiatric abnormality seems to attach to users of diverse drugs; a study by M. Gossop (personal communication) would seem to bear this out. Gossop studied fifty-nine patients attending the drug clinic as outpatients at the Maudsley Hospital. Thirty-nine subjects were intravenous users, all except two being narcotics addicts, and twenty were oral users, dependent on a wider range of drugs. The two groups did not differ with respect to age (mean age of all patients was 28 years), and they did not differ on E or L. The oral users did, however, have significantly higher P and N scores (8.05 vs. 5.39 for P; 19.35 vs. 13.97 for N). Combining the two groups gives the total drug-taking group P and N means

TABLE 51   Psychoticism, extraversion, neuroticism and anxiety scores (means) of cannabis users (from Wells and Stacey, 1976)

Sex	Cannabis Group	PEN scores			Anxiety scores	Number of subjects
		P	E	N	A	
Male	Non-misusers	2.95	13.25	9.33	6.47	697
	Occasional takers*	3.02	13.65	10.13	6.91	113
	Regular takers	5.01	12.78	11.96	7.38	78
	All takers**	4.58	13.77	11.09	7.21	352
Female	Non-misusers	2.75	12.26	10.38	6.68	659
	Occasional takers	2.42	12.15	11.82	7.40	61
	Regular takers	3.50	11.92	13.92	8.64	24
	All takers	2.89	12.16	12.37	7.42	123

*Who have never tried any other illegal drug.
**Who include, in addition to the above two groups, other takers who occasionally or regularly use one or more additional drugs.

significantly higher than standardization controls. This study thus agrees with the others cited in suggesting that drug users are characterized by a P+N+ personality. The possibility that the drug taking came first, and caused the personality deviation from normal, must of course be considered; it seems somewhat less likely than the alternative hypothesis, namely that the personality of the patient, in interaction with problems arising from interpersonal and environmental causes, was responsible for the use of drugs. The variety of drugs, use of which has been linked with this type of personality, is too great to make it likely that they would have had the same pronounced effect on personality. However, there is no conclusive answer to this question as yet, and the possibility of drug effects influencing personality remains.

Alcoholism may be regarded as a kind of drug addiction, and consequently it might be hypothesized that alcoholics, too, would be characterized by a P+N+ personality. A study by Shaw *et al.* (1975) suggests that this may be true, although the numbers of alcoholics used in this study are not sufficient to make the answer definitive. Included in the same study were depressed patients (unipolar depressions) of presumably endogenous pathology; some of these were retested after recovery, and the scores for these are also available after recovery. The alcoholics studied were primary alcoholics, and patients with sociopathic traits were excluded, as were those with concurrent depression. This selection ensures a lowering of P scores, and probably of N scores, in the selected population. All alcoholics had been off alcohol for a minimum of two weeks at time of testing. Table 52 shows the main results.

As far as the alcoholics are concerned, they have clearly elevated P scores among the males, but not the females; for N, both males and females have elevated scores. The N score differences are highly significant ($p < .001$), but for P the differences fall short of significance. It would seem likely that this is due to the small number of cases, but repetition of the study would be needed to establish this point. There

TABLE 52 Scores of alcoholics and depressives on P, E and N (from Shaw *et al.*, 1975)

	Male				Female			
	n	P	E	N	n	P	E	N
Controls	(415)	2.15	11.80	6.68	(279)	1.73	11.70	7.62
Alcoholics	(24)	4.33	11.50	11.71	(15)	1.52	10.90	11.30
Depressives Recovered	(18)	3.89	8.94	12.50	(28)	3.29	9.57	14.10
Depressives	(14)	2.29	12.00	7.50	(20)	1.75	12.60	7.75

may be a marked difference between males and females in this respect; there is no suggestion among the females that enlarging the group would make their scores on P different from the control group. There is no suggestion that E is related to alcoholism in any way for either sex, although for both sexes the alcoholics have slightly lower scores. It is not impossible that with larger groups these differences might become significant statistically.

For both males and females, the depressed patients have elevated P scores. The differences are not significant individually, but they become so when combined. Thus we have here some evidence that high P is found not only in schizophrenia, but may be characteristic also of endogenous depression. After recovery, P and N values are significantly lower, and E values higher, in both sexes; this suggests that the inventory might with advantage be used as an objective index of recovery.

A rather different study of excessive alcohol intake has been carried out by M. Hilton (personal communication), using prisoners as her subjects. Her subjects were all recidivists, tested in Wandsworth prison in London. Two groups were used: 123 medium-term prisoners, serving from twelve months to five years, and 96 long-term prisoners, serving five years and over. The following questionnaires were administered: (1) the Hilton Questionnaire on Drinking Behaviour (a Guttman scale measuring the extent to which drinking presented a problem); and (2) the EPQ. These tests were included in a routine battery given to all men shortly after their reception into prison. The two groups were analysed separately. Taking the medium-term prisoners first, the correlations between drinking behaviour and the personality scales were insignificant, but, as Burgess (1972) has pointed out, for the analysis of antisocial behaviour, theory suggests that some form of zone analysis is required. In other words, it is the combination of N+ and E+ which produces the antisocial behaviour, not E or N alone. Combining these scores into an E+N+ group, and dividing the Drinking Behaviour scale scores into high (11+) and low, Hilton showed a relationship which was significant at the $p < .01$, i.e. E+N+ prisoners drank significantly more. P even in combination did not significantly add to the discrimination, although the evidence suggested that heavy drinkers were under-represented in the P−E− and the P−N− quadrants.

Long-term prisoners gave a significant correlation between drinking and P ($r = .29$). Testing E and N in combination (neither of these traits was significantly related to heavy drinking on its own) failed to give a significant result, although the tendency was in the same direction as before. Combining P and N produced a highly significant prediction of drinking behaviour. Hilton has attempted to explain the differences between the groups in terms of the distinction between alcoholic criminals and criminal alcoholics (Glatt, 1965). As the terms imply, the former is defined as someone whose drinking is simply another facet of his antisocial, delinquent behaviour, whereas the latter's delinquent behaviour results from his alcoholism, and bears no essential relationship to his pre-alcoholic personality: 'If it is accepted that on average the length of sentence given to a man reflects to some degree the seriousness of his offence, and therefore the extent of criminal involvement, then it follows that long termers are on average more involved criminally than medium termers. That is, heavy drinkers in the medium-term group are more likely to be in prison because of their drinking than are heavy drinkers in the long-term group.'

Hilton suggested a major deduction from this set of premises, namely that criminal alcoholics are more likely to have experienced drunkenness before conviction than are alcoholic criminals. To test this hypothesis, Hilton took from her extensive data 'age first drunk' for each subject to whom this notation applied, took this figure away from age at first conviction, and added 50. This means that all those scoring more than 50 had experienced drunkenness before experiencing conviction, and so are more likely to be criminal alcoholics than alcoholic criminals. Setting this figure against the score on the drinking questionnaire, she found a significant relationship for the medium-term prisoners, but not for the long-term prisoners: 'This supports our . . . prediction that criminal alcoholics are more likely to have experienced drunkenness before conviction than alcoholic criminals.' This in turn suggests that P is more involved in criminality than in alcoholism as such, although the chain of deduction is perhaps somewhat lengthy for a decision on such an important question. This ingenious study may, however, suggest the complexity of the problem under investigation.

The observation of high P scores among criminals, drug users, alcoholics and other deviant groups suggests that similarly high P scores might be found among patients at a V.D. clinic, although it is of course realized that many such patients have acquired the disease, not through profligacy and concupiscence, but from erring husbands and other legitimate sources. Wells (1970) studied the responses to the PEN scales obtained from 161 men and 115 women, consitituting successive patients newly admitted to a clinic for venereal disease; only patients having acceptable L scores were admitted to the sample. The pattern of responses is so different for the two sexes that they must be discussed separately. Male patients differ from the standardization group only in that they are much more extraverted ($p < .001$). On P and N there are no significant differences. Female patients, however, are more introverted, and very substantially more neurotic ($p < .001$). On P, the female patients were much higher than the controls; they even exceeded the male patients ($p < .001$), although in the general population females have lower P scores than males. The mean of the male patients for P was 2.48, that of the female patients was 4.39; this difference is found both among innocent wives and promiscuous women.

Personality differences were also observed in the reaction of the patients to treatment. Among the men, high N and high P scorers were significantly more likely to default and leave treatment; E did not play a significant part. For the women, defaulting was associated with high E scores, not with P or N. Thus on all counts, male behaviour and female behaviour seems to follow quite different paths, and correlate quite differently with personality. It would seem very promising to study prostitutes with the EPQ; it would be very unexpected if their P scores did not reach considerable heights. The fact that female prisoners, many of whom had in private life been prostitutes, have been found to have such high P scores lends credence to this prediction.

Higher P scores for females, and a failure to find elevation of P scores, was also observed in another sample of an odd and unusual kind, namely persons enrolling in a course of 'transcendental meditation' (P. Williams, A. Francis, and R. Durham, personal communication). Thirty-nine male and twenty-seven female subjects, mean age 26, completed the EPQ, and their age norms were compared with the standardization data. The males were found to have significantly higher N and significantly lower E scores; in other words, they were largely dysthymic as a group. This was not true of the females, who however had significantly higher P scores as a group. Follow-up studies revealed that regular meditators had a significantly lower P score than did infrequent meditators (regular, 2.67±0.94; infrequent, 6.38±2.55; $p < .005$). These figures apply to the males; the number of females followed up was too small for meaningful analysis. These men also showed a large drop in N over the six-months period of the follow-up, from 14.44 to 6.11 ($p < .0005$). It is difficult to frame any generalizations from these data, but the failure of the high P scorers to practise regularly would seem to indicate a failure to follow through, to persevere, which we have found characteristic of high P scorers in other connections.

(b) Experimental studies

When we turn next to a series of experimental studies, we find that interpretation is both easier and more difficult. Experimental studies, as compared with clinical, have certain obvious advantages. In the first place, the investigation has a precise target; this enables the formulation of null hypotheses which can be disproved (or fail to be disproved) quite unequivocally. In the second place, the procedure involves laboratory manipulation; this in turn makes it possible to control many variables which in clinical investigations remain uncontrolled. And in the third place, the techniques and paradigms used have psychological meaning in terms of well-established theories, so that results can be evaluated more safely than would be possible in less well explored regions. The disadvantages are, perhaps, that laboratory investigations are much more removed from everyday life than are clinical studies, so that their relevance may not be obvious. In being linked with precise hypotheses, such studies may be premature—the possibility of framing precise hypotheses may not yet exist. Last, the theories in terms of which results of such experiments are evaluated may be erroneous, so that results are in fact misinterpreted. These are not reasons for abandoning either clinical or experimental studies; these two types of investigations complement each other, so that both may throw light on the nature of emerging concepts. Gradually, no doubt, the weight of investigation will shift from purely clinical to experimental, but it is clearly too early to suggest this as a feasible strategy for research on P.

The first study in this section (Thompson, 1973) investigated the hypothesis that high P scorers have difficulties in preserving set. The literature (already briefly summarized in an earlier chapter) shows fairly uniformly that schizophrenics (1) have longer reaction times than controls, and (2) benefit less than controls by having warning signals precede the RT stimulus. Thompson tested 103 male subjects in a complex design involving differences in the intensity of the auditory warning signal, and differences in the length of the preparatory interval (50 to 950 msecs.). Signal detection theory was used in the analysis of the data. Most of the results are of no interest in connection with the theme of this book, but two sets of data are relevant. Thompson found (as had Hendrickson, 1972, before) that high P scorers gave shorter, rather than longer reaction times. Whether this contradicts the findings on schizophrenics depends on the interpretation of the psychiatric data. It is possible that the slowness of the psychotics is due to institutionalization or to drug administration; this would be a trivial cause. It is possible that it is due to interference from psychotic symptomatology; this would not contradict our main hypothesis, although it would also not support it. Or of course it could be that psychotics have genuinely slower reaction times; this would contradict our hypothesis. At present, no final verdict is possible on this point.

The second set of data is concerned with the effects of warning signals as opposed to having no signals to indicate the arrival of the stimulus. Thompson concluded that 'psychoticism showed relationships suggesting that high P scorers may have difficulty in processing information as complexity and intensity increase'. This conclusion was based on the fact that warning signals, at all preparatory intervals, seemed to affect high P scorers inversely. As already noted, P correlates negatively with unsignalled reaction times (high P—fast reactions), but shows no relationship with either of the mean reaction time scores when warning signals are given. This suggests that high P scorers are hampered by the addition of the warning signal, as compared with low P scorers. The percentages of improvement from the unsignalled trials to the short and long PI (preparatory interval with warning signal) trials are shown in Figure 44, at four levels of P (low, medium low, medium high, high). As can be seen, none of the curves overlap; the higher the P score, the poorer is the improvement at all PIs. This regularity is quite marked, and suggests that the phenomenon is a very stable one. Thompson's interpretation of the results has already been quoted; it fits in well with our interpretation of P as psychoticism. Not dissimilar would be an explanation in terms of failure to preserve set; this failure can only occur when warning signals are present. The difference in reaction time produced by the addition of warning stimuli is thus a fair measure of the presence and importance of set, and its preservation over time. In this respect, then, Thompson's results are favourable to the theory which is being tested.

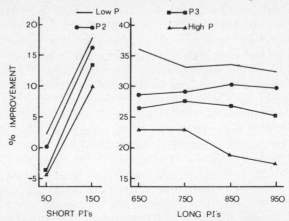

Figure 44 The effects of P on the percentage improvement from unsignalled stimuli to short and long warning signals in reaction time experiment (from Thompson, 1973)

Related to the Thompson experiment is a study by Stroh (1969). We have already noted that failure to preserve set is one of the most noticeable and widely replicated characteristics of the psychotic (particularly the schizophrenic) patient; if P is indeed related to psychosis in the manner postulated, then we would expect high P scorers to be also characterized by poor preservation of set. One experimental paradigm which mediates such predictions is that associated with vigilance tasks (Stroh, 1971). In tasks of this kind, subjects have to pay attention (preserve set) for lengthy periods of time to repetitive, low-intensity stimuli. Occasional stimuli diverge from the usual pattern, and have to be signalled; omission of such signals indicates lack of attention on the part of the subject. The prediction in such an experiment would be, therefore, that high P scorers would show poor vigilance. Falsification of such a prediction would not entirely invalidate the theory, but would certainly weaken it considerably.

In his experiment, Stroh (1969) used a one-hour visual vigilance task on seventy-two subjects. The task consisted of detecting light flashes of unusual intensity (either brighter or dimmer) in a regular series of light flashes. There were three levels of signal frequency (6, 18, and 60 per hour), and three levels of stimulus frequency (360, 1200, and 3600 per hour) in a factorial design. Analysis used signal detection theory, thus yielding two scores: d', a measure of sensory threshold, and β a measure of the subject's cautiousness, or subjective evaluation of the criterion required for response. Differences in β would be of little interest in connection with our hypothesis, which requires differences to be d'. The experimenter also took EEG, pulse rate and skin-conductance recordings during eighteen approximately equally spaced ten-second intervals, spread throughout the vigilance session. Basal recordings were also taken immediately prior to the beginning of the vigilance session.

P scores, taken from the PEN inventory, were correlated with both d' and β: only the former turned out to be significant ($r = -.30$, $p < .01$). The higher an individual's P score, the lower is his visual sensitivity; there is no evidence of any differences in subjects' criteria of judgment as a function of personality. This result bears out the prediction, and must therefore be regarded as verification of the general theory. It is supported by incidental evidence of a rather curious kind. Of the four subjects who scored higher than six on the P scale, three aborted (data could not be used; session was terminated prematurely for reasons other than equipment failure), and the fourth did extremely poorly, having detected less that 20 per cent of the signals presented during the hour. The three subjects who aborted had the highest three P scores of any of the subjects who were tested.

The method of rejecting the situation was different for each of the three subjects. After some twenty minutes on the task, Mr F suddenly began pounding all four of the response keys at once. He kept this up until the experimenter entered the subject's room. Mr H, on the other hand, insisted on being let out in order to go to the lavatory. Insistence, accompanied by demands for immediate release, brought about his release after some forty minutes on the task. Mr B's approach was by far the most passive; after displaying adequate ability on the practice trials, he sat through the hour without making a single response, either correct or incorrect. These three high P scorers were the only subjects whose data had to be omitted from the analysis for any reason other than equipment failure. Experimentalists who have worked with subjects on laboratory tasks will realize how odd and unusual such reactions are; they suggest that high P scorers probably found the task more disturbing than low P scorers (perhaps because of the inability to preserve set), and did not mind creating a scene in order to get out of the situation, or at least behave in an unusual manner. Their reactions certainly demonstrated an unusual lack of cooperation.

The physiological data did not throw much light on the behaviour of high P scorers. Extraverts, as expected, showed a lower level of cortical arousal (higher alpha incidence) than did introverts or ambiverts (at least at low levels of N); similarly, low N individuals showed less cortical arousal than did high or medium N subjects (at least at levels of E other than low). These results are not unexpected, but there is no suggestion that the poor performance of high P scorers is due to specific arousal defects.

High P scorers have been shown to have poor vigilance and poor set preservation; we have also seen that there is some indication that they may compensate by having high originality, defined as unusual associative ability. This hypothesis has been tested in an experimental manner by D.W. Kidner (personal communication), in a study using thirty-seven male and thirty-one female subjects, mostly students,nurses and teachers. They were administered the EPQ, as well as the following tests: (1) Acceptance of Culture scale—an eighteen-item scale intended to measure the degree to which a person accepted the prevailing British culture; (2) 'creativity' or 'originality' tests—this set contained three of the Wallach and Kogan (1965) tests (unusual uses, similarities, and pattern meaning), scored for both associational fluency and originality, to give a total of six scores; (3) two IQ tests, viz. the advanced Matrices and the Mill Hill Vocabulary scale; and (4) an education scale, relating to the amount of education experienced, and the enjoyment and acceptance of the experience. These items were correlated and factor analysed, but in addition an index of 'creativity relative to intelligence' was computed, using standard scores on the Wallach and Kogan tests, and subtracting from their sum the standardized and summed intelligence test scores. This 'creativity index' was not included in the factor analysis, as it was based on scores already included.

The raw correlations indicate that the index of creativity was correlated significantly with P ($r = .31$); the correlation with L was negative ($r = -.23$). The correlation with E was .21, that with N .09. P also correlated with the creativity tests, values of r ranging from .16 to .33, all positive, and with acceptance of culture, $r = -.52$! L showed negative correlations with the creativity tests, values ranging from $-.18$ to $-.30$; the correlation with acceptance of culture was .44. These correlations suggest that high P scorers are original and unsocialized, while high L scorers are unoriginal and socialized, a conclusion which agrees well enough with our previous discussion. The results of the factor analysis bear out this provisional conclusion; two factors were extracted which were clearly recognizable as *originality* (loaded on all the creativity tests, and also, much less highly, the IQ tests), and *socialization* (loaded on acceptance of culture, education, and vocabulary). Figure 45 shows the pattern of loadings.

It will be seen that P and L are situated just where theoretical considerations suggest they ought to be. P combines originality with lack of socialization, while L combines socialization with lack of originality. Note that L and acceptance of culture have almost identical loadings on the two factors, while P has loadings identical in size, but opposite in sign, to those of L and acceptance of culture. N is clearly not related to either factor; E is characterized by lack of socialization, which again agrees with prediction. Kidner concludes his discussion by saying that 'the

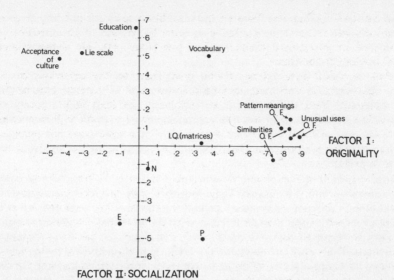

Figure 45 Two-factor solution of analysis of originality, intelligence and personality test intercorrelations (drawn after figures supplied by Kidner, personal communication)

analysis supports the viewpoint that the element common to "creativity" and psychoticism concerns the associational mode of thought, whilst a crucial difference concerns the success or otherwise of socialization processes'.

In another experiment, Kidner was concerned with performance on a tachistoscopic Reaction Time task in which the subject had to decide whether or not the word shown was a member of a particular category. There were sixty-two subjects, and they were administered a series of scales, including most of those used in the preceding experiment. Among tests not used previously was an 'adjective relevance' test; this was intended to measure the subject's ability and willingness to think metaphorically. It was in the form of an Adjective Checklist with the six nouns and eight adjectives arranged in grid fashion. The subject simply had to tick each grid space where he thought that the adjective was relevant to the noun. High scores on the test might perhaps be considered evidence of 'over-inclusiveness', a psychotic symptom studied in detail by Payne and Hewlett (1960). P was found to correlate with acceptance of culture ($r = -.53$), with the Wallach and Kogan originality tests (values all positive, but rather lower than before), authoritarianism ($-.57$), adjective relevance (.34), and average reaction time (.33). These results to some extent confirm those of the previous experiment, and add over-inclusiveness and slowness in categorization. But of course the main finding, corroborating several studies already mentioned, is that high P scorers have unusual associative processes, resembling in this typical psychotic (particularly schizophrenic) patients.

A rather different approach to the experimental study of P and psychotic reactivity is represented by the work of Hinton (1975, and personal communication). The hypothesis under examination postulated that 'if P is an index of psychoticism . . . then an index of one central feature of so-called psychotics, namely attention difficulty while decision making, should correlate positively with

P'. Thirty-nine university students constituted the population tested in three two-hour sessions. The experimenter used tests of sensory discrimination which were dependent on intra-sensory inhibition mechanisms, and tests of selective perception under conditions of inter-sensory interference. Auditory, visual and tactile stimuli were used. A measure relating to attentional effort was also recorded through the EMG; it is the increase in EMG in response to the task that constitutes the main measure of attentional difficulty. It was found that high P scorers did in fact, as postulated, exhibit consistently greater increases in EMG with attention to a task. The correlation between P and this measure of EMG percentage change with attention was .54, which is significant at the $p < .001$ level. Correlations of the index with N and E were insignificant.

Hinton repeated the experiment with male patients in a maximum security prison for the criminally insane. These patients gave a higher percentage EMG increase during the attentional tasks than had the students (211 per cent *vs.* 178 per cent), but the correlation of their P scores with the EMG percentage score was now −.66, i.e. significant in the opposite direction as compared with the students. An explanation for this curious reversal may be found in the fact that the patients had much higher L scores (6.8 *vs.* 2.0), and that the L scale, which had not shown any significant correlation with EMG percentage in the student group, now correlated very significantly with this score ($r = .63$). It may be useful to quote Hinton's own conclusions in their entirety:

'It is claimed that the EMG index is an objective measure of increase in muscle action potentials in response to simple perceptual decision making tasks, and this response cannot be faked under the controlled conditions of subject naivete. On the other hand, the personality test scores are open to faking—but the L scale gives the indication of the extent to which the individual is faking socially good. High L scorers might therefore be expected to be generally defensive in responses especially to the P scale. In the case of the P scale it is easy to identify items relating to paranoia or suspiciousness, sadism, extrapunitiveness and non-conformity in social attitudes. Students tested under conditions of anonymity have no reason to feel threatened and are not likely to be defensive, while many patients detained in a security hospital see good reason for responding defensively on questionnaires—showing themselves in a socially desirable light. Thus, students show low lie scores and detained patients show significantly higher scores. Also, the results show clearly that the higher the patient's L score, the more likely he is to give a low P score.

It may be argued that those patients who, if they were honest, would give the highest P scores go to the extreme to ensure that they do not endorse P items—they probably interpret endorsement of these items as likely to decrease their chances of discharge from the institution. This conclusion would be merely reasonable conjecture were it not for the correlations of P and L with the objective EMG index: the highly significant correlations of P with EMG percentage change is positive in students and negative in detained patients. Also, only in the Broadmoor sample is the L score significantly correlated with the EMG index. These patterns of correlations in the two groups clinch the argument given above. Thus, it is probable that detained patients who are really the most paranoid, suspicious, sadistic, extrapunitive and negatively evaluative of normal social attitudes are the patients who are the most defensive and fake socially desirable in answering questionnaires.'

If we accept this argument, which is well documented, we see again how important the inclusion of an L scale is for the evaluation of questionnaire responses; without it, evaluation of scores on the other scales can be very much mistaken. We also see that the hypothesis with which Hinton started out on his work is on the whole borne out by the data; psychotics and high P scorers among the normal controls show difficulties in attending for long periods of time, and have to muster reserves in order to do so. The calling up of such reserves can be indexed in terms of electromyographic responses, and the EMG percentage increase is found to correlate highly with P (or with L when dissimulation is very marked). Perhaps this 'attention effort' is only another aspect of vigilance, and its poor development among high P scorers; all these different studies seem to reflect the same underlying reality, along their different paths.

The various experiments mentioned in this section have attempted to verify predictions made on some sort of theoretical basis, e.g. the hypothesis that psychotics (particularly schizophrenics) are characterized by unusual associative connections, or that they have poor control over their 'sets'. A study by Maclean (personal communication) uses in a more primitive form the paradigm outlined at the beginning of this section, namely that P+ as opposed to P− subjects perform as psychotics as compared to normals. This means that, in the general conspectus afforded us by Figure 42, these studies are located more to the left, and represent a somewhat more primitive line of research. The difference is not absolute, of course; such theories as those mentioned are rather tenuous, and ultimately based on the behaviour of psychotics vs. normals; the difference is mainly that the theory is based on generalizations from several different studies, using divergent methodologies and tests, whereas the a-theoretical, purely empirical study is based on single tests. This means that artifacts (institutionalization, drug treatment effects, etc.) are less controlled for, and that consequently positive effects are probably more difficult to achieve, and negative ones more likely to occur.

Maclean administered the PI questionnaire to 569 male recidivists serving medium-term sentences at Wandsworth Prison, and to 595 male trainee drivers at a London Transport training centre. This control group was chosen because it resembled the prison group closely in sex, social class, and age. Table 53 shows the mean scores of the two groups on P, E and N; it will be seen that, as predicted, prisoners score more highly on all three variables.* From these populations, 200 men were selected to undergo testing on the objective test battery. The sole criterion for selection was that their P scores should be extreme enough to fall outside one standard deviation from the mean for their respective populations; this gives us fifty P+ and fifty P− prisoners, and fifty P+ and fifty P− controls. Each experiment compares these four groups, the optimum result expected being that if a given test had previously differentiated between psychotics and normals, then it would now (1) discriminate between prisoners and controls, (2) between P+ and P− prisoners, and (3) between P+ and P− controls, in the same direction. As an example of the methodology, consider the results on the dotting test.

Penrose and Wilson (1942) have shown that when subjects are instructed to tap with a pencil on a sheet of paper, schizophrenics show a significantly larger dispersion of dots and a greater patterning than do normals. Eysenck (1952a)

*Maclean also subdivided the E scale into two subscales, dealing respectively with Impulsiveness and Sociability. Prisoners were significantly more impulsive than controls, and P+ subjects than P− subjects. No differences were observed on sociability.

TABLE 53   Scores on the PI of prisoners and controls (from A. Maclean, unpublished)

	n	P	E	N
Prisoners:	569	6.65±3.12	12.47±3.67	11.77±4.98
Controls:	595	4.38±2.32	11.54±3.62	8.82±4.50
Significance Level:		$p<.001$	$p<.001$	$p<.001$

replicated this result, as did S.B.G. Eysenck (1956a). Foulds (1961) has demonstrated that paranoid patients scatter dots significantly more than non-paranoid patients. We would therefore expect P+ subjects (in both groups) to have higher scatter scores than P– subjects, and we would expect prisoners to have higher scatter scores than controls. The actual scores are 49mm and 32mm for the prisoners, and 53mm and 41mm for the controls. The only significant result is that P+ subjects have greater scatter than P– subjects ($p < .001$); the difference between prisoners and controls is not significant, and if anything in the wrong direction.

On another test, the U.S.E.S. pinboard test of finger dexterity, S.B.G. Eysenck (1956a) showed that psychotics performed worse than neurotic and normal controls in assembling and disassembling the washers and rivets which make up this test. In the Maclean study, there were no significant differences in assembling the pieces; but in disassembling, controls were significantly better (more pieces assembled), and P+ scorers made significantly more errors. In this partial fashion the P score replicates the original findings. On another set of tests, using expressive movements (S.B.G. Eysenck, 1956a; Eysenck, Granger and Brengelmann, 1957), no significant differences were observed. On yet another task, the Weigl colour-form sorting test, Keehn (1953) had found that psychotics tended to choose colour as the basis for discrimination significantly more frequently than did normals. Maclean found that P+ as compared with P– subjects, and prisoners as compared with controls, chose colour more frequently, but these differences failed to reach the $p < .05$ level of significance. A common elements test, similar in nature to the Weigl and also used by Keehn, failed to show any significant differences. On the Gibson Spiral Maze (Gibson, 1964) high P scorers were found to make significantly more errors.

Another test used was the Gottschaldt figures. There are two sets, A and B; Eysenck, Granger and Brengelmann (1957) had found psychotics to perform worse on these tests than normals and neurotics. In Maclean's investigation, P+ subjects were significantly differentiated from P– subjects on all measures, in that they made fewer correct and more uncorrected drawings. Prisoners also did worse than controls on Part B. These results are in line with prediction, although of course there is no good theoretical reason for making these predictions, other than the purely empirical findings mentioned above.

Two tests of memory were included in the battery; this seemed permissible because, although such tests usually correlate with intelligence (Eysenck and Halstead, 1945), the groups did not differ significantly on IQ. The tests used were the Graham and Kendall (1960) Memory for Designs test, and a recall/recognition test on which Nachmani and Cohen (1969) found that schizophrenics were significantly worse than normals. It was found that on the first test, prisoners scored significantly worse than controls; on the second test, prisoners were found to be more over-inclusive than controls. These differences are in the expected direction, but the failure of P+ and P— subjects to be differentiated is not. A word association test was more successful in that prisoners gave significantly more

TABLE 54 Test performance of high P scorers (as compared with low P scorers) and prisoners (as compared with controls) (from A. Maclean, unpublished)

Test	High P Scorers	Prisoners
Gibson Spiral Maze Error Score	More errors	—
Tapping Test Scatter	More dispersion	—
U.S.E.S. Pinboard Disassemble Disassemble errors	— More errors	Less disassembled —
Expressive Movements Wavelength Three Squares Time	— Quicker	Shorter —
Gottschaldt Figures Set A Set B Set A errors Set B errors	Fewer correct Fewer correct More errors More errors	— Fewer correct — —
Perception of Quantities Orderly Random	— —	Overestimation Overestimation
Span of Apprehension Single target letters	—	Fewer recognized correctly
M.F.D. Errors	—	More errors
Recognition/Recall Over-inclusion Errors	— —	— More
Word Association Uncommon Responses	—	More

unusual responses than did controls; there was also a significant tendency for P+ prisoners to make more unusual responses than P− prisoners, a tendency which was not, however, apparent among controls. A last test, the Mittenecker (1951, 1958) test of rigidity, failed to yield significant differences on any score. Maclean has provided a Table which lists the observed significant differences between P+ and P− subjects, and between prisoners and controls (Table 54). It will be seen that while quite a number of significant differences appear, and while most of these are in the expected direction, there is certainly no one-to-one correspondence between P+/P− and prisoners/controls. On the whole these results give mild support to the general hypothesis, but the simple argument by analogy is clearly less strongly borne out than the arguments from general theory previously considered. This may be a consequence of the natural superiority of the more widely based theoretical generalizations, as previously suggested, or it may be due in part to artifacts introduced by the use of prisoners whose conditions of life are so different to those of the controls. It is difficult at this point of time to pinpoint the cause of the difference.

(c) Correlational studies

In one sense, all the studies so far summarized might be called correlational; they all relate performance on a given task or set of tasks to psychoticism. However, the studies in the clinical section compare the performance of normal and psychiatrically ill subjects, while the studies in the experimental section compare the performance of P+ and P− subjects on a task selected to test a particular hypothesis about the behaviour of such persons. Correlational studies summarized here are more concerned with the observed correlations between P and some other scale which in theory ought to be related to P. The correlation between P and the Acceptance of Culture scale (negative) which we reported earlier on would be an example of such a study, had that correlation been observed by itself; the study was grouped with the experimental ones because this was only one of several relationships explored, some of which at least seemed to be nearer the explicit theory-testing paradigm. The nature of the distinction intended will be clear, even though there are no very definite boundaries between the studies included in these three sections.

Some of these correlational studies have already been noted in previous chapters, e.g. the connection between P and the Hostility scale and P and toughmindedness (Eaves and Eysenck, 1974). Nias (1973a) found similar correlations with toughmindedness on fifty-five male and forty female students, and fifty-five male and sixty-four female non-students who constituted a random sample of the general population. Correlations between P and toughmindedness were .37, .45, .30, and .40 respectively. Correlations between P and conservatism were negative: −.41, −.38, −.39, and n.s., respectively. The L scale, as expected, had negative correlations with toughmindedness (−.41, −.34, respectively for male and female students, and n.s. for the general population samples). The correlations between L and conservatism were significant for all but the male students (.45, .30, and .41, respectively, for the other three groups). Thus, overall, P correlates with radical toughmindedness, L with tenderminded conservatism.

Nias used as his measure of social attitudes the Wilson-Patterson scale (Wilson, 1973). In another study, using children, he found similar results, although the correlations are smaller (Nias, 1973b). Some 200 boys and the same number of girls were used, and correlations are reported for the sub-scales of the social attitude inventory. P correlated negatively with religious attitudes ($r = -.31$), and positively with ethnocentrism ($r = .17$), punitiveness ($r = .15$), and permissive attitudes to sex ($r = .19$). L correlated positively with religion ($r = .52$), and negatively with permissiveness ($r = -.50$). These correlations are all in the same direction as those for adults, suggesting that the relationship between personality and social attitudes is already present in eleven- to twelve-year-old children.

Wilson (1973) himself, using the PEN questionnaire, failed to find a correlation between P and toughmindedness on ninety-seven female student teachers. (Wilson prefers to call the second factor which emerges from his inventory when factor analysed 'realism'; we have for the sake of simplicity preferred to retain the older term.) He did, however, discover a significant correlation with conservatism ($r = .23$). He also reported that E correlated significantly with both conservatism ($r = -.35$) and toughmindedness ($r = .33$). This is the only study to fail in finding a significant correlation between P and toughmindedness among those surveyed; the reason is not obvious, although it may be that the special format of the Wilson-Patterson inventory may result in factors slightly different from the original Eysenck R and T social attitude factors (1954). The correlations between L and toughmindedness, however, are preserved ($r = -.26$), although in a somewhat weakened form. L also correlates with conservatism ($r = .26$). On the whole, the evidence suggests that P and toughmindedness are correlated positively, particularly when the original Eysenck scales are used for measuring T.

In a particularly impressive study, Forbes (1973) had his students fill in the PEN, the Comrey Personality Scale (Comrey, 1970), and the Hostility and Direction of Hostility Questionnaire (Caine et al., 1967). There were 201 students in this study, and the analysis of twenty-eight scales in all produced three major factors, easily identified as E, N and P. The loading of the E scale on the extraversion factor was .78, that of the N scale on the neuroticism factor was .68, and that of the P scale on the psychoticism factor was .64. (There were, in addition, three minor factors of little psychological interest.) The percentage of the variance contributed by these three major factors was 15, 15 and 14 per cent, suggesting roughly equal importance. None of the remaining factors exceeded half this value. This paper also includes an interesting discussion of the nature of P, as evidenced by the PEN scale; in view of the changes that have taken place in the composition of the scale it would not be useful to go into detail regarding its psychological interpretation.

A somewhat different approach was used by D.E. Grayson (personal communication), who employed the semantic differential technique, and related results from its application to the PEN scale; he also applied the Cattell 16PF scales to his subjects. His sample was made up of adolescent offenders. Fourteen concepts were chosen, supposedly relevant to the experience of the group, and to delinquency in general. These were evaluated along twenty bipolar adjectival scales, seventeen of which were taken from Osgood's original work, with three new ones added (rich—poor; fair—unfair; strange—familiar). Factor analysis showed that a major evaluative component was the only one having wide generality over all concepts, and scores for P+ and P− subjects were compared, there being fifty-eight P+ and fifty-one P− scorers. In general, the evaluative scores of the P+ group were lower than those of the P− group, suggesting perhaps that the P+ group were less well adjusted than were those with lower scores. The more significant differences were those relating to evaluations of human beings (father, mother, police, child, myself) rather than to things or concepts, although 'law' figures were significantly, and perhaps not unexpectedly, among the highly discriminative items. It is interesting to note that when subjects were subdivided by score on Cattell's superego factor, those low on this factor showed similar reactions to P+ scorers; this confirms our suggestion in an earlier chapter that P+ may be simply the obverse of super-ego mentality.

Brown (1972) demonstrated some value correlates of P. His sample consisted of 306 school children aged between 13:00 and 13:11 years. They and their parents were administered a composite questionnaire of value statements with a Likert-type response format, as well as the JEPQ and various other ratings, occupational aspiration, and awareness of role conflict scales. Factor analysis of the value items disclosed six main factors, of which two correlated significantly with P. P+ scorers emerged as less trusting and optimistic, and as lower in family loyalty; the correlations, although significant, were quite small. L+ scorers also emerged as lacking in trust or optimism, but high on family loyalty; they also scored high on drive/ambition, but had a poor adjustment to work. The study of values promises to be an interesting area for further assessment of personality correlates and differences, even though the results so far emerging do not show very high correlations.

A study similar in some ways to that of Brown is an investigation by Nias (1975) into the interests of school children and their parents. His sample was made up of 588 boys and 572 girls, with a mean age of thirteen and a half, and 603 male and 654 female parents, mean age forty-three. (For the most part, the parents were of course related to the children in question, but occasional failure to fill in forms, absence through illness, etc., makes the figures disagree.) The children and the parents were administered a lengthy interests questionnaire, as well as the EPQ, and inventories concerning personal details. A number of interesting relationships emerged between P and certain responses. There was a slight but significant correlation between parents' P score and occupational level ($r = -.15$ and $-.12$, for men and women respectively); in other words, P+ is (slightly) more characteristic of lower-class subjects. School absences are also correlated with parents' P+ scores ($r = .12$ and $.20$, respectively for fathers and mothers).

An interesting comparison was made between the P scores of children whose parents completed the questionnaire ('cooperative') and those who did not ('uncooperative'). In both sexes, the cooperative parents had children with significantly lower P scores than did non-cooperative parents, the mean P scores for boys and girls being 8.7 *vs.* 9.6 for boys, and 6.7 *vs.* 7.0 for girls. For both sexes combined, $p < .01$. Child-parent correlations for P were rather low; boys correlated with father and mother .03 and .04, midparent .07, while girls correlated .10 and .20, midparent .18. These low correlations are not due to low reliability of the P scores; over a test-retest interval of four months, retest reliability was .70 for boys and girls.

The interest items were factor analysed, and factor scores correlated with P. For both sexes, the major outcome was that P correlated negatively with academic interests ($-.15$ and $-.16$), and positively with sport (.21 and .25); there were also positive correlations with crime and horror (.08 and .19) and war (.21 and .06) films and TV shows. P correlated negatively with general interests ($-.22$ and $-.23$). For the adults also there was a negative correlation with academic interests ($-.16$

and −.14). In addition, women who had been interested in sport when young had daughters high on P. These general findings can be extended by looking at individual items, and their correlations with P. For boys and girls respectively, the leisure-time correlations are as follows: outdoor sports, .13, .27; indoor sports, .14, .25; watching sports, .03, .15; shopping, −.18, −.13. School interests show the following correlations: English, −.15, −.03; games, .18, .25; P.E., .19, .23; scripture, −.13, −.16. For TV viewing, correlations are as follows: horror films, .28, .26; war films, .22, .10; sports programmes, .06, .23; educational programmes, −.23, −.16. Similar correlations are found for reading interests: newspaper sport, .10, .18; horror stories, .19, .24; war stories, .18, .14. (In all these comparisons, correlations of .15 are at the $p < .01$ level of significance.) What stands out in all these comparisons is that P+ scorers are interested in sport and 'manly' pursuits, while P− scorers are interested in reading, learning, and scholastic pursuits generally.* It is of considerable interest here that Sollenberger (1940) has shown that high-androgen hormone groups of boys are more interested in heterosexual activities, personal adornment, and strenuous competitive sports than are low-androgen boys; this clearly forms a link between P+ and masculinity, similar to the relationship we have already established in earlier chapters.

One more study may be used to complete this section. In it, ratings were made of a group of sixty long-term prisoners (mean age 25 years) by three independent raters (wing psychologist, senior officer, landing officer). Extreme groups were formed in terms of these ratings, and their EPQ scores compared. The traits used for rating were chosen so as to be relevant to the situation, and applicable to the ratees, as well as intelligible to the raters. The study was carried out by D. Thornton (personal communication). The following ratings were found significantly associated with high P scores: immature and irresponsible; anti-authority and difficult; independent of inmates; independent of staff. Interestingly enough, high L scorers were found to be conformist, influenceable by staff; they also were found to hang on the fringe of social groups (unlike extraverts who were rated as being right in the social groups) and to avoid staff.

Thornton's comments are of interest: 'Immature and irresponsible correlates with anti-authority and difficult. This seems to refer to that subgroup of the wing whom the staff find hard to handle, and who are seen as being against prison authority. However, the independent ratings showed the strongest relationship to P, especially the independent of inmates rating; this implies that although this group (P+) are anti-authority, etc., it is not because they are part of the prison sub-culture which supports these attitudes. My hypothesis is that the staff find them difficult to understand or influence, and that consequently the high P scorers tend to run foul of the control system.' It is further suggested that 'the E scale had the fewest significant correlates, but the two involved suggest both the social and behavioural side of extraversion, emphasising being the centre of social groups and responding to frustration in an under-controlled, uninhibited way'. It is concluded that 'the Lie-scale correlates make a pattern consistent with avoidance of social disapproval by (a) conforming when socially visible, and (b) trying to avoid the limelight when possible'.

A final study, also using ratings, was concerned with the personality of male

---

*Correlations between P and sports interests are higher for girls than for boys, presumably because it is considered more 'natural' for boys to have such interests!

nurses (Brown and Stones, 1972). These authors investigated some four hundred male nurses who were followed up, rated, and questioned regarding difficulties and dissatisfactions during training. The PEN was used for personality investigation; intelligence was measured by means of the Progressive Matrices. The major findings concerning the P scale were as follows. Those who continued in a nursing career had significantly lower P scores than those who did not. Tutors' assessments tended to favour those with low P scores; in particular, 'those who were categorized as potentially good members of the nursing profession had lower P scores on average than those categorized as potentially poor'. When P scores were compared with comments on the first year's training, 'we found that only those men with low P scores claimed that they had liked the responsibility of nursing. Those with high P scores were more inclined to say they had not liked anything specific about their first year's training, although they did say that they had more trouble in getting on with other groups of staff, including women.' It was found that 'none of the high P scorers said they liked working under a woman. More of them complained that they could not rely on senior nurses for help and that not enough attention was paid to students' suggestions.' These results suggest that high P scorers have a querulous, non-conformist personality, get on poorly with colleagues, are not suited to a 'helping' profession which involves much social intercourse, and do not like social responsibility. These findings fit in well with our general view of the high P scorer. So do the findings from a follow-up study after qualification (Brown, 1974). P scores of those who abandoned training averaged 3.27; of those who left the profession after qualifying, 2.90; of those who were still nursing two years after qualification, 2.29. High P scorers are clearly a poor bet for nursing training courses, and may be so for other types of courses as well.

These correlational studies are all in principle 'validation' studies; an attempt is made to discover significant correlations with other indicants (tests, ratings, etc.) of traits or behaviours which theoretically should be associated with P. The last set of studies to be reviewed is concerned with quite a different aspect of P, namely its lack of national or cultural limitation. We have already seen that psychotic disorders are not culture-bound (even though some of the specific delusions encountered may be); it would seem to follow that P factors very similar to the one discussed here should be found in cultures very different from the Anglo-American-European culture in which the test was developed. We shall now turn to a consideration of several such inter-cultural comparison studies; some of these contain further information related to the validation of the inventory, and this will be considered in passing.

The first of these transcultural studies, done specifically for the purpose of comparison between different groups, was concerned with an investigation of English and Nigerian subjects (personal communication; O. Adelaja). The Nigerian sample consisted of 430 civilians of various trades. All the subjects had a basic minimum qualification of West African School Certificate, with at least a pass in English. All were tested in connection with examinations or interviews for selection into the Armed Forces Short Services; they were told explicitly that the questionnaire was unconnected with their selection or their medical fitness (some of the subjects were officer cadet pilots waiting for their medical). In spite of these assurances, it cannot be assumed that these subjects were not motivated to dissimulate, and consequently another sample of 246 male soldiers was administered the questionnaire on a random basis, under conditions of complete anonymity; these soldiers were not involved in any selection procedure. The English sample consisted of 404 men and 544 women; they were taken from the standardization group in such a way as to equate the age of the white sample with the samples of Nigerians. In addition, another comparison of 81 male British soldiers were used, in order to rule out the possible influence of occupation.

A factor analysis was carried out on the scores of the Nigerian men and women (101 of the Nigerians were female). Principal components analysis was followed by Promax rotation to oblique simple structure; four factors were extracted and rotated. The results obtained from the Nigerian sample were compared with the results of the standardization analysis of the EPQ. Of major interest here are the results of the factor comparisons which were carried out using a method described in H.J Eysenck and S.B.G. Eysenck (1969). For the males, the indices of factor comparison were: $P = .98$; $E = .99$; $N = .99$; $L = .98$. For the women, they were: $P = .66$; $E = .91$; $N = .92$; $L = .93$. Results for the women are less reliable than for the men, because the sample was much smaller; two items had to be left out of the P scale as all the women answered in the same direction; and in addition the women, as in England, had much lower P scores than the men. On the whole the results (particularly for the men) support the view that the structure of personality in Nigerians is very similar to that in English subjects. Reliability of the scales is lower, but not much lower, for the Nigerians; the correlations between the scales are somewhat higher, but not much higher, for the Nigerians. As regards the mean values, the Nigerians are characterized by high P and high L values, even for the anonymous group (which for our purpose is the most useful). They have a mean P value of 6.81, as compared with 3.60 for the British soldiers; they have a mean L value of 14.04, as compared with 8.13 for the British soldiers. Correction for dissimulation would of course raise the already high P values still higher.

In addition to these normal samples, a group of fifty-five male schizophrenics was also tested in order to determine whether among Nigerian nationals we would find the same elevated P and L scores usually found in British samples of schizophrenics. The mean score of these psychotics was 11.64, very much higher than any comparable mean ever found in white schizophrenic samples for P. The mean L score was 11.42, which is also significantly higher than comparable schizophrenic L scores in Britain. E and N scores are not particularly different from those we have found in British psychotic samples. Thus among Nigerians, extremely high P values (even when compared with the elevated P values common in Nigeria) are characteristic of schizophrenics. So are extremely high L values, although the fact that L values are very high even among normals makes this a characteristic of the national community, rather than of schizophrenics alone. It is impossible to know, without further study, whether the observed P values should be corrected upwards by taking L scores into account. Such a correction would merely paint the lily, and would seem unnecessary at the moment.

In an unpublished study, Saburo Iwawaki (personal communication) tested 284 male and 273 female college students in Japan with the PEN; he also tested 53 male and 57 female Japanese psychotics, mainly schizophrenics. His findings are of interest both in comparing two different civilizations, and also in discovering similar reactions of psychotic individuals in both, as compared with non-psychotic individuals. The Japanese students, as compared with English students, are more introverted (by over half a SD), more neurotic (also by over half a SD), and higher on P (by more than one SD). Japanese psychotics are characterized by higher P scores than Japanese students (by between half and one SD), and also by much higher P scores than English psychotics; in fact, English psychotics are at about the level of Japanese students, as far as P scores are concerned. L scores of Japanese psychotics are very elevated, as compared with Japanese students, by almost 1½ SD; in this respect also they resemble English psychotics. The data should not be overinterpreted, particularly as far as the national comparisons are concerned, but they do show quite clearly that psychotics in Japan show identical characteristics to psychotics in England, as far as scores on P and L scales are concerned.

A somewhat similar study was undertaken by Stanley and Watkins (1972), using an Australian population of 245 university students, males and females mixed, and with an average age of 19. (It may not be advisable to mix male and female subjects in studies of this kind, as it is not axiomatic that identical factor patterns can be obtained from the two sexes). Some of the subjects answered Form A of the EPI, plus a twenty-item P scale; others answered Form B, plus the twenty P items. Factor analysis disclosed a very similar pattern to that usually found in England for Form B, but a rather distorted one for Form A. It is difficult to account for this failure of one form to replicate the results obtained with the other; it is not likely that national differences can be responsible. It is more likely that the very small number of subjects enabled odd and unusual results to appear; small samples are contraindicated in factor-analytic work. There is also the point, of course, that Stanley and Watkins used a very early version of the P, E and N inventories; it was precisely because these did not give too good a fit that the EPQ was developed. On the whole, their work does not suggest that Australian samples would react differently to English ones, or give alternative solutions to the factorial problem.

Verma and Wig (1972) reported on the application of the PEN to seventy-eight normal and thirty-seven psychiatric patients in Chandigarh (India). The normals did not score in a very dissimilar manner to the standardization group, although their P and L scores were higher, and their E and N scores lower. This conclusion would not be worth reporting for such small groups were it not that the same trends were observed for males and females. Psychiatric patients (psychotic) were found to have much elevated P scores, lowered E scores, and high N and L scores; in this they resembled the English samples described in earlier chapters. On the whole, results from this Indian group are compatible with the view that cultural differences did not affect the scale to any marked extent.

Also in India, Prasad, Verma and Pershad (1974) administered the MPI, the PEN, the Personality Trait Inventory of Sen (1966), and the PGI Health Questionnaire (Wig and Verma, 1973) to sixty-four psychiatric patients referred for psychological testing. These scales measured altogether fifteen traits, including activity, cyclothymia, superego, dominance, paranoid tendency, depressive tendency, emotional instability, etc. Linkage analysis was carried out (McQuitty, 1959) on the matrix of intercorrelations, and three clusters were obtained which were identified as neuroticism, extraversion and psychoticism. The major correlates of P were paranoid and depressive tendencies, dominance and emotional instability.

The 'anti-educational' proclivities of high P-scoring children were explored in a study of sixty-four boys with extremely high IQs, taught in a special school for such boys in India (U. Khire, personal communication). The personality scales were correlated with school marks, reading-test scores, and intelligence (Progressive Matrices). P correlated −.56 with school attainment, but insignificantly with reading and with intelligence. Clearly, personality factors connected with P have a profound (negative) influence on scholastic performance, even when all the children involved have already uniformly high IQs. This study thus bears out for an Indian population the results we have already reported for English populations.

C. Plug (personal communication) used an Afrikaans version of the scales in South Africa on 306 students. He reported means, variances, and correlations between the scales. The means are not dissimilar to the English means, and show the usual sex differences, males having higher P scores than females. The correlations between the scales are all low, and similar to those reported in earlier chapters. Clearly, translation into Afrikaans and application to a South African population has not materially affected the basic characteristics of the test.

Rather more substantial is a study by Shultz, Miley and Evans (1976) on Caucasian- and Japanese-American college students in Hawaii, using the PEN. Altogether some five hundred subjects were used, and independent factor analyses were done for the two racial groups. A principal axes analysis yielded similar factor structures for males compared to females, and for Caucasian-Americans compared to Japanese-Americans. Furthermore, orthogonal rotations of the first three factors derived from these data revealed close correspondence with the P, E and N scales, and similar factor structures for the American subjects compared to the British scoring key matrix. These analyses justified reporting, for these two different samples, normative PEN scores which proved quite similar to those of British students. One major difference appeared between the two American samples—Japanese-Americans had higher P and N scores than Caucasian-Americans. This may be a simple sampling effect; as the study was not designed to look at racial differences, those that emerge may be the result of uncontrolled factors not related to race. In this study, too, males had higher P scores than females.

A Persian version of the PI has been used on a large scale by Mehryar, Khajavi, Razavieh and Hosseini (1973), in an attempt to replicate English work on the correlation of personality with scholastic achievement. Subjects were 18—19-year-old students taking the Pahlavi University Entrance Examination; 23,000 students were tested, but only a smaller sample is reported on. The major outcome was (1) that P was found to be correlated negatively with scholastic achievement, and (2) that 'on the whole, the personality patterns of more intelligent and academically successful Iranian students would appear to be more like those of younger British pupils (below 15 years) than their own age-mates'. The finding that P is negatively correlated with academic success coincides with the findings of Nias, already reported, as well as with studies by Savage (1972) and Brown and Stones (1972). Iranian results, too, thus give similar conclusions to those obtained in this country.

Ireland is perhaps too similar to England to make possible a trans-cultural comparison, but even between countries geographically close together important personality differences may appear. Bamber (1973) has published an account of the use of the Junior PEN in Ireland, using 14—15-year-old Grammar School girls (n = 107) and boys (n = 72), and Secondary Intermediate School girls (n = 74) and boys (n = 88). Means comparable with English norms were found for all groups, but there were also some surprises. Grammar School girls emerged with very high P scores, as compared with Grammar School boys, who had the lowest P scores of all groups; in the Secondary School samples, boys had the usual higher P scores, as compared with the girls. No suggestion springs to mind to explain this unusual finding for the Grammar School girls, but the overall finding is that the Irish groups do not differ in any other significant way from the English samples.

A very careful study of the P scale, in conjunction with E and N, in a German version has been undertaken by Baumann and Dittrich (1975a,b). This would not be the place to discuss in detail the very extensive work done by these authors, which included not only factor analysis, but also item analysis, taking into account difficulty level and discrimination of items. The results are very similar indeed to those obtained in England with the early version of the P scale in question; there appears to be little doubt that the psychometric properties of the P, E and N scales (and the L scale) do not change by crossing the Channel.

In Israel, I. Montag (personal communication) has correlated the P scale with the MMPI on 200 normal subjects. He reports correlations of .30 with the psychopathic deviate scale, .38 with the schizophrenia scale, .33 with the hypomania scale, and .42 with the F (validity) scale; these are very much like correlations found in Britain. He also found, in other samples, that men had higher P scores than women. In yet another study, he tested 100 males under standard instructions, and 100 males under special 'honesty' instructions (Eysenck, Eysenck and Shaw, 1974), correlating their P, E, N and L scores with Cattell's 16PF scales.* The major correlations for P were with ego strength (−.10 and −.27, for standard and special instructions, respectively); superego strength (−.45 and −.37); parmia (−.06 and −.32); self-sufficiency (.24 and .20); self-sentiment control (−.33 and −.35); and ergic tension (.25 and .38). On the whole, these correlations agree well with what would be expected on the basis of British work, particularly the negative correlation with superego strength. Extraversion correlated with cyclothymia (.30 and .33); ego strength (.34 and .27); dominance (.46 and .31); surgency (.60 and .62); parmia (.77 and .65); guilt proneness (−.46 and −.28); self-sufficiency (−.34 and −.34); and ergic tension (−.38 and −.32). Neuroticism correlated with ego strength (−.53 and −.66); surgency (−.32 and −.32); parmia (−.53 and −.44); guilt proneness (.58 and .63); self-sentiment control (−.19 and −.47); and ergic tension (.46 and .75). The L scale correlated with ego strength (.27 and .49); dominance (−.24 and −.21); superego strength (.46 and .33); shrewdness (.20 and .24); self-sufficiency (−.21 and −.26); self-sentiment control (.44 and .45); and ergic tension (−.35 and −.53). These values also are much as expected. It is worth noting that the complex structure of Cattell's factors can be reduced to our four major factors to a surprising degree. Ego strength, for instance, is not a simple 'source trait', as Cattell contends; it is made up of low P, high E, low N, and high L. Using the results from the 'honesty instructions', we find that a combination of P, E, N and L reproduces the Cattell score with as great accuracy as the reliability of that score permits.

Using another sample, Montag correlated the EPQ with the PSI factor scales (Overall, Johnson and Lanyon, 1974). Again the sample consisted of 100 subjects tested under ordinary instructions, and 100 subjects tested under special 'honesty' instructions. P correlated with 'major psychopathology' (.26 and .57) and social maladjustment (.20 and .31); E correlated with extraversion, not perhaps unexpectedly (.70 and .65), N with neuroticism (.54 and .67), and L with social desirability (.57 and .63). The correlations for E, N and L are of course more in the nature of reliabilities than substantive findings, considering that the scales were

---

*The use of these 'honesty' instructions had actually been pioneered by Montag, whose technique was taken over by Eysenck, Eysenck and Shaw (1974).

designed to measure the same personality traits; however, the correlations of psychopathology and social maladjustment confirm two aspects of our interpretation of the P scale for an Israeli population.

In a last study, Montag found a correlation of $-.17$ $(p < .01)$ between P and IQ as measured on the Progessive Matrices, for a population of 311 adult referrals for psychological assessment for manual and technical vocational placement. This slight but significant correlation agrees with other studies cited, both British and foreign.

A final study in this section is a report by Neumann and Kunftová (1974) from Czechoslovakia. They tested fifty criminals (most aged 25 to 30) with the PEN scales, and found that these offenders had significantly higher scores on P than the British standardization group (8.3 vs. 6.3). It is of course possible that this difference is produced by the national difference involved, and not by the comparison between criminals and normals; the study is of interest mainly because it was apparently possible to apply the scales in Czechoslovak language without difficulty. To prove the existence of a relationship between criminality and P in that country would require a more controlled study. Such a study was in fact carried out by I. Münnich, from the Hungarian National Institute of Criminality and Criminology; we have already discussed this in a previous chapter. He clearly demonstrated that when a proper control group is in fact used, differences between criminals and controls are found which are very similar to those discovered in Britain.

This survey of trans-cultural studies completes our evaluation of the literature on P; as far as these studies go, they seem to indicate that the scales constructed in Britain apply pretty much in the same way in a variety of other countries—Nigeria, Czechoslovakia, Hawaii, Israel, Hungary, Iran, etc. Most of these studies were not designed to test trans-cultural hypotheses, but where such comparisons could be made, they did not suggest that the applicability of the scales was seriously questioned. This must remain a fruitful and interesting area of study for the future; very little is known about racial and national differences in personality, and if the major dimensions of personality can be shown to be as fundamental in other cultures as in ours, then meaningful comparisons become possible.

Summary and conclusions

The major thesis of this book was that it would be feasible and useful to posit the existence of a major dimension of personality, independent of E and N, and also of L, which could be assumed to underlie the personality features so floridly exposed in psychiatric cases of psychosis. This dimension, labelled P for short, was posited to have a strong genetic basis, to run through the normal range of personality manifestations, and to be measured by reference to behavioural traits, rather than to psychiatric symptoms. We have discussed in great detail a variety of studies carried out in an effort to create and validate such a scale; what are the major conclusions, however tentative, to which this evidence gives rise?

1. It is possible to construct a reliable P scale, on a factor-analytic basis; this scale is independent from E, N and L. It discriminates clearly between men and women, men having much higher scores, and values of P decline with advancing age.
2. The psychological meaning of the scale, as expressed in the surviving items from a lengthy series of factor analyses, suggests that the P+ personality is solitary, troublesome, cruel, lacking in feeling, lacking in empathy, hostile to others, sensation-seeking, and liking odd and unusual things.
3. The P scale correlates with a wide variety of inventories and sub-scales from inventories such as the MMPI, the Cattell 16PF, the Foulds Hostility scale, the Jesness scale, toughmindedness, (non)acceptance of culture, and various others, in a predictable direction. It also correlates with ratings of such traits as immature, irresponsible, anti-authority, difficult to handle, and independent.
4. Experimental studies show P+ scorers to be non-cooperative, to have poor vigilance, to preserve set poorly, to have high 'creativity' or 'originality', as defined by unusual associative responses, and to have difficulties in attending.
5. Concerning the value and interest systems of P+ scorers, it is found that they undervalue people, particularly people in authority. Their interests tend to be in impersonal sex, war and horror films and TV shows, and in sport; education and cultural pursuits have a negative valence for them. Their artistic productions tend towards the bizarre, and their artistic preferences towards the unusual.
6. Clinically, P+ scorers are found in unusual abundance among psychotics (mostly schizophrenics, but also other functional psychotic types), and among psychopaths and criminals. Among neurotics, P+ scorers are characterized by poor response to therapy, whether psychotherapy or behaviour therapy. P-scale scores require correction by L-scale scores; psychotics have unusually high L scores, psychopaths do not, and neither do criminals.
7. Within psychotic groups, those most seriously ill, and showing the most virulent symptons (incoherent speech, incongruity of affect, hallucinations, coherent

delusions), tend to have the highest P scores. Improvement in psychotic disorder is usually accompanied by a lowering of P scores.

8. Genetically, P has a high heritability which is purely additive; there is no dominance and no assortative mating. D_R and E_1 are the major components of the phenotype; there is an absence of E_2 effects. The model for P is almost identical with the model which has been found the best fit for psychosis (in particular schizophrenia). The absence of E_2 (between-families effects) rules out certain cherished environmental hypotheses, such as the influence of psychotogenic mothers, etc.

9. P, like E and N, is not culture-bound. Factor-analytic and other studies in various cultures (Iran, India, Nigeria, Israel, Hawaii, etc.) have shown that the same major dimensions of personality apply there as here. Such trans-cultural differences as may exist are likely to be relatively minor, although of course still of interest.

10. Personality description in terms of a dimensional system, such as here advocated, is not *complementary* to the categorical psychiatric system of nosology, but is suggested to be an *alternative* to it. People are seen as unique configurations of positions on several dimensions, not as representative of diagnostic classifications grouping them together in categories.

11. P scores cannot be interpreted without regard to other aspects of personality. A P+ personality will have quite different impact when associated with very high or very low intelligence, or with an extraverted or an introverted personality. A P+ person who is highly gifted may, because of his originality and unusual associative responses, reach the 'genius' level in science or the arts; another P+ person, with a low IQ, may join the large army of the 'inadequates', particularly when also possessed of a low E, and a high N.

12. While there are causal theories regarding E and N, linking the behavioural manifestations of these personality dimensions with such physiological and anatomical structures as the ascending reticular formation and the visceral brain, the only link between P and more basic physiological concepts appears to be with *maleness*, and through it possibly with the androgen/oestrogen balance and hormonal secretions generally. There is too little evidence directly bearing on this hypothesis at the moment to advance it with any confidence.

These and other findings suggest that the concept of P as a psychoticism dimension (with psychopathy as a half-way stage towards psychosis) is well supported by a great variety of findings, observational, correlational, and experimental. The genetic determination of P is clearly established, and it is of particular interest that the model which best fits P also fits psychosis. These findings do not establish the existence of P as a *fact*; P is a *concept*, and concepts do not exist in the sense that material things do. Scientific concepts are judged in terms of their usefulness, their fruitfulness in generating research hypotheses, and their success in finding confirmation for such predictions. Along all these lines, we would suggest that P constitutes a fitting addition to the better established personality dimensions E and N. P complements these other dimensions in a unique manner, and extends their sway to a new range of behaviours, associated with psychosis, psychopathy and criminality. We believe that further research in this direction is likely to unearth many interesting and novel facts.

References

AFFLECK, D.C. and GARFIELD, S.L. (1960) The prediction of psychosis with the MMPI. *J. clin. Psychol.*, 16, 14-26.

ALANEN, Y.O. (1966) The family in the pathogenesis of schizophrenia and neurotic disorders. *Acta psychiat. Scand. Supp.*, 189, 1.

ALEX, C. (1965) *How to Beat Personality Tests*. New York: Arc.

ALLSOPP, J.F. (1975) Investigations into the applicability of Eysenck's theory of criminality to the antisocial behaviour of schoolchildren. London: unpublished Ph.D. thesis.

ALLSOPP, J.F. and FELDMAN, M.P. (1974) Extraversion, neuroticism, psychoticism and antisocial behaviour in schoolgirls. *Soc. Beh. Pers.*, 2, 184-90.

ALLSOPP, J.F. and FELDMAN, M.P. (1975) Item analysis of questionnaire measures of personality and antisocial behaviour in schoolboys. *.Br. J. Crim.*, in press.

ARIETI, S. (1956) *Interpretation of Schizophrenia*. New York: Bruner.

ARMSTRONG, H.E., JOHNSON, M.H., RIES, H.A. and HOLMES, D.S. (1967) Extraversion-introversion and process-reactive schizophrenia. *Br. J. Soc. Clin. Psychol.*, 6, 69.

ASH, P. (1949) The reliability of psychiatric diagnosis. *J. abnorm. Soc. Psychol.*, 44, 272-6.

AX, A.F., BECKETT, P.G.S., COHEN, B.D., FROHMAN, C.E., TOURNEY, C. and GOTTLIEB, J.S. (1961) Psychophysiological patterns. Paper presented at the meeting of the Social Biological Psychiatry Conference.

BAMBER, J.H. (1973) The Junior PEN Inventory in Ireland. *Irish J. Psychol.*, 2, 1-8.

BAUMANN, U. and DITTRICH, A. (1975) Kunstruktion einer deutschsprachigen Psychotizismus-skala. *Z. exp. angew. Psychol.*, 22, 421-43.

BAUMANN, U. and DITTRICH, A. (1976) Uberprufung der Fragebogendimension P (Psychotizismus) im Vergleich zu Extraversion und Neurotizismus. *Z. klin. Psychol.*, 5, 1, 5, 1-23.

BECK, A.T., WARD, C.H., MENDELSON, M., MOCK, J.E. and ERBAUGH, J.K. (1962) The reliability of psychiatric diagnoses: 2. A study of consistency of clinical judgements and ratings. *Am. J. Psychiat.*, 119, 351-7.

BLEULER, E. (1911) *Dementia Praecox or the Group of Schizophrenias*. Trans. J. ZINKIN (1950) New York: International Universities Press.

BLEULER, M. (1931) A contribution to the problem of heredity among schizophrenics. *J. nerv. ment. Dis.*, 74, 393-467.

BOHMAN, M. (1972) A study of adopted children, their background, environment and adjustment. *Acta paed. Scand.*, 61, 90-7.

BORISLOW, B. (1958) The Edwards Personal Preference Schedule (EPPS) and fakeability. *J. appl. Psychol.*, **42**, 22-7.

BRAUN, J.L. and GOMEZ, B.J. (1966) Effects of faking instructions on the Eysenck Personality Inventory. *Psychol. Rep.*, **19**, 388-90.

BRAUN, J.R. and LA FARO, D. (1968) Fakeability of the Sixteen Personality Factor Questionnaire, Form C. *J. Psychol.*, **68**, 3-7.

BROMLEY, D.B. (1956) Some experimental tests on the effect of age on creative intellectual output. *J. Geront.*, **11**, 74-82.

BROMLEY, D.B. (1957) Some effects of age on the quality of intellectual output. *J. Geront.*, **12**, 318-23.

BROOKS, G.W. and MUELLER, E. (1966) Serum urate concentration among university professors: relation to drive, achievement and leadership. *J. Am. med. Ass.*, **195**, 415-18.

BROWN, G. (1972) Concomitants of adolescent achievement values. Paper delivered to British Psychological Society Conference.

BROWN, R.G.S. (1974) *Male nurses—careers after registration.* Hull: Institute of Health Studies, University of Hull.

BROWN, R.G.S. and STONES, R.W.H. (1972) Personality and intelligence characteristics of male nurses. *Int. J. nurs. Stud.*, **9**, 167-77.

BÜHLER, C., BÜHLER, K. and LEFEVER, D.W. (1949) *Development of the Basic Rorschach Score.* California: Copyright 1949. Quoted from H.J. EYSENCK, 1970a.

BURGESS, P.K. (1972) Eysenck's theory of criminality: a new approach. *Br. J. Crim.*, **12**, 74-82.

BUTCHER, J.N. (1969) *MMPI: Research Developments and Clinical Applications.* New York: McGraw-Hill.

CADORET, R.J. (1973) Toward a definition of the schizoid state: evidence from studies of twins and their families. *Br. J. Psychiat.*, **122**, 679-85.

CAINE, T.M., FOULDS, G.A. and HOPE, K. (1967) *Manual of Hostility and Direction of Hostility Questionnaire.* London: University of London Press.

CALLAWAY, E., III, and DEMBO, E. (1958) Narrowed attention: a psychological phenomenon that accompanies a certain physiological change. *Archs Neurol. Psychiat.*, **79**, 74-90.

CARSON, R.C. (1969) Interpretive manual of the MMPI. In J.N. BUTCHER (Ed.) *MMPI: Research Developments and Clinical Applications.* New York: McGraw-Hill.

CARTER, C.O. (1969) An ABC of medical genetics. VI. Polygenic inheritance and common diseases. *Lancet*, **1**, 1252-6.

CARTER, M. and WATTS, C.A.H. (1971) Possible biological advantages among schizophrenics' relatives. *Br. J. Psychiat.*, **118**, 453-60.

CATTELL, R.B. (1946) *Description and Measurement of Personality.* London: Harrap.

CATTELL, R.B. (1965) Higher order factor structures and reticular-vs-hierarchical formulae for their interpretation. In C. BEECH and G.L. BROADHURST (Eds.) *Studies in Psychology.* London: University of London Press.

CATTELL, R.B. and BOLTON, L.S. (1969) What pathological dimensions lie beyond the normal dimensions of the 16PF? *J. consult. clin. Psychol.*, **33**, 18-29.

CATTELL, R.B. and BUTCHER, H.J. (1968) *The Prediction of Achievement and Creativity.* Indianapolis: Bobbs-Merrill.

CATTELL, R.B., DELHEES, K.H. and NESSELROADE, J.R. (1971) Personality structure checked in primary objective test factors, for a mixed normal and psychotic sample. *Multivariate Behaviour Research*, **6**, 187-214.

CATTELL, R.B. and DREVDAHL, J.E. (1955) A comparison of the personality profile of eminent researchers with that of eminent teachers and administrators and of the general population. *Br. J. Psychol.* **46**, 248-61.

CATTELL, R.B., DUBIN, S.S. and SAUNDERS, D.R. (1954) Personality structure in psychotics by factorization of objective clinical tests. *J. ment. Sci.*, **100**, 154-76.

CATTELL, R.B., EBER, H.W. and TSATSUOKA, M.M. (1970) *Handbook for the Sixteen Personality Factor Questionnaire.* Champaign: Institute for Personality and Ability Testing.

CATTELL, R.B. and SCHEIER, I.N. (1961) *The Meaning and Measurement of Neuroticism and Anxiety.* New York: Ronald Press.

CATTELL, R.B. and SCHMIDT, L.R. (1972) Clinical diagnosis by the objective-analytic personality batteries. *J. clin. Psychol.*, Monograph Supplement No. 34.

CATTELL, R.B. and TATRO, D.F. (1966) The personality factors, objectively measured, which distinguish psychotics from normals. *Behav. Res. Ther.*, **4**, 39-51.

CATTELL, R.B. and TSUJIOKA, B. (1964) The importance of factor-trueness and validity versus homogeneity and orthogonality in test scales. *Educ. psychol. Measur.*, **24**, 330-8.

CEPELÁK, J. (1973) 'Psychoticism' in toxicomans—imprisoned delinquents. *Activitas Nervosa Superior*, **15**, 155-6.

CHAMOVE, A.S., EYSENCK, H.J. and HARLOW, H.F. (1972) Personality in monkeys: factor analysis of rhesus social behaviour. *Q. J. exp. Psychol.*, **24**, 496-504.

CLARIDGE, G.S. (1967) *Personality and Arousal.* Oxford: Pergamon Press.

CLARIDGE, G.S. (1972) The schizophrenias as nervous types. *Br. J. Psychiat.*, **121**, 1-17.

CLARIDGE, G.S. and CHAPPA, H.J. (1973) Psychoticism: A study of its biological basis in normal subjects. *Br. J. soc. clin. Psychol.*, **12**, 175-87.

CLARIDGE, G.S. and HUME, W.I. (1966) Comparison of effects of dexamphetamine and LSD-25 on perceptual and autonomic function. *Percept. mot. Skills*, **23**, 456-8.

CLEMENTS, J.C. (1970) The effects on performance of behavioural manipulation of arousal in schizophrenics and controls. London: unpublished M.Phil. thesis.

CLONINGER, C.R., REICH, T. and GUZE, S.B. (1975a) The multifactorial model of disease transmission: II Sex differences: the familial transmissions of sociopathy (antisocial personality). *Br. J. Psychiat.*, **127**, 11-22.

CLONINGER, C.R., REICH, T. and GUZE, S.B. (1975b) The multifactorial model of disease transmission: III Familial relationships between sociopathy and hysteria (Briquet's syndrome). *Br. J. Psychiat.*, **127**, 23-32.

COAN, R.W. (1974) *The Optimal Personality.* London: Routledge & Kegan Paul.

COHEN, J. (1960) A coefficient of agreement for nominal scales. *Educ. psychol. Measur.*, **20**, 37-46.

COMREY, A.L. (1970) *The Comrey Personality Scales.* San Diego: Educational and Industrial Testing Service.

COMREY, A.L. and DUFFY, K.E. (1968) Cattell and Eysenck factor scores related to Comrey personality factors. *Multivariate Behavioural Research*, **3**, 379-92.

CONKLIN, E.S. (1937) Three diagnostic scorings for the Thurstone Personality Schedule, *Ind. University Publ. Sci. Ser.* No. 6.

COOLEY, W.W. and LOHNES, P.R. (1971) *Multivariate Data Analysis.* London: Wiley.

COOPER, J.E., KENDELL, R.E., GURLAND, B.J., SHARPE, L. and COPELAND, J.R.M. (1972) *Psychiatric Diagnosis in New York and London,* London: Oxford University Press.

CORAH, N.L. (1964) Neuroticism and extraversion in the MMPI: empirical validation and exploration. *Br. J. soc. clin. Psychol.,* **3**, 168-74.

COWIE, V. (1961) The incidence of neurosis in the children of psychotics. *Acta psychiat. Scand.,* **37**, 37-87.

CROOKS, R. and McNULTY, G. (1966) Autonomic response specificity in normal and schizophrenic subjects. *Can. J. Psychol.,* **20**, 280-95.

CROSS, P., CATTELL, R.B. and BUTCHER, H.J. (1967) The personality pattern of creative artists. *Br. J. educ. Psychol.,* **37**, 292-9.

CUNNINGHAM, L., CADORET, R.J., LOFTUS, R. and EDWARDS, J.E. (1975) Studies in adoptees from psychiatrically disturbed biological parents: psychiatric conditions in childhood and adolescence. *Br. J. Psychiat.,* **126**, 534-49.

DAHLSTROM, W.G. and WELSH, G.S. (1960) *An MMPI Handbook: A Guide to Use in Clinical Practice and Research.* Minneapolis: University of Minnesota Press.

DAVIS, H. (1974) What does the P scale measure? *Br. J. Psychiat.,* **125**, 161-7.

DELAY, J., DENIKER, P. and GREEN, A. (1957) Le milieu familial des schizophrènes. *Encéphale,* **46**, 189.

DEUTSCH, J.A. and DEUTSCH, D. (1966) *Physiological Psychology.* Homewood, Illinois: Dorsey Press.

DEVADASAN, K. (1964) Cross-cultural validity of twelve clinical diagnostic tests. *Journal of Indian Academy of Applied Psychology,* **1**, 55-7.

DE VAULT, S.H. (1955) Physiological responsiveness in reactive and process schizophrenia. Michigan State University: unpublished Ph.D. dissertation.

DICKEN, C.F. (1959) Simulated patterns on the Edwards Personal Preference Schedule. *J. appl. Psychol.,* **43**, 372-8.

DI LORETO, A.O. (1971) *Comparative Psychotherapy.* New York: Aldin-Atherton.

DOLL, R.E. (1971) Item susceptibility to attempted faking as related to item characteristics and adopted fake set. *J. Psychol.,* **77**, 9-16.

DRAKE, L.E. (1946) A social IE scale for the MMPI. *J. appl. Psychol.,* **30**, 51-4.

DREVDAHL, J.E. (1956) Factors of importance for creativity. *J. clin. Psychol.,* **12**, 21-6.

EASTERBROOK, J.A. (1959) The effect of emotion on cue utilization and the organization of behaviour. *Psychol. Rev.,* **66**, 183-201.

EAVES, L.J. (1973) The structure of genotypic and environmental covariation for personality measurements: an analysis of the PEN. *Br. J. soc. clin. Psychol.,* **12**, 275-82.

EAVES, L.J. and EYSENCK, H.J. (1974) Genetics and the development of social attitudes. *Nature,* **249**, No. 5454, 288-9.

EAVES, L.J. and EYSENCK, H.J. (1975) The nature of extraversion: a genetical analysis. *J. Pers. soc. Psychol.,* **32**, 1, 102-12.

EAVES, L.J. and EYSENCK, H.J. (1976) A genetic model for psychoticism. In press.

EDWARDS, J.H. (1969) Familial predispostion in Man. *Br. med. Bull.*, **25**, 58-64.

EHRENKRANZ, E.B. and SHEARD, M.H. (1974) Plasma testosterone: correlation with aggressive behaviour and social dominance in man. *Psychosom. Med.*, **36**, 469-75.

ELLIS, H. (1904) *A Study in British Genius.* London: Hurst and Blackett.

ELSTON, R.C., KRINGLEN, E. and NAMBOUDIRI, K.K. (1973) Possible linkage relationships between certain blood groups and schizophrenia or other psychoses. *Behav. Genet.*, **3**, 101-6.

ERLENMEYER-KIMLING, L. and PARADOWSKI, W. (1966) Selection and schizophrenia. *American National Academy*, **100**, 651-65.

ESSEN-MOLLER, E. (1941) Psychiatrische Untersuchungen an einer Serie von Zwillingen. *Acta Psychiatrica et Neurologica*, Supplement 23, 1-200.

EYSENCK, H.J. (1950a) Criterion analysis: an application of the hypothetico-deductive method to factor analysis. *Psychol. Rev.*, **57**, 38-53.

EYSENCK, H.J. (1950b) Schizothymia-cyclothymia as a dimension of personality. I. Historical Review. *J. Personality*, **19**, 123-52.

EYSENCK, H.J. (1952a) *The Scientific Study of Personality.* London: Routledge & Kegan Paul.

EYSENCK, H.J. (1952b) Schizothymia-cyclothymia as a dimension of personality. II. Experimental. *J. Personality*, **20**, 345-84.

EYSENCK, H.J. (1954) *The Psychology of Politics.* London: Routledge & Kegan Paul.

EYSENCK, H.J. (1955a) Psychiatric diagnosis as a psychological and statistical problem. *Psychol. Rep.*, **1**, 3-17.

EYSENCK, H.J. (1955b) *Psychology and the Foundations of Psychiatry.* London: H.K. Lewis.

EYSENCK, H.J. (1956) The questionnaire measurement of neuroticism and extraversion. *Revista di Psicologia*, **50**, 113-40.

EYSENCK, H.J. (1957) *The Dynamics of Anxiety and Hysteria.* London: Routledge & Kegan Paul.

EYSENCK, H.J. (1958) A short questionnaire for the measurement of the dimensions of personality. *J. appl. Psychol.*, **42**, 14-17.

EYSENCK, H.J. (1960) Classification and the problem of diagnosis. In H.J. EYSENCK (Ed.) *Handbook of Abnormal Psychology.* London: Pitman.

EYSENCK, H.J. (1964) (Ed.) *Experiments in Motivation.* London: Pergamon Press.

EYSENCK, H.J. (1967a) Personality patterns in various groups of businessmen. *Occup. Psychol.*, **41**, 449-50.

EYSENCK, H.J. (1967b) *The Biological Basis of Personality.* Springfield: C.C. Thomas.

EYSENCK, H.J. (1970a) *The Structure of Human Personality*, 3rd edn. London: Methuen.

EYSENCK, H.J. (1970b) A dimensional system of psychodiagnostics. In A.R. MAHRER (Ed.) *New Approaches to Personality Classification and Psycho-diagnosis.* New York: Columbia University Press.

EYSENCK, H.J. (1970c) The classification of depressive illness. *Br. J. Psychiat.*, **117**, 241-50.

EYSENCK, H.J. (1970d) Personality and attitudes to sex: a factorial study. *Personality*, **1**, 355-76.

EYSENCK, H.J. (1970e) *Crime and Personality*, 2nd edn. London: Paladin Press.

EYSENCK, H.J. (1971a) On the choice of personality tests for research and prediction. *J. behav. Sci.*, **1**, 85-9.

EYSENCK, H.J. (1971b) Personality and sexual adjustment. *Br. J. Psychiat.*, **118**, 593-608.

EYSENCK, H.J. (1971c) Masculinity-femininity, personality and sexual attitudes. *J. sex. Res.*, **7**, 83-8.

EYSENCK, H.J. (1971d) Hysterical personality and sexual adjustment, attitudes and behaviour. *J. sex. Res.*, **7**, 274-81.

EYSENCK, H.J. (1972a) An experimental and genetic model of schizophrenia. In A.R. KAPLAN (Ed.) *Genetic Factors in Schizophrenia.* Springfield: C.C. Thomas.

EYSENCK, H.J. (1972b) Personality and sexual behaviour. *J. psychosom. Res.*, **16**, 141-52.

EYSENCK, H.J. (1972c) Primaries or second-order factors: a critical consideration of Cattell's 16PF battery. *Br. J. soc. clin. Res.* **11**, 265-9.

EYSENCK, H.J. (1972d) The development of aesthetic sensitivity in children. *J. child Psychol. Psychiat.*, **13**, 1-10.

EYSENCK, H.J. (1973a) Personality, Learning and 'Anxiety'. In H.J. EYSENCK (Ed.) *Handbook of Abnormal Psychology.* London: Pitmans.

EYSENCK, H.J. (1973b) The questionnaire measurement of psychoticism. *International Research and Communications Systems*, **1**, 44.

EYSENCK, H.J. (1973c) Personality and attitudes to sex in criminals. *J. sex. Res.*, **9**, 295-306.

EYSENCK, H.J. (1974a) *The Measurement of Intelligence.* Lancaster: Medical and Technical Publishing Co.

EYSENCK, H.J. (1974b) Personality, premarital sexual permissivenesss and assortative mating. *J. sex. Res.*, **10**, 47-51.

EYSENCK, H.J. (1974c) Crime and personality reconsidered. *Bull. Br. psychol. Soc.*, **27**, 23-4.

EYSENCK, H.J. and BROADHURST, P.L. (1964) Experiments with animals. In H.J. EYSENCK (Ed.) *Experiments in Motivation.* Oxford: Pergamon Press.

EYSENCK, H.J. and CLARIDGE, G.S. (1962) The position of hysterics and dysthymics in a two-dimensional framework of personality description. *J. abnorm. soc. Psychol.*, **64**, 46-55.

EYSENCK, H.J., EASTINGS, G. and EYSENCK, S.B.G. (1971) Personality measurement in children: a dimensional approach. *J. special Educ.*, **4**, 261-8.

EYSENCK, H.J. and EYSENCK, S.B.G. (1968) A factorial study of psychoticism as a dimension of personality. *Multivariate Behaviour Research, Special Issue*, 15-31.

EYSENCK, H.J. and EYSENCK, S.B.G. (1969) *Personality Structure and Measurement.* London: Routledge & Kegan Paul.

EYSENCK, H.J. and EYSENCK, S.B.G. (1971) The orthogonality of psychoticism and neuroticism: a factorial study. *Percept. mot. Skills*, **33**, 461-2.

EYSENCK, H.J. and EYSENCK, S.B.G. (1972) Prisoners of XYY constitution. *Br. J. Psychiat.*, **120**, 124.

EYSENCK, H.J. and EYSENCK, S.B.G. (1976) Psychopathy, Personality and Genetics. In press.

EYSENCK, H.J., GRANGER, G.W. and BRENGELMANN, J.C. (1957) *Perceptual Processes and Mental Illness.* London: Oxford University Press.

EYSENCK, H.J. and HALSTEAD, H. (1945) The memory function: a factorial study of fifteen clinical tests. *Am. J. Psychiat.*, **102**, 174-80.

EYSENCK, S.B.G. (1956a) Neurosis and psychosis: an experimental analysis. *J. ment. Sci.*, **102**, 517-29.

EYSENCK, S.B.G. (1956b) An experimental study of psychogalvanic reflex responses of normal, neurotic and psychotic subjects. *J. psychosom. Res.*, **1**, 258-72.

EYSENCK, S.B.G. (1960) Social class, sex and response to a five-part personality inventory. *Educ. psychol. Measur.*, **20**, 47-54.

EYSENCK, S.B.G. (1962) The validity of a personality questionnaire as determined by the method of nominated groups. *Life Sci.*, **1**, 13-18.

EYSENCK, S.B.G. (1965a) A new scale for personality measurement in children. *Br. J. educ. Psychol.*, **35**, 362-7.

EYSENCK, S.B.G. (1965b) *The Junior Eysenck Personality Inventory.* London: University of London Press.

EYSENCK, S.B.G. (1966) *Manual of the Eysenck-Withers Personality Inventory for Subnormal Subjects.* London: University of London Press.

EYSENCK, S.B.G., ADELAJA, O. and EYSENCK, H.J. (1976) A comparative study of personality in Nigerian and English subjects. *J. soc. Psychol.*, to appear.

EYSENCK, S.B.G. and EYSENCK, H.J. (1963a) Acquiescence response set in personality questionnaires. *Life Sci.*, **2**, 144-7.

EYSENCK, S.B.G. and EYSENCK, H.J. (1963b) An experimental investigation of 'desirability' response set in a personality questionnaire. *Life Sci.*, **2**, 343-55.

EYSENCK, S.B.G. and EYSENCK, H.J. (1963c) The validity of questionnaire and rating assessments of extraversion and neuroticism, and their factorial stability. *Br. J. Psychol.*, **54**, 51-62.

EYSENCK, S.B.G. and EYSENCK, H.J. (1964a) Acquiescence response set in personality inventory items. *Psychol. Rep.*, **14**, 513-14.

EYSENCK, S.B.G. and EYSENCK, H.J. (1964b) An improved short questionnaire for the measurement of extraversion and neuroticism. *Life Sci.*, **3**, 1103-9.

EYSENCK, S.B.G. and EYSENCK, H.J. (1966) The personality of judges as a factor in the validity of their judgement of extraversion-introversion. *Br. J. soc. clin. Psychol.*, **3**, 141-4.

EYSENCK, S.B.G. and EYSENCK, H.J. (1968) The measurement of psychoticism: a study of factor stability and reliability. *Br. J. soc. clin. Psychol.*, **7**, 286-94.

EYSENCK, S.B.G. and EYSENCK, H.J. (1969a) Scores on three personality variables as a function of age, sex and social class. *Br. J. soc. clin. Psychol.*, **8**, 69-76.

EYSENCK, S.B.G. and EYSENCK, H.J. (1969b) 'Psychoticism' in children: a new personality variable. *Research in Education*, **1**, 21-37.

EYSENCK, S.B.G. and EYSENCK, H.J. (1970a) A factor-analytic study of the lie scale of the JEPI. *Personality*, **1**, 3-10.

EYSENCK, S.B.G. and EYSENCK, H.J. (1970b) Crime and personality: an empirical study of the three-factor theory. *Br. J. Crim.*, **10**, 225-39.

EYSENCK, S.B.G. and EYSENCK, H.J. (1971a) Crime and personality: item analysis of questionnaire responses. *Br. J. Crim.*, **11**, 49-62.

EYSENCK, S.B.G. and EYSENCK, H.J. (1971b) Attitudes to sex, personality and Lie Scale scores. *Percept. mot. Skills*, **33**, 216-18.

EYSENCK, S.B.G. and EYSENCK, H.J. (1971c) A comparative study of criminals and matched controls on three dimensions of personality. *Br. J. soc. clin. Pyschol.*, **10**, 362-6.

EYSENCK, S.B.G. and EYSENCK, H.J. (1972) The questionnaire measurement of psychoticism. *Psychol. Med.*, **1**, 50-5.

EYSENCK, S.B.G. and EYSENCK, H.J. (1973a) Test-retest reliabilities of a new personality questionnaire for children. *Br. J. educ. Psychol.,* **43**, 126-30.

EYSENCK, S.B.G. and EYSENCK, H.J. (1973b) The personality of female prisoners. *Br. J. Psychiat.*, **122**, 693-8.

EYSENCK, S.B.G. and EYSENCK, H.J. (1974) Personality and recidivism in Borstal Boys. *Br. J. Crim.*, **14**, 385-7.

EYSENCK, S.B.G. and EYSENCK, H.J. (1975) *Manual of the EPQ* (Personality Questionnaire). London: Hodder and Stoughton Educational; San Diego: Educational and Industrial Testing Service.

EYSENCK, S.B.G., EYSENCK, H.J. and SHAW, L. (1974) The modification of personality and lie scale scores by special 'honesty' instructions. *Br. J. soc. clin. Psychol.*, **13**, 41-50.

EYSENCK, S.B.G., NIAS, D.K.B. and EYSENCK, H.J. (1971) The interpretation of Children's Lie Scale scores. *Br. J. educ. Psychol.*, **41**, 23-31.

EYSENCK, S.B.G., RUSSELL, T. and EYSENCK, H.J. (1970) Extraversion, intelligence and ability to draw a person. *Percept. mot. Skills*, **30**, 925-6.

FAERGEMANN, P.M. (1963) *Psychogenic Psychoses.* London: Butterworth.

FARLEY, F.H. (1966) Social desirability, extraversion and neuroticism: a learning analysis. *J. Psychol.*, **64**, 113-18.

FARMER, E.W. (1974) Psychoticism and person-orientation as general personality characteristics of importance for different aspects of creative thinking. Glasgow: unpublished B.Sc. thesis.

FEIFEL, A. (1949) Qualitative differences in the vocabulary response of normals and abnormals. *General Psychol. Monographs*, **39**, 151-204.

FENZ, W.D. and VELNER, J. (1970) Physiological concomitants of behavioural indices in schizophrenia. *J. abnorm. Psychol.*, **76**, 27-35.

FISCHER, M. (1972) Umweltfaktoren bei der Schizophrenie. *Der Nervenarzt*, **43**, 230-8.

FLEISS, J.L. and COHEN, J. (1973) The equivalence of weighted Kappa and the intra-class correlation coefficient as measures of reliability. *Educ. psychol. Measur.*, **33**, 613-19.

FLOR-HENRY, P. (1969) Psychosis and temporal lobe epilepsy: a controlled investigation. *Epilepsia*, **10**, 367-95.

FORBES, A.R. (1973) Some correlates of psychoticism. *New Zealand Psychologist*, **2**, 2-14.

FOULDS, G.A. (1955) The reliability of psychiatric, and the value of psychological diagnoses. *J. ment. Sci.*, **101**, 851-62.

FOULDS, G.A. (1961) The scatter of tapping in mental patients. *J. clin. Psychol.*, **7**, 168-9.

FOULDS, G.A. (1965) *Personality and Personal Illness.* London: Tavistock.

FRANKENHAEUSER, M., DUNNE, E. and LUNDBERG, U. (1974). *Sex differences in catecholamine excretion in response to different stressors.* Stockholm: Reports from the Psychological Laboratories, Number 436.

FRITH, C.D. and NIAS, D.K.B. (1974) What determines aesthetic preferences? *J. gen. Psychol.*, **91**, 163-73.

211

FULKER, D.W. (1973) A biometrical genetic approach to intelligence and schizophrenia. *Social Biology*, 20, 266-75.

FULKER, D.W. (1974) Applications of biometrical genetics to human behaviour. In J.H.F. van AHEELEN (Ed.) *The Genetics of Behaviour*. Amsterdam: North Holland Publishing Co.

GELLHORN, E. (1953) *Physiological Foundations of Neurology and Psychiatry*. Minneapolis: University of Minnesota Press.

GELLHORN, E. (1967) *Autonomic Imbalance and the Hypothalamus*. Minneapolis: University of Minnesota Press.

GIBSON, H.B. (1964) The Spiral Maze. A psychomotor test with implications for the study of delinquency. *Br. J. Psychol.*, 55, 219-25.

GLATT, M.M. (1965) Crime, alcohol and alcoholism. *Howard Journal*, 11, 274.

GOLDBERG, L.R. (1965) Diagnosticians vs. diagnostic signs. *Psychol. Monogr.*, Whole No. 602.

GOLDSTEIN, I.B. (1965) Relationship of muscle tension and autonomic activity to psychiatric disorders. *Psychosom. Med.*, 27, 39-52.

GOMEZ, B.J. and BRAUN, J.R. (1967) Effects of 'salesman candidate' sets in the Eysenck Personality Inventory. *Psychol. Rep.*, 20, 192.

GOODMAN, R., SILBERSTEIN, R. and MANDELL, W. (1963) Adopted children brought to a child psychiatric clinic. *Archs. gen. Psychiat.*, 9, 451-6.

GOORNEY, A.B. (1970) MPI and MMPI scores, correlations and analysis for a military air crew population. *Br. J. soc. clin. Psychol.*, 9, 164-70.

GORDON, K.K. and GORDON, R.E. (1967) Birth order, achievement, and blood chemistry levels among college nursing students. *Nurs. Res.*, 16, 234-6.

GORDON, L.V. and STAPLETON, E.S. (1956) Fakeability of a forced-drive personality test under realistic high school employment conditions. *J. appl. Psychol.*, 40, 258-62.

GORDON, R.E., LINDEMAN, R.H. and GORDON, K.K. (1967) Some psychological and biochemical correlates of college achievement. *Journal of the American College Health Association*, 15, 326-31.

GORHAM, D.R. (1956) A proverbs test for clinical and experimental use. *Psychol. Rep. Monogr. Supp.*, 2, 1-12.

GOTTESMAN, I.I. and SHIELDS, J. (1966) Contributions of twin studies to perspectives in schizophrenia. In B.A. MAHER (Ed.) *Progress in Experimental Personality Research*. New York: Academic Press.

GOTTESMAN, I.I. and SHIELDS, J. (1972a) A polygenic theory of schizophrenia. *Int. J. ment. Hlth.*, 1, 107-15.

GOTTESMAN, I.I. and SHIELDS, J. (1972b) *Schizophrenia and Genetics*. London: Academic Press.

GOTTESMAN, I.I. and SHIELDS, J. (1973) Genetic theorizing and schizophrenia. *Br. J. Psychiat.*, 122, 15-30.

GOUGH, H.G. (1946) Diagnostic patterns on the Minnesota Multiphasic Personality Inventory. *J. clin. Psychol.*, 2, 23-7.

GRAHAM, F.K. and KENDALL, B.S. (1960) Manual for the Memory for Designs Test. *Percept. mot. Skills*, 11, 147-88.

GRAVES, M. (1946) *Design Judgement Test*. New York: Psychology Corp.

GRAY, J.A. (1964) *Pavlov's Typology*. Oxford: Pergamon Press.

GRAY, J.A. (1973) Causal theories of personality and how to test them. In J.R.

ROYCE (Ed.) *Multivariate Analysis and Psychological Theory.* London: Academic Press.

GREEN, R.F. (1951) Does a selection situation induce testees to bias their answers on interest and temperament tests? *Educ. psychol. Measur.,* **11,** 503-15.

GREIF, S. (1970) Untersuchungen zur deutschen Übersetzung der 16PF Fragebogen. *Psychologische Beiträge,* **12,** 186-213.

GRIFFITHS, A.W. (1971) Prisoners of XYY constitutions: psychological aspects. *Br. J. Psychiat.,* **119,** 193-4.

GRIFFITHS, J. (1975) Personality and symptomatology in psychiatric patients. London: unpublished Ph.D. thesis.

GUILFORD, J.P. and ZIMMERMAN, W.S. (1956) Fourteen dimensions of temperament. *Psychol. Monogr.,* **70,** 417.

HARTSHORNE, H. and MAY, M.A. (1928) *Studies in Deceit.* New York: Macmillan.

HARVALD, B. and HAUGE, M. (1965) Hereditary factors elucidated by twin studies. In J.V. NEEL, M.W. SHAW and V.J. SHULL (Eds.) *Genetics and Epidemiology of Chronic Diseases.* Washington D.C.: Public Health Service Publishing Corp., No. 1163.

HEBB, D.O. (1955) Drives and the CNS (conceptual nervous system). *Psychol. Rev.,* **62,** 243-54.

HENDRICKSON, A. and WHITE, P.O. (1964) Promax: a quick method for rotation to oblique simple structure. *Br. J. statist. Psychol.,* **17,** 65-70.

HENDRICKSON, D.E. (1972) An examination of individual differences in cortical evoked responses. London: unpublished Ph.D. thesis.

HERON, A. (1956) The effects of real life motivation on questionnaire responses. *J. appl. Psychol.,* **40,** 65-8.

HERRINGTON, R.N. and CLARIDGE, G.S. (1965) Sedation threshold and Archimedes' spiral after-effect in early psychosis. *J. psychiat. Res.,* **3,** 159-70.

HESTON, L.L. (1966) Psychiatric disorders in foster home reared children of schizophrenic mothers. *Br. J. Psychiat.,* **112,** 819-25.

HILL, H.E., HAERTZEN, C.A. and DAVIS, H. (1962) An MMPI factor analytic study of alcoholics, narcotic addicts and criminals. *Q. J. Alcohol.,* **23,** 411-31.

HINTON, J.W. (1975) Individual differences in perceptual discrimination, personality and arousal—with special reference to sensory inhibition and the effects of induced stress. Southampton: unpublished Ph.D. thesis.

HIRSCH, S.R. and LEFF, J.P. (1975) *Abnormalities in Parents of Schizophrenics.* London: Oxford University Press.

HOCH, P.H. and ZUBIN, J. (1961) (Eds.) *Comparative Epidemiology of the Mental Disorders.* New York: Grune and Stratton.

HODGSON, R.J. and RUNDALL, P. *The relationship between personality, ability to draw a person and the content of drawings.* To appear.

HOFFMANN, H. (1921) *Die nachkommenshaft bei endogenen Psychosen.* Berlin: Springer.

HOLLINGSHEAD, A.B. and REDLICH, F.C. (1958) *Social Class and Mental Illness.* New York: Wiley.

HOLZINGER, K.J. (1929) The relative effect of nature and nurture influences on twin differences. *J. educ. Psychol.,* **20,** 245-8.

HORN, J.L. (1975) Psychometric studies of ageing and intelligence. In S.

GERSHON and A. RASKIN (Eds.) *Geriatric Psychopharmacology*. New York: Raven Press.

HORN, J.L. and KNAPP, J.R. (1973) On the subjective character of the empirical base of Guildford's structure-of-intellect model. *Psychol. Bull.*, **80**, 33-43.

HOWARTH, E. and BROWNE, A. (1971) An item-factor analysis of the 16PF. *Personality*, **2**, 117-39.

HOWE, E. (1958) GSR conditioning in anxiety states, normals and chronic functional schizophrenic subjects. *J. abnorm. soc. Psychol.*, **56**, 183-94.

HOYT, C. (1941) Test reliability estimated by analysis of variance. *Psychometrika*, **6**, 153-60.

HUME, W.I. (1970) An experimental analysis of 'arousal'. University of Bristol: unpublished Ph.D. thesis.

HUME, W.I., and CLARIDGE, G.S. (1965) A comparison of two measures of 'arousal' in normal subjects. *Life Sci.*, **4**, 545-53.

HUNDLEBY, J.P. and CONNOR, W.H. (1968) Interrelationships between personality inventories: the 16PF, the MMPI and the MPI. *J. consult. clin. Psychol.*, **32**, 152-7.

HUNDLEBY, J.P., PAWLIK, K. and CATTELL, R.B. (1965) *Personality Factors in Objective Test Devices*. San Diego: R.R. Knapp.

HUNT, W.A., WILTSON, C.L. and HUNT, E.B.A. (1953) A theoretical and practical analysis of the diagnostic process. In P.H. HOCH and J. ZUBIN (Eds.) *Current Problems in Psychiatric Diagnosis*. New York: Grune and Stratton.

HUTCHINGS, B. and MEDNICK, S. (1973) Registered criminality in the adoptive and biological parents of registered male criminal adoptees. *Proceedings of 63rd annual meeting of the American Psychopathological Association*.

HUXLEY, J., MAYR, E., OSMOND, H. and HOFFER, A. (1964) Schizophrenia as a genetic morphism. *Nature*, **204**, 220-1.

INOUE, E. (1970) Personality deviations seen in monozygotic co-twins of the index cases with clinical schizophrenia. *Acta Psychiat. Scand. Supp.*, **219**, 90-6.

JESNESS, C. (1966) *Manual: The Jesness Inventory*. California: Consulting Psychologists' Press.

JESNESS, C. (1969) *The Preston Typology study*. California Youth Authority and American Justice Institute: Final Report.

JINKS, J.L. and FULKER, D.W. (1970) Comparison of the biometrical genetical MAVA and classical approaches to the analysis of human behaviour. *Psychol. Bull.*, **73**, 311-49.

JONES, M.B. and OFFORD, D.R. (1975) Independent transmission of IQ and schizophrenia. *Br. J. Psychiat.*, **126**, 185-90.

JUDA, A. (1953) *Höchstbegabung: Ihre Erbverhältnisse sowie ihre Beziehungen zu psychischen Anormalien*. Munich: Urban und Schwarzenberg.

KAHLBAUM, K. (1890) Uber Heboidophrenie. *Allg. Z. Psychiat.*, **46**, 461.

KAHN, E. (1923) *Schizoid und schizophrenie im Erbgang*. Berlin: Springer.

KALLMANN, F.J. (1938) *The Genetics of Schizophrenia*. New York: Augustin.

KAPLAN, A.R. (1972) (Ed.) *Genetic Factors in 'Schizophrenia'*. Springfield: C.C. Thomas.

KARLSSON, J.L. (1973) An Icelandic family study of schizophrenia. *Br. J. Psychiat.*, **123**, 549-54.

KARSON, S. and FREUD, S.C. (1956) Predicting psychiatric diagnosis with MMPI. *J. clin. Psychol.*, **17**, 376-9.

KAY, D.W.K., ROTH, M., ATKINSON, M.W., STEPHENS, D.A. and GARSIDE, R.F. (1975) Genetic hypotheses and environmental factors in the light of psychiatric morbidity in the families of schizophrenics. *Br. J. Psychiat.*, **127**, 109-18.

KEEHN, J.D. (1953). An experimental investigation into the validity of the use of attitude to colour and form in the assessment of personality. London: unpublished Ph.D. thesis.

KELLEY, T.L. (1947) *Fundamentals of Statistics.* Cambridge: Harvard University Press.

KENDELL, R.E. (1968) *The Classification of Depressive Illness.* London: Oxford University Press.

KENDELL, R.E. and GOURLAY, J. (1970) The clinical distinction between psychotic and neurotic depression. *Br. J. Psychiat.*, **117**, 257-66.

KETY, S.S., ROSENTHAL, D., WENDER, P.H. and SCHULSINGER, F. (1968) The types and prevalence of mental illness in the biological and adoptive families of adopted schizophrenics. In D. ROSENTHAL and S.S. KETY (Eds.) *The Transmission of Schizophrenia.* Oxford: Pergamon Press.

KILOH, L.G. and GARSIDE, R.F. (1965) The independence of neurotic depression and endogenous depression. *Br. J. Psychiat.*, **109**, 451-63.

KLING, A. (1973) Testosterone and aggression. Paper presented at APA meeting, Hawaii, June 1973. Quoted by Ehrenkranz and Sheard, 1974.

KRAEPELIN, E. (1913) *Psychiatrie*, Vol. III, 8th edn. Leipzig: Barth.

KRAMER, M., POLLACK, E.S. and REDICK, R.W. (1961) Studies of the incidence and prevalence of hospitalized mental disorders in the United States: current status and future goals. In P.H. HOCH and J. ZUBIN (Eds.) *Comparative Epidemiology of the Mental Disorders.* New York: Grune and Stratton.

KRAULIS, W. (1939) Zur Klinik der Erbpsychosen. *Allg. Z. Psychiat.*, **113**, 32.

KREITMAN, N. (1961) The reliability of psychiatric diagnosis. *J. ment. Sci.*, **107**, 876-86.

KRETSCHMER, E. (1929) *Geniale Menschen.* Berlin: Springer.

KRETSCHMER, E. (1948) *Körperbau und Charakter.* Berlin: Springer.

KREUZ, L.E. and ROSE, R.M. (1972) Assessment of aggressive behaviour and plasma testosterone in a young criminal population. *Psychosom. Med.* **34**, 331-6.

KRINGLEN, E. (1966) Schizophrenia in twins: an epidemiological study. *Psychiatry*, **29**, 172-84.

KRINGLEN, E. (1967a) Hereditary and social factors in schizophrenic twins. In ROMANO, J. (Ed.) *Origins of Schizophrenia.* Amsterdam: Excerpta Medica Foundation.

KRINGLEN, E. (1967b) *Heredity and Environment in the Functional Psychoses.* Oslo: Universitetsforlaget.

KRINGLEN, E. (1968) An epidemiological-clinical twin study on schizophrenia. In D. ROSENTHAL and S.S. KETY (Eds.) *The Transmission of Schizophrenia.* Oxford: Pergamon.

KRISHNAMOORTI, S.R. and SHAGASS, C. (1964) Some psychological test correlates of sedation threshold. In J. WORTIS (Ed.) *Recent Advances in Biological Psychiatry.* New York: Plenum.

KUDER, G.F. (1950) Identifying the faker. *Personnel Psychol.*, **3**, 155-67.

LAKATOS, I. and MUSGRAVE, A. (1971) *Criticism and the Growth of Knowledge.* London: Cambridge University Press.

LEVONIAN, F. (1961a) A statistical analysis of the 16 Personality Factors Questionnaire. *Educ. psychol. Measur.*, 21, 589-96.

LEVONIAN, F. (1961b) Personality measurement with items selected from the 16PF Questionnaire. *Educ. psychol. Measur.*, 21, 937-46.

LEWIS, A.J.(1934) Melancholia: a clinical survey of depressive states. *J. ment. Sci.*, 80, 277-378.

LEWIS, A.J. (1974) Psychopathic personality: a most elusive category. *Psychol. Med.*, 4, 133-40.

LIDZ, T., WILD, C., SCHAFER, S., ROSMAN, B. and FLECK, S. (1963) Thought disorders in the parents of schizophrenic patients: a study utilizing the object sorting test. *J. psychiat. Res.*, 1, 193-200.

LIGHT, R.J. (1971) Measures of agreement for qualitative data: some generalizations and alternatives. *Psychol. Bull.*, 76, 365-73.

LIN, T.Y. and SARTORIUS, N. (1974) *Report of the International Pilot Study of Schizophrenia.* Geneva: World Health Organization.

LITTLE, B.R. (1972) (Ed.) *New Perspectives in Personality.* Harmondsworth: Penguin.

LONGSTAFF, H.P. and JURGENSEN, C.E. (1953) Fakeability of the Jurgensen Classification Inventory. *J. appl. Psychol.*, 37, 86-9.

LORR, M., KLETT, C.J., McNAIR, D.M. and LASKY, J.J. (1963) *Inpatient Multidimensional Psychiatric Scale: Manual.* Palo Alto: Consulting Psychologists' Press.

LUBIN, A. (1951) Some contributions to the testing of psychological hypotheses by means of statistical multivariate analysis. London: unpublished Ph.D. thesis.

LYKKEN, D.T. and MALEY, M. (1968) Autonomic versus cortical arousal in schizophrenics and non-psychotics. *J. psychiat. Res.*, 6, 21-32.

LYKKEN, D.T. and ROSE, R. (1963) Psychological prediction from actuarial tables. *J. clin. Psychol.*, 19, 139-51.

LYKKEN, D.T., ROSE, R., LUTHER, B. and MALEY, M. (1966) Correcting psychophysiological measures for individual differences in range. *Psychol. Bull.*, 66, 481-4.

LYNN, R. (1963) Russian theory and research in schizophrenia. *Psychol. Bull.*, 60, 486-98.

McALLISTER, J. (1968) Fould's 'Continuum of personal illness' and the 16PF. *Br. J. Psychiat.*, 114, 53-6.

McCONAGHY, N. (1959) The use of an object sorting test in elucidating the hereditary factor in schizophrenia. *J. Neurol. Neurosurg. Psychiat.*, 22, 243-6.

McCONAGHY, N. (1960) Modes of abstract thinking and psychosis. *Am. J. Psychiat.*, 117, 106-10.

McCONAGHY, N. and CLANCY, M. (1968) Familial relationships of allusive thinking in university students and their parents. *Br. J. Psychiat.*, 114, 1079-87.

McCONAGHY, N., JOFFE, J.D. and MURPHY, B. (1967) The independence of neurotic and endogenous depression. *Br. J. Psychiat.*, 113, 479-84.

McGILVERY, R.W. (1970) *Biochemistry.* Philadelphia: W.B. Saunders.

McGUIRE, R.J. (1973) Classification and the problem of diagnosis. In H.J. EYSENCK (Ed.) *Handbook of Abnormal Psychology.* London: Pitman.

MacKINNON, D.W. (1962) The personality correlates of creativity. In *Proceedings of the Fourteenth Congress on Applied Psychology*, vol. 2. Copenhagen: Munksgaard.

McMULLEN, T. (1967) Personality questionnaires of differential psychiatric diagnosis. Sydney: unpublished Ph.D. thesis.

McPHERSON, F.M., PRESLEY, A.S., ARMSTRONG, J. and CURTIS, R.H. (1974) 'Psychoticism' and psychotic illness. *Br. J. Psychiat.*, **125**, 152-60.

McQUITTY, L.L. (1959) Elementary linkage analysis for isolating orthogonal and oblique types and typal relevancies. *Educ. psychol. Measure.*, **17**, 207-14.

MASSERMAN, J.W. and CARMICHAEL, H.T. (1938) Diagnosis and prognosis in psychiatry: with a follow-up study of the results of short term general hospital therapy of psychiatric cases. *J. ment. Sci.*, **84**, 893-946.

MATHER, K. and JINKS, J.L. (1971) *Biometrical Genetics.* London: Chapman and Hall.

MAYER-GROSS, W., SLATER, E. and ROTH, M. (1969) *Clinical Psychiatry*, 3rd. edn. London: Baillière, Tindall and Cassell.

MEDNICK, S.A. (1958) Learning theory approach to research in schizophrenia. *Psychol. Bull.*, **55**, 316-27.

MEDNICK, S.A. and SCHULSINGER, F. (1968) Some pre-morbid characteristics related to breakdown in children with schizophrenic mothers. In D. ROSENTHAL and S.S. KETY (Eds.) *The Transmission of Schizophrenia.* Oxford: Pergamon Press.

MEDNICK, S.A., SCHULSINGER, F., HIGGINS, J. and BELL, B. (1974) (Eds.) *Genetics, Environment and Psychopathology.* New York: American Elsevier Publishing Co.

MEDOW, W. (1914) Zur Erblichkeit in der Psychiatrie. *Z. ges. neurol. Psychiat.*, **26**, 493.

MEEHL, P.E. (1956) Profile analysis of the MMPI in differential diagnosis. In A.S. WELSH and W.C. DAHLSTROM (Eds.) *Basic Readings on the MMPI in Psychology and Medicine.* Minneapolis: University of Minnesota Press.

MEGGENDORFER, F. (1921) Klinische und genealogische Untersuchungen über 'Moral Insanity'. *Z. ges. neurol. Psychiat.*, **66**, 208.

MEHLMAN, B. (1952) The reliability of psychiatric diagnosis. *J. abnorm. soc. Psychol.*, **47**, 577-8.

MEHRYAR, A.H., KHAJAVI, F., RAZAVIEH, A. and HOSSEINI, A. (1973) Some personality correlates of intelligence and educational attainment: Iran. *Br. J. educ. Psychol.*, **43**, 8-16.

MICHAEL, C.M., MORRIS, D.P. and SOROKER, E. (1957) Follow-up studies of shy withdrawn children. II: Relative incidence of schizophrenia. *Am. J. Orthopsychiat.*, **27**, 331-7.

MICHAELIS, W. and EYSENCK, H.J. (1971) The determination of personality inventory factor patterns and intercorrelations by changes in real-life motivation. *J. genet. Psychol.*, **118**, 223-34.

MIKKELSEN, W.M., DODGE, H.J. and VALKENBURG, U. (1965) The distribution of serum uric acid values in a population unselected as to gout or hyperuricemia. *Am. J. Med.*, **39**, 242-51.

MITTENECKER, E. (1951) Eine neue quantitative Methode in der Sprachanalyse und ihre Anwendung bei Schizophrenen. *Monatsschrift für Psychiatrie und Neurologie*, **6**, 364-75.

MITTENECKER, E. (1958) Die Analyse 'zufälliger' Reaktionsfolgen. *Z. exp. angew. Psychol.*, **5**, 45-64.

MOON, A.F., MEFFERD, R.B., WIELAND, B.A., POKORNY, A.D. and

FALCONER, G.A. (1968) Perceptual dysfunction as a determinant of schizo-phrenic word associations. *J. nerv. ment. Dis.,* **46,** 80-4.

MORRIS, W.W. (1947) A preliminary evaluation of the Minnesota Multiphasic Personality Inventory. *J. clin. Psychol.,* **3,** 370-4.

MOSHER, L. POLLIN, W. and STAHENAN, J. (1971) Identical twins discordant for schizophrenia. *Archs gen. Psychiat.,* **24,** 422-30.

NACHMANI, G. and COHEN, B.D. (1969) Recall and recognition in free learning in schizophrenics. *J. abnorm. Psychol.,* **74,** 511-16.

NEEL, J.V. and SCHULL, W.J. (1954) *Human Heredity.* Chicago: University of Chicago Press.

NEUMANN, J. and KUNFTOVÁ, J. (1974) Dimenze psychoticismu H.J. Eysenck av Kriminologickém vyzkumu. *Ceskoslovenska Psychiatrie,* **70,** 37-41.

NIAS, D.K.B. (1972a) A note on the effects of administration conditions upon personality scores in children. *J. child Psychol. Psychiat.,* **13,** 115-19.

NIAS, D.K.B. (1972b) The effects of providing a warning about the Lie Scale in a personality inventory. *Br. J. educ. Psychol.,* **42,** 308-12.

NIAS, D.K.B. (1973a) Attitude to the Common Market: a case study of conservatism. In G.D. WILSON (Ed.) *The Psychology of Conservatism,* 239-55. London: Academic Press.

NIAS, D.K.B. (1973b) Measurement and structure of children's attitudes. In G.D. WILSON (Ed.) *The Psychology of Conservatism,* 93-113. London: Academic Press.

NIAS, D.K.B. (1975) Personality and other factors determining the recreational interests of children and adults. London: unpublished Ph.D. thesis.

NICHOLS, R.C. (1965) National Merit twin study. In S.G. VANDENBERG (Ed.) *Methods and Goals in Human Behaviour Genetics.* New York: Academic Press.

NORMAN, W.T. (1963) Personality measurement, faking and detection: an assessment method for use in personnel selection. *J. appl. Psychol.,* **47,** 225-41.

ÖDEGARD, Ö. (1963) The psychiatric disease entities in the light of a genetic investigation. *Acta psychiat. Scand. Supp.,* **169,** 94.

ÖDEGARD, Ö. (1972) The multifactorial theory of inheritance in predisposition to schizophrenia. In R.A. KAPLAN (Ed.) *Genetic Factors in 'Schizophrenia'.* Springfield: C.C. Thomas.

O'DONOVAN, D. (1969) An historical review of the Lie Scale—with particular reference to the Maudsley Personality Inventory. *Papers in Psychology,* **3,** 13-19.

OFFORD, D.R., APONTE, J. and CROSS, L.A. (1969) Presenting symptomatology of adopted children. *Archs gen. Psychiat.,* **20,** 110-16.

OVERALL, J.E., JOHNSON, J.H. and LANYON, R.I. (1974) Factor structure and scoring of the PSI: an application of marker variable analysis. *Multivariate Behavioural Research,* **9,** 407-22.

PAGE, J. (1934) Introversion-extraversion and the functional psychoses. *J. appl. Psychol.,* **18,** 478-88.

PAINTAL, A.S. (1951) A comparison of the galvanic skin responses in normals and psychotics. *J. exp. Psychol.,* **41,** 425-8.

PAWLIK, K. (1973) Right answers to wrong questions? A re-examination of factor analytic personality research and its contribution to personality theory. In J.R. ROYCE (Ed.) *Multivariate Analysis and Psychological Theory,* 17-44. London: Academic Press.

PAYNE, R.W. (1955) Experimentelle Untersuchungen zum Spaltungsbegriff von Kretschmer. *Z. exp. angew. Psychol.*, **3**, 65-97.

PAYNE, R.W. and HEWLETT, J.H.G. (1960) Thought disorder in psychotic patients. In H.J. EYSENCK (Ed.) *Experiments in Personality*, Vol. II. London: Routledge & Kegan Paul.

PENROSE, L.S. and WILSON, D.J. (1942) The spatial dispersion of psychotic responses in the tapping test. *J. abnorm. soc. Psychol.*, **27**, 131-3.

PERSKY, H., SMITH, K.D. and BASU, G.K. (1971) Relation of psychologic measures of aggression and hostility to testosterone production in man. *Psychosom. Med.*, **33**, 265-71.

PFEIFFER, C.C., ILIEV, V., NICHOLS, R.E. and SUGARMAN, A.A. (1969) The serum urate level reflects degree of stress. *J. clin. Pharmac.*, **9**, 384-92.

PHILLIPS, J.E., JACOBSEN, N. and TURNER, W.M. (1965) Conceptual thinking in schizophrenics and their relatives. *Br. J. Psychiat.*, **111**, 823-39.

PICKERING, R. (1975) *Creative Malady.* London: Oxford University Press.

PLANANSKY, K. (1966a) Phenotypic boundaries of schizophrenia in twins. *Mutation in Population, Proceedings of a Symposium held in Prague, 1965.* Prague: Academia.

PLANANSKY, K. (1966b) Schizoidness in twins. *Acta genet. Med. Gemel,* **15**, 151.

PLANANSKY, K. (1972) Phenotypic boundaries and genetic specificity in schizophrenia. In R.A. KAPLAN (Ed.) *Genetic Factors in 'Schizophrenia'.* Springfield: C.C. Thomas.

POWELL, A., THOMSON, N., HALL, D.J. and WILSON, L. (1973) Parent-child concordance with respect to sex and diagnosis in schizophrenia and manic-depressive psychosis. *Br. J. Psychiat.*, **123**, 653-8.

POWER, R.P. (1968) Simulation of stable and neurotic personalities by subjects warned of the presence of Lie Scales in inventories. *Br. J. Psychol.*, **59**, 105-9.

POWER, R.P. and O'DONOVAN, P. (1969) Detection of simulation on the MPI by subjects given the rationale of the Lie Scale. *Br. J. Psychol.*, **60**, 535-41.

PRASAD, M., VERMA, S.K. and PERSHAD, D. (1974) Inter-relationships among some measures of personality in psychiatric patients. *Ind. J. Psychiat.*, **16**, 244-51.

QUAY, N. and POWELL, J.T. (1955) The validity of a schizophrenic screening scale of the MMPI. *J. clin. Psychol.*, **11**, 92-3.

RADCLIFFE, J.A. (1966) A note on questionnaire faking with 16 PFQ and MPI. *Austral. J. Psychol.*, **18**, 154-7.

RAPAPORT, D. (1945) *Diagnostic Psychological Testing.* Chicago: Year Book Publishers.

RAY, T.S. (1963) Electrodermal indications of level of psychological disturbance in chronic schizophrenia. *Am. J. Psychol.*, **18**, 393.

REED, S.C., HARTLEY, C., ANDERSON, V.E., PHILLIPS, V.P. and JOHNSON, N.A. (1973) *The Psychoses: Family Studies.* London: W.B. Saunders.

REES, L. (1973) Constitutional factors and abnormal behaviour. In H.J. EYSENCK (Ed.) *Handbook of Abnormal Psychology*, 487-539. London: Pitman.

REICH, T., CLONINGER, C.R. and GUZE, S.B. (1975) The multifactorial model of disease transmission: I. Description of the model and its use in psychiatry. *Br. J. Psychiat.*, **127**, 1-10.

REISBY, N. (1967) Psychoses in children of schizophrenic mothers. *Acta psychiat. Scand.*, **43**, 8-20.

RENNIE, T.A.C. (1953) Prognosis in the psychoneuroses: Benign and malignant developments. In P.H. HOCH and J. ZUBIN (Eds.) *Current Problems in Psychiatric Diagnosis.* New York: Grune and Stratton.

RIE, H.E. (1963) An exploratory study of the CMAS Lie Scale. *Child Dev.,* **34,** 1003-17.

RIEDEL, H. (1937) Zur empirischen Erbprognose der Psychopathie. *Z. ges. neurol. Psychiat.,* **159,** 597.

ROMNEY, D. (1969) Psychometrically assessed thought disorder in schizophrenic and control patients and in their parents and siblings: Part I—Patients; Part II—Relatives. *Br. J. Psychiat.,* **115,** 999-1002.

ROSENTHAL, D. (1963) (Ed.) *The Genain Quadruplets.* New York: Basic Books.

ROSENTHAL, D. (1970) *Genetic Theory and Abnormal Behaviour.* London: McGraw-Hill.

ROSENTHAL, D., WENDER, P.W., KETY, S.S., SCHULSINGER, F., WELNER, J. and ÖSTERGAARD, L. (1968) Schizophrenics' offspring reared in adoptive homes. *J. psychiat. Res.,* **6,** 377-92.

ROSENTHAL, D. and VAN DYKE, J. (1970) The cure of monozygotic twins discordant as to schizophrenia in the search for an inherited characterological defect. *Acts psychiat. Scand. Supp.,* **219,** 183-9.

ROSMAN, B., WILD, C., RICCI, J., FLECK, S. and LIDZ, T. (1964) Thought disorders in the parents of schizophrenic patients: a further study utilizing the object sorting test. *J. psychiat. Res.,* **2,** 211-21.

ROUSELL, C.H. and EDWARDS, C.N. (1971) Some developmental antecedents of psychopathology. *J. Pers.,* **39,** 362-77.

ROYCE, J.R. (1973) The conceptual framework for a multi-factor theory of individuality. In J.R. ROYCE (Ed.) *Multivariate Analysis and Psychological Theory.* London: Academic Press.

RUBIN, H. (1954) Validity of a critical item scale for schizophrenics on the MMPI. *J. consult. Psychol.,* **18,** 219-20.

RÜDIN, E. (1916) *Zur Vererbung und Neuentstehung der Dementia praecox.* Berlin: Springer.

RUESCH, J. and BOWMAN, K. (1945) Prolonged post-traumatic syndromes following head injury. *Am. J. Psychiat.,* **102,** 145-63.

RUSSELL, M.A.H., ARMSTRONG, E. and PATEL, U.A. (1975) Temporal contiguity in electric aversion therapy for cigarette smoking. *Behav. Res. Ther.,* in press.

SALES, S.M. (1969) Differences among individuals in affective, behavioral, biochemical, and physiological responses to variations in work load. Michigan: unpublished Ph.D. thesis. Quoted by Stevens, 1973.

SALZMAN, L.F., GOLDSTEIN, R.H., ATKINS, R. and BABIGIAN, H. (1966) Conceptual thinking in psychiatric patients. *Arch gen. Psychiat.,* **14,** 55.

SANDIFER, M.G., HORDERN, A., TIMBURY, G.C. and GREEN, L.M. (1968) Psychiatric diagnosis: a comparative study in North Carolina, London and Glasgow. *Br. J. Psychiat.,* **114,** 1-9.

SAVAGE, R.D. (1972) An exploratory study of individual characteristics associated with attainment in medical school. *Br. J. med. Educ.,* **6,** 68-77.

SCHAFER, R. (1951) *The Clinical Application of Psychological Tests.* New York: International University Press.

SCHMIDT, H.O. and FONDA, C.P. (1956) The reliability of psychiatric diagnosis: a new look. *J. abnorm. soc. Psychol.,* **52,** 262-7.

SCHULZ, B. (1940) Kinder manisch-depressiver und anderer affektiv-psychotischer Elternpaare. *Z. ges. neurol. Psychiat.*, **169**, 311.

SEEMAN, W. (1953) Psychiatric diagnosis. *J. nerv. ment. Dis.*, **118**, 541-4.

SEGRAVES, R.T. (1970) Personality, body build and adrenocortical activity. *Br. J. Psychiat.*, **117**, 405-11.

SELLS, S.B., DEMAREE, R.G. and WILL, D.P. (1968) *A Taxonomic Investigation of Personality*. Texas Christian Institute of Behavioral Research.

SELLS, S.B., DEMAREE, R.G., and WILL, D.P. (1971) Dimensions of personality: II. Separate factor structures in Guilford and Cattell trait markers. *Multivariate Behavioral Research*, **5**, 135-85.

SEN, N.N. (1966) *Personality Trait Inventory*. New Delhi: Psychological Foundation, NCERT.

SHAW, D.M., MacSWEENEY, D.A., JOHNSON, A.C. and MERRY, J. (1975) Personality characteristics of alcoholic and depressed patients. *Br. J. Psychiat.*, **126**, 56-9.

SHIELDS, J. (1971) Concepts of heredity for schizophrenia. In M. BLEULER and J. ANGST (Eds.) *The Origin of Schizophrenia*. Bern: Hans Huber.

SHIELDS, J. (1973) Heredity and psychological abnormality. In H.J. EYSENCK (Ed.) *Handbook of Abnormal Psychology*. London: Pitman.

SHIELDS, J. and GOTTESMAN, I.I. (1971) Cross-national diagnosis and the heritability of schizophrenia. *Encerpta Medica, International Congress. Series No: 274, Symposium 27*, 1153-8.

SHIELDS, J. and GOTTESMAN, I.I. (1973) Genetic studies of schizophrenia as signposts to biochemistry. *Biochemical Society*, Special Publication,1, 165-74.

SHULTZ, T.E., MILEY, A.D. and EVANS, I.M. (1976) Factor similarities and normative scores for the PEN administered to Caucasian and Japanese-American college students in Hawaii. *Br. J. soc. clin. Psychol.*, to appear.

SINCLAIR, I. and CHAPMAN, B. (1973) A typological and dimensional study of a sample of prisoners. *Br. J. Crim.* **13**, 341-53.

SLADE, P.D. (1975) An experimental approach to the study of auditory hallucinations. London: unpublished Ph.D. thesis.

SLATER, E. (1947) Genetical causes of schizophrenic symptoms. *Monatschr. Psychiat. Neurol.*, **113**, 50.

SLATER, E. (1953) *Psychotic and Neurotic Illnesses in Twins*. London: H.M. Stationery Office.

SLATER, E. (1958) The monogenic theory of schizophrenia. *Acta genetica et statistics Medica*, **8**, 50-6.

SLATER, E. and COWIE, V. (1971) *The Genetics of Mental Disorder*. London: Oxford University Press.

SLATER, E. and ROTH M. (1969) In W. MAYER-GROSS, E. SLATER and M. ROTH, *Clinical Psychiatry*, 3rd edn. London: Baillière, Tindall & Cassell.

SLATER, P. (1960) Experiments in psychometrics. In H.J. EYSENCK (Ed.) *Experiments in Personality, Vol. 2.* London: Routledge & Kegan Paul.

SMITH, D.E. (1974) Relationship between the Eysenck and Jesness Personality Inventories. *Br. J. Crim.*, **14**, 376-84.

SOLLENBERGER, R.T. (1940) Some relationships between the urinary excretion of male hormone by maturing boys and their expressed interests and attitudes. *J. Psychol.*, **9**, 179-89.

SPENCE, J.T. and SPENCE, K.W. (1966) The motivational components of manifest anxiety; drive and drive stimuli. In C.P. SPIELBERGER (Ed.) *Anxiety and Behaviour.* London: Academic Press.

SPICER, C.C., HARE, E.H. and SLATER, E. (1973) Neurotic and psychotic forms of depressive illness: evidence from age-incidence in a national sample. *Br. J. Psychiat.,* **123**, 535-41.

SPITZER, R.L. and FLEISS, J.L. (1974) A re-analysis of the reliability of psychiatric diagnosis. *Br. J. Psychiat.,* **125**, 341-7.

STANLEY, G. and WATKINS, D. (1972) A factorial study of Eysenck and Eysenck's Psychoticism, Extraversion and Neuroticism Scales. *Austral. Psychol.,* **7**, 26-32.

STEPHENS, D.A., ATKINSON, M.W., KAY, D.N.K., ROTH, M. and GARSIDE, R.F. (1975) Psychiatric morbidity in parents and sibs of schizophrenics and non-schizophrenics. *Br. J. Psychiat.,* **127**, 97-108.

STEVENS, H.A. (1973) Serum uric acid: a biochemical factor in learning. Saskatchewan: unpublished Ph.D. thesis.

STEWART, R.A., POWELL, G.E. and ALLSOPP, J.F. (1975) The effects of personality and deviancy on the social attitudes and goals of male and female adolescents. Paper presented at postgraduate conference in the Behavioural Sciences, Sheffield, England, April, 1975.

STORR, A. (1972) *The Dynamics of Creation.* London: Secker and Warburg.

STROH, C.M. (1969) Vigilance, arousal and personality. London: unpublished Ph.D. thesis.

STROH, C.M. (1971) *Vigilance: The Problem of Sustained Attention.* Oxford: Pergamon Press.

STUMPFL, F. (1935) *Erbanlage und Verbrechen.* Berlin: Springer.

TEASDALE, J.P. (1973) Drug dependence. In H.J. EYSENCK (Ed.) *Handbook of Abnormal Psychology,* 97-130. London: Pitman.

TEASDALE, J.P., SEGRAVES, R.T. and ZACUNE, J. (1971) 'Psychoticism' in drug-users. *Br. J. soc. clin. Psychol.,* **10**, 160-71.

THAYER, J. and SILBER, D.E. (1971) Relationship between levels of arousal and responsiveness among schizophrenics and normal subjects. *J. abnorm. Psychol.,* **77**, 162-73.

THODAY, J.M. (1961) Location of polygenes. *Nature,* **191**, 368-70.

THODAY, J.M. (1967) New insights into continuous variation. In J.F. CROW and J.V. NEEL (Eds.) *Proceedings of the 3rd International Congress in Human Genetics.* Baltimore: John Hopkins Press.

THOMPSON, A.H. (1973) Reaction time, signal processing and personality. London: unpublished Ph.D. thesis.

THOMSON, Sir G. (1961) *The Inspiration of Science.* London: Oxford University Press.

TIENARI, P. (1963) Psychiatric illnesses in identical twins. *Acta psychiat. Scand.,* **39**, Supplement 171, 1-195.

TIMM, U. (1968) Reliabilität und Faktorenstruktur von Cattell's 16PF Test bei einer deutschen Stichprobe. *Z. exp. angew. Psychol.,* **15**, 354-73.

TOBIN, J. and HALGRIMSON, H. (1969) Personal communication, quoted in Pfeiffer *et al.*

TROUTON, D.S. and MAXWELL, A.E. (1956) The relation between neurosis and psychosis. *J. ment. Sci.,* **102**, 1-21.

VEE, S. (1969) And a little child shall lead them. *J. Am. med. Ass.,* **209**, 269.

VENABLES, P.H. (1963) The relationship between level of skin potential and fusion of paired light flashes in schizophrenic and normal subjects. *J. psychiat. Res.*, 1, 279-87.

VENABLES, P.H. (1964) Input dysfunction in schizophrenia. In B.A. MAHER (Ed.) *Progress in Experimental Personality Research.* New York: Academic Press.

VENABLES, P.H. (1967) The relation of two flash and two click thresholds to withdrawal in paranoid and non-paranoid schizophrenics. *Br. J. soc. clin. Psychol.*, 6, 60-2.

VENABLES, P.H. and WING, J.K. (1962) Level of arousal and the subclassification of schizophrenia. *Archs gen. Psychiat.*, 7, 114-19.

VERMA, R.M. and EYSENCK, H.J. (1973) Severity and type of psychotic illness as a function of personality. *Br. J. Psychiat.*, 122, 573-85.

VERMA, S.K. and WIG, N.N. (1972) Some experiences with PEN. *Psychol. Stud.*, 17, 11-14.

WAKEFIELD, J.A., BRADLEY, P.E., DOUGHTIE, E.B. and KRAFT, I.A. (1975) The influence of overlapping and nonoverlapping items on the theoretical interrelationships of MMPI scales. To appear.

WAKEFIELD, J.A. and DOUGHTIE, E.B. (1973) The geometric relationship between Holland's personality model and the Vocational Preference Inventory. *J. counsel. Psychol.*, 20, 513-18.

WAKEFIELD, J.A., YAM, B.H.L., BRADLEY, P.E., DOUGHTIE, E.B. and COX, J.A. (1974) Eysenck's personality dimensions: a model for the MMPI. *Br. J. soc. clin. Psychol.*, 13, 413-20.

WALLACH, M. and KOGAN, N. (1965) *Modes of Thinking in Young Children.* London: Holt, Rinehart and Winston.

WECHSLER, D. (1945) *A Standardized Memory Scale for Clinical Use.* New York City: Bellevue Hospital.

WELLS, B.W.P. (1970) Personality study of VD patients. *Br. J. ven. Dis.*, 46, 498-501.

WELLS, B. and STACEY, B. (1976) A further comparison of Cannabis (Marijuana) users and non-users. *Br. J. Addict.*, in press.

WELNER, J. and STROMGREN, E. (1958) Clinical and genetic studies on benign schizophreni-form psychoses based on a follow-up. *Acta psychiat. Scand.*, 33, 377.

WERMAN, A.G. (1952) Faking personality test scores in a simulated employment situation. *J. appl. Psychol.*, 36, 112-13.

WEST, P.J. and FARRINGTON, D.P. (1973) *Who Becomes Delinquent?* London: Heinemann.

WIG, N.N. and VERMA, S.R. (1973) PGI Health Questionnaire, N-1: a simple neuroticism scale. *Ind. J. Psychiat.*, 15, 80-4.

WIGNER, E.P. (1964) Events, laws of nature and invariance principles. *Science*, 145, 995-9.

WILLIAMS, N. (1953) Psychophysiological responsiveness to psychological stress in early chronic schizophrenic reactions. *Psychosom. Med.*, 15, 456-62.

WILLIAMS, P., FRANCIS, A. and DURHAM, R. (1976) Personality and meditation. *J. psychosom. Res.*, in press.

WILSON, G.D. (1973) (Ed.) *The Psychology of Conservatism.* London: Academic Press.

WINTER, W.P. and STORTROEN, M. (1963) A comparison of several MMPI indices to differentiate psychotics from normals. *J. clin. Psychol.*, 19, 220-3.

WOLPE, J. (1970) The discontinuity of neurosis and schizophrenia. *Behav. Res. Ther.*, 8, 179-87.

YACORZYNSKI, G.K. (1941) An evaluation of the postulates underlying the Babcock deterioration test. *Psychol. Rev.*, 48, 261-7.

ZAHN, T.P. (1964) *Autonomic Activity and Behaviour in Schizophrenia.* Washington: American Psychiatric Association, Psychiatric Research Report, 19.

ZAHN, T.P. (1968) Electrodermal and heart rate orienting reactions in chronic schizophrenia. *J. psychiat. Res.*, 6, 117-34.

ZUBIN, J. (1967) Classification of the behaviour disorders. In P.R. FARNSWORTH and Q. McNEMAR (Eds.) *Annual Review of Psychology.* Palo Alto: Consulting Psychologists' Press.

ZUBIN, J., EVANS, L.D. and SCHEIER, F. (1965) *An Experimental Approach to Projective Techniques.* London: Wiley.

Author Index

Subject Index

RC
512
E97

0

Eysenck, Hans J.
    Psychoticism as a dimension
of personality.

RC512 E97
+Psychoticism as +Eysenck, Hans Ju

0 00 02 0229182 9
MIDDLEBURY COLLEGE

DEMCO